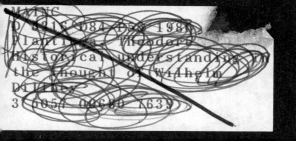

Theodore Plantinga received his PHD from the University of Toronto in 1975. He is a freelance editor and translator, and executive director of the Ontario Christian College Association.

Wilhelm Dilthey (1833–1911), a philosopher who has influenced twentieth-century intellectual history via such thinkers as Heidegger, Jaspers, Ortega y Gasset, and Max Scheler, is subjected to careful analysis in this book. What emerges is a reinterpretation of his theory of understanding (*Verstehen*) and historical knowledge.

The concept of understanding for which Dilthey became famous was developed only after 1900, in the third and final phase of his career, but it was an approach to the problem or set of problems that had preoccupied him throughout his entire intellectual career. To delineate this doctrine and its place in Dilthey's thinking on history, the author discusses Dilthey's early views on history as a science, his efforts to divide the various sciences into two major types, and his attempt to develop a psychology that would serve as a foundation for the *Geisteswissenschaften*.

The decisive shift in Dilthey's post-1900 thought came when he began to look beyond psychology to culture, to meaning-laden expressions of the human spirit. The understanding of these expressions in the outer public world, he decided, was the basic cognitive operation on which the *Geisteswissenschaften*, including the historical sciences, could be built.

Dilthey's analysis of understanding, the core of his later philosophy, draws on the hermeneutic tradition and advances it. His philosophical outlook also has important existential applications that have stimulated twentieth-century thought. The central problem for him was that of the relation between the individual and the whole or wholes with which his life is interwoven, and his solution was 'understanding,' an ability which enables the individual to transcend the confines of self and to seek communion with a more encompassing whole.

THEODORE PLANTINGA

Historical Understanding
in the Thought
of Wilhelm Dilthey

UNIVERSITY OF TORONTO PRESS
Toronto Buffalo London

Library of Congress Cataloging in Publication Data

Plantinga, Theodore, 1947–
    Historical understanding in the thought of Wilhelm
    Dilthey.

    Bibliography: p.
    Includes index.
    1. Dilthey, Wilhelm, 1833-1911.   2. History – Phi-
    losophy.   I. Title.
    B3216.D84P55   193   79–19240
    ISBN 0-8020-5475-7

Contents

vi Contents

Short Forms of Titles

Aufbau
Der Aufbau der geschichtlichen Welt in den Geisteswissenschaften (The Construction of the Historical World in the *Geisteswissenschaften*). This treatise of 1910, which appears in Vol. VII of the *Gesammelte Schriften* (pp. 79–188), is the most important work of Dilthey's final years.

Briefwechsel
Briefwechsel zwischen Wilhelm Dilthey und dem Grafen Paul Yorck v. Wartenburg, 1877–1897 (Correspondence Between Wilhelm Dilthey and Count Paul Yorck von Wartenburg). This volume of letters affords us a more informal glimpse of Dilthey. The correspondence is also revealing because of Yorck's influence on Dilthey and his commentary on Dilthey's ideas and plans.

Der junge Dilthey
Der junge Dilthey: Ein Lebensbild in Briefen und Tagebüchern, 1852–1870 (The Young Dilthey: A Biographical Sketch in Letters and Diaries). These excerpts from Dilthey's letters and diaries furnish considerable evidence about his early hopes and convictions.

Einleitung
Einleitung in die Geisteswissenschaften (Introduction to the *Geisteswissenschaften*). This book is the earliest (1883) of Dilthey's major systematic works. It forms Vol. I of the *Gesammelte Schriften* and is the first instalment of a longer work that was never completed.

Erlebnis
Das Erlebnis und die Dichtung (Lived Experience and Poetry). This book of collected essays deals with four major German writers. It is the most widely read of Dilthey's works but is only of secondary importance for this study.

Fortsetzung
Plan der Fortsetzung zum Aufbau der geschichtlichen Welt in den Geisteswissenschaften (Plan for a Continuation of 'The Construction of the Historical World in the *Geisteswissenschaften*'). These notes, which appear in Vol. VII (pp. 191–291), are in unfinished form and were never published by Dilthey himself. They are of great importance for establishing where Dilthey was headed during the final years of his life.

Ideen
Ideen über eine beschreibende und zergliedernde Psychologie (Ideas Concerning a Descriptive and Analytical Psychology). This treatise of 1894, which appears in Vol. V (pp. 139–237), is the key to Dilthey's 'psychological period.'

Individualität
Ueber vergleichende Psychologie: Beiträge zum Studium der Individualität (On Comparative Psychology: Contributions Towards the Study of Individuality). This treatise of 1895–96 follows up the line of thought begun in *Ideen* and comes right after it in Vol. V (pp. 241–316).

Philosophie
Das Wesen der Philosophie (The Essence of Philosophy). This essay of 1907 also appears in Vol. V (pp. 339–416) and was originally published in a book devoted to systematic philosophy.

Poetik
Die Einbildungskraft des Dichters: Bausteine für eine Poetik (The Imaginative Power of the Poet: Building Blocks for a Theory of Poetry). This treatise of 1887, which appears in Vol. VI (pp. 103–241), is Dilthey's most extensive treatment of literature in a systematic context.

Weltanschauung
Die Typen der Weltanschauung und ihre Ausbildung in den metaphysischen Systemen (The Types of Worldviews as Developed in the Metaphysical Systems). This essay, which appears in Vol. VIII (pp. 75–118), was originally published in 1911 in a book on worldview, philosophy, and religion. It is Dilthey's major statement on worldviews and philosophies as historical phenomena.

Preface

This study, which has been ten years in the making, owes much to people whose names are not mentioned, including my professors at Calvin College, the Johns Hopkins University, and the University of Toronto. I hope they will regard the book as fruit from their pedagogical labours. Three of them deserve special mention. It was Professor H. Evan Runner who introduced me to philosophy at Calvin College and first suggested that I focus on Dilthey in my doctoral research. Professor E.L. Fackenheim helped steer this study towards its goal and contributed generously by his stimulating questions and constructive criticism. Finally, Professor T.D. Langan presided over the book's birth by serving as my dissertation supervisor. I shall always be grateful to him for the energy, personal concern, and spiritual sensitivity he manifested as he guided me in my work and constantly held before me the profound significance of philosophical inquiry.

I would also take this occasion to thank the Canada Council in Ottawa and the Deutscher Akademischer Austauschdienst in Bonn for providing the financial support that enabled me to spend a year at the University of Freiburg (West Germany), where this study was written. The book has been published with the help of a grant from the Canadian Federation for the Humanities, using funds provided by the Social Sciences and Humanities Research Council of Canada, and a grant to University of Toronto Press from the Andrew W. Mellon Foundation.

To keep down the number of notes in the book, I have referred to Dilthey's most important works by way of abbreviated titles. A list of those abbreviated titles follows the Contents. Titles mentioned in the notes include publication data only if they do not appear in the bibliography. As for the bibliography, it reflects my reading and preparation and is not meant to be exhaustive.

The translations from German, French, and Dutch are my own, except in cases where an English title is cited for the foreign-language work. Because the German philosophical vocabulary includes various words that have no exact English equivalent, in certain cases I have added the original German in parentheses, hoping that something of the flavour of Dilthey's thinking would come through even when it was discussed in English.

HISTORICAL UNDERSTANDING
IN THE THOUGHT OF WILHELM DILTHEY

Introduction

Wilhelm Dilthey is well known as a man of unfinished projects, of first volumes never followed by second volumes. Critics and sympathizers alike complain that there are no 'answers' in his work. Is this assessment just? Did Dilthey give no answers to the great questions that have plagued mankind throughout the ages? Was he unusual as a thinker only because of the impressive range of disciplines to which he applied his penetrating mind?

Dilthey would have been the first to admit that he did not finish what he started as a thinker, but he would also have been the first to *deny* that he was unconcerned with giving answers to existential questions. His stand on this matter comes to clear expression in some notes he prepared for remarks to a circle of well-wishers on his seventieth birthday. In these notes Dilthey declares that although he has no answer to the 'riddle of life,' he does want to share with his assembled friends a message about life. He finds this difficult, for a systematic formulation of that message involves certain limitations: every expression of a doctrine is somehow too cold and heavy. He therefore begs the indulgence of his audience and proposes to pass on his message in poetic form. This he proceeds to do by relating the content of a dream he claims to have had years before.[1]

Dilthey's message for Western civilization is reflected in this dream, but it is also to be found in his other works. Unfortunately, this has not been properly recognized by students of his thought, who have generally been thrown off the track by the diversity of his writings and the shifts in his thinking. To appreciate Dilthey properly, one must begin by facing some of the obstacles to the study of his thought.

One of these difficulties is the sheer length of his intellectual career. Dilthey was born in 1833, at about the time when Goethe, Hegel, and Schleiermacher died. As a student and young scholar, he lived in an atmosphere dominated by such nineteenth-century movements as positivism and the historical school, and he felt attracted to both. In the later years of his life he sought his own way to an increasing degree, and a new philosophical position began to emerge from his labours. During the crucial years after his formal retirement, i.e., the early years of the twentieth century, he moved well beyond many of the nineteenth-century concerns reflected in his earlier writings. He lived long enough to greet the publication of Husserl's first major work, the *Logical Investigations*, with enthusiasm. Some years after his death in 1911, he was praised by Heidegger for his 'pioneering work'[2] and hailed by Ortega y Gasset as the most important philosopher of the second half of the nineteenth century.[3]

Ortega's estimate is no doubt exaggerated, but it is no exaggeration to call Dilthey one of the founders of twentieth-century philosophy. Traces of his influence – whether direct or indirect – are to be found in the works of numerous twentieth-century thinkers. When we survey the path that leads from the thinking of Ranke and Trendelenburg to the portal of the philosophies of Heidegger, Jaspers, Ortega, and Scheler, we see that Dilthey had come a long way. Perhaps we can best pay tribute to him by acknowledging this.

If we are to get at Dilthey's message for Western civilization, we must focus on his doctrine of understanding as developed in the post-1900 writings. This can best be done by examining his views on historical knowledge. This approach, however, brings us to another difficulty in the study of Dilthey: it is a characteristic of his writings that they almost invariably deal with a wider range of topics than their titles suggest. Hence the search for his views on historical knowledge cannot be confined to the writings in which he deals with the foundations of the sciences of man. Many of the texts to which I shall refer in my efforts to get at his doctrine of understanding and his views on history are drawn from seemingly peripheral writings.

Although it was not my original intention to undertake a reinterpretation of Dilthey's thought, it slowly became apparent to me that much of the Dilthey literature is misleading and inadequate, and that there is at present no reliable guide to the main outlines of his thought. This is a third significant difficulty in the study of Dilthey. Since the overall view of Dilthey's work that emerged from my own reading differs in various important respects from the account of his thinking offered in the secondary literature, I have indicated some of my points of disagreement.

There are reasons, of course, why the Dilthey literature is somewhat less enlightening than one might expect. One of them is that his thinking is accessible only through a large and diffuse collection of writings, many of which were first published after his death. Dilthey has written no central work that would introduce the student of his philosophy to the main outlines of his thought and would then indicate the place and function of the other writings within this larger scheme. The works of Dilthey include numerous concrete historical investigations, various studies in aesthetics and literature, and a number of important essays and treatises on psychological and philosophical topics – to say nothing of the many notes, drafts, and unfinished works he left behind. The arrangement of the *Gesammelte Schriften* (Collected Writings), which now include the bulk of his work, does not reveal what is essential and what is secondary. Thus, those who wish to 'read Dilthey' usually find themselves choosing somewhat arbitrarily, often on the basis of their own interests.

I hope to bring some order into the confusion by presenting a distinct interpretation of Dilthey's thought and its development. This interpretation, however, has not been reached by a deductive process; it should not be viewed as a necessary consequence of any one philosophical doctrine which he affirmed. Neither does my interpretation rest on one or a few key passages or statements in Dilthey's writings.

This study does not proceed by analysing and explicating one or a few key texts, for I have found no single passage in Dilthey that adequately sums up the various facets of his doctrine of understanding. The argument for my interpretation of Dilthey should instead be seen as cumulative. Within the framework of my reading of the development of his thought, various texts cited below seem to me to point towards a certain conception of understanding and its role in life. My procedure in this study is to sketch the historical framework (the development of Dilthey's thought) and the systematic framework (his views on other, related topics) that together shed a revealing light on a number of statements from various writings.

My interpretation of Dilthey is reached by a somewhat circuitous route, then. To avoid possible misunderstandings, I will set out my major contentions before we turn to Dilthey's early writings.

To begin with, it is important to note that Dilthey did not get around to placing his doctrine of understanding in a larger epistemological context. One might be led to think that understanding represents the mode of knowledge corresponding to the cultural realm, while there is another mode of knowledge corresponding to the natural realm. This is certainly the direction in which Dilthey moved in his earlier thinking, but in his later writings he stopped short of embracing such a view. Because an interpreter must pay attention not only to what an author says but also to what he *refrains* from saying, the temptation to lead Dilthey to a destination he did not actually reach must be resisted.

Moreover, the doctrine of understanding present in the later writings is not to be equated with what Dilthey says about understanding in his pre-1900 writings. Although there is indeed a doctrine of understanding in the earlier writings, it is less specific. Since 'understanding' (*Verstehen*) is a popular word in German as well as in English, it was already used in a non-technical way in the earliest of Dilthey's writings. It retained a variety of meanings in his subsequent writings, but during the last years of his life, a new doctrine of understanding emerged.

Understanding as sketched by Dilthey in his later writings is not a mysterious or mystifying process based on some sort of inner contact between two minds. On the contrary, understanding can take place only if expressions of mind are present, and these expressions of mind form the first and most important object of the operation of understanding. To understand is first of all to grasp something meant – and not to probe or sympathize with events and processes in someone else's mind. Understanding as such is interested not so much in what lies behind expressions as in what they mean.

This process of understanding must be seen as a mode of contact between human beings made possible by what the two or more persons involved have in common. It is not a scientific method or technique invented by scholars at some point in the history of scholarship. Understanding is a part of daily life. When historians and cultural scientists use understanding as a tool, they are only refining a procedure used without reflection by all members of the human community.

Understanding, according to Dilthey, admits of degrees. In principle it is possible for something that is understood to be even better understood. To understand something means (among other things) to grasp it in context. Since expressions and what they mean can usually be put in ever broader contexts, in most cases there is no end to the process of understanding. And since the author of an expression is usually not aware of all those contexts, it must be possible – in some cases, at least – to understand expressions and what they mean better than their authors understood them. Thus understanding is not a mere reception of something given but involves an active process of interpretation.

To understand an expression in terms of a larger context is not necessarily to understand it in terms of its origin or genesis. Dilthey's 'understanding' is not reductionistic, for it does not relativize expressions by analysing meaning in terms of origin. The material from which an expression is shaped is drawn from experience, but its meaning is not to be sought solely in an investigation of its origin.

Finally, understanding as practised by the historian involves a certain neutrality or detachment. To understand the other is not to affirm what he has affirmed. Dilthey was well aware that understanding requires a fundamental openness to the thinking and experience of others, but he did not regard this openness as tantamount to agreement. On this point, too, Dilthey's views differ from those of various other thinkers who have written on 'understanding.'

Although the understanding of the historian engaged in scholarship involves detachment and reserve, the process of understanding also serves to enlarge our selfhood – if only we will open ourselves to others and the past. Tennyson declared: 'I am a part of all that I have met.' Dilthey would reverse this by saying that all that I have met and lived has become a part of me, and that I have become a fuller, richer, larger self as a result. Dilthey sees the drive for meaning in life as an effort to reach out to others and make what they have lived part of our own existence. We ingest and digest the other by reliving the events of human history, enjoying works of art, and steeping ourselves in other cultures, religions, and societies through the fruits of scholarship.

Mircea Eliade, the famous historian of religion, has a keen sense of what it means to move in the direction of a larger self. Eliade is a student of many different religious traditions and has lived in various countries. In his journal he writes that the meaning of much that he had lived and studied suddenly came home to him one day:

I suddenly felt, not older, but extraordinarily rich and full; expanded – bringing together in me, concomitantly, both the Indian, Portuguese, and Parisian 'time' and the memories of my Bucharest childhood and youth. As if I had acquired a new dimension of depth. I was 'larger,' 'rounder.' An immense inner domain – where, not so long ago, I was penetrating only fragmentarily by trying to relive such-and-such an event – was revealed in its totality: I'm able to see it from end to end and, at the same time, in all its depth.

A vigorous, strong feeling. Historical human life suddenly takes on meaning and significance. Optimism.[4]

Such words could well have been written by Dilthey, who also saw the movement towards a larger self as a basis for optimism. Perhaps his optimism, which was not subjected to the trials of two world wars and technological totalitarianism, is the reason he is so misunderstood today.

1

The Question of History

In an era of rapid change, the value of studying the past can easily be called into question. Dilthey lived in such an era. He responded to the challenge to history by pointing out the existential significance of historical understanding. His initial goal with regard to history, however, was more limited: he wanted to show that history is a legitimate and independent scientific discipline. His conception of historical understanding grew slowly out of his defence of history as an autonomous discipline. Hence we begin with a consideration of the question of history as Dilthey faced it when he was a young scholar.

SOME DOUBTS ABOUT HISTORICAL KNOWLEDGE

The history of philosophical thought includes a number of arguments that support a skeptical attitude towards the possibility of reliable historical knowledge. Although some of those arguments can be disposed of without much difficulty, there are certain basic objections that should cause every practitioner of the historical sciences some anxious moments. Most of them have been in circulation for quite some time, and we have good reason to suppose that Dilthey himself had come across them in one form or another. Although he never wrote a refutation of historical skepticism, his view of history can be regarded as answering some of the major objections, three of which will be dealt with in this section.

Arthur Schopenhauer, whose works were read widely during the period of Dilthey's youth, was a creative thinker in his own right, but he also had a gift for absorbing the ideas of others and reformulating them in a fresh and often amusing fashion. The second edition of his major work *The World as Will and Representation*, which was published in 1844, included a number of essays in which the ideas already contained in the first edition of 1819 were further explicated and illustrated. Among these additions was a short essay entitled 'On History,' which represents an admirable statement of the case against historical science.

Schopenhauer begins by affirming the old thesis that history is inferior to poetry. But a much more serious charge – in view of the growing esteem of history in the eyes of many nineteenth-century Germans – is that it is not and cannot be a science in the proper sense of the term, that is, that '... it lacks the fundamental characteristic of science, the subordination of what is known ...' (pp. 439–40). Schopenhauer elaborates as follows: 'As the sciences are systems of concepts, they always speak of species; history speaks of individuals. History would accordingly be a science of individual things, which implies a contradiction' (p. 440). Schopenhauer was not simply measuring history by criteria derived from the natural sciences; he made it clear that his critique of history's claim to the status of science is rooted in a Platonic conception of knowledge according to which the object of our knowledge is the unchangeable and permanent. Thus he writes: '... we should try to understand what *exists*, what actually *is*, today and always, in other words, to know the *Ideas* (in Plato's sense)' (p. 443). His critique, then, is tied to a particular ontological outlook – which in turn suggests how his argument might be countered. It is meaningful to speak philosophically about history, on Schopenhauer's view, but what we are allowed to say must remain general: 'The true philosophy of history thus consists in the insight that, in spite of all these endless changes and their chaos and confusion, we yet always have before us only the same, identical, unchangeable essence, acting in the same way today as it did yesterday and always' (p. 444).

Schopenhauer's argument does not rule out historical knowledge entirely; it simply denies it the title of reliable knowledge, science, *epistémé*. Memory of the past plays an undeniable role in human life, and history can be regarded as the 'rational self-consciousness of the human race' (p. 445). But this is only a pale shadow of the exalted view of history held by the nineteenth-century historical thinkers whom Dilthey so much admired and by whom he was inspired.

A second objection, which is reflected in Schopenhauer's essay but not explicitly formulated, is that the object of historical knowledge is a *past* event and is therefore not open to our direct inspection. We cannot perform experiments on it or confirm our observation by taking a second look. Again, this does not rule out the possibility of historical knowledge altogether, but it does cast the idea of history as a science into doubt. F.H. Bradley writes: 'That the object of knowledge must be present is a truism ...'[1] Science requires objectivity in some sense or other, and objectivity, in turn, is only possible if the object of our knowledge or the evidence on which we base our knowledge is somehow present to us and can be inspected by two or more investigators. If history is bound entirely to memory, it would appear that it cannot be much more objective and scientific than a private revelation.

A third objection to historical knowledge arises from philosophical considerations closer to the outlook of the nineteenth-century German historians and theorists of history. Yet it is perhaps the most troublesome of the three. The idea that history is in some sense a 'whole' is an old one, and Schopenhauer, too, reflects it in his essay. If history is indeed a 'whole,' then it would seem that an individual past event can be known and grasped properly only if it is regarded as part of a sequence of events forming a whole. Since there is no basic, atomic definition of an 'event,' the events of which the past is composed can be reduced to such minute proportions that they become wholly meaningless in themselves. Clearly, historical knowledge requires some sort of arranging and co-ordinating of events to form sequences and larger wholes: the fuller the sequence, the better our grasp of the particular events that comprise it. In order to understand an event in the recent past as fully as possible, then, we must have a virtually complete knowledge of the past, for the entire history of the Western world could be regarded as a huge sequence and context in which the event in question must be situated. Yet a knowledge of all of the past, or of a substantial proportion of it, cannot be gained all at once; it must rather be built up on the basis of a knowledge of particular events. Thus, historical knowledge seems to presuppose itself, or at least to require a circular method.

This objection can also be developed in another direction. The sequence in which we locate a particular event in the recent past is continually growing and unfolding; that is to say, the future is relentlessly becoming the past. Later events often cast an important light on earlier events and cause us to re-evaluate or reinterpret them. As E.H. Carr observes: 'To learn about the present in the light of the past means also to learn about the past in the light of the present.'[2] Dilthey himself liked to point out that in our reflection on the course of our own lives, we are sometimes forced to reinterpret the past in the light of more recent events. For similar reasons, historians are regularly forced to rewrite the histories of nations. In a significant sense, therefore, our knowledge of the past seems to be dependent on knowledge of the future, of events that have not yet occurred and cannot (at present) be foreseen. 'One would first have to await the end of history in order to possess all the material necessary to determine its meaning,' wrote Dilthey in recognition of this problem (*Fortsetzung*, 233). Thus it appears that there is something essentially incomplete and provisional about historical knowledge.

DILTHEY'S INITIAL APPROACH TO HISTORICAL KNOWLEDGE

It is important to remember that Dilthey was both a historian and a philosopher. It was as a historian that he first grappled with the question of history; in fact, he did not begin to write about the methods and foundation of history and the *Geisteswissenschaften* until he had been a practising historian for quite some time. His first major historical work, the biography of Schleiermacher, was published in 1870, some thirteen years before the publication of his first major philosophical work, the *Einleitung in die Geisteswissenschaften*.

Although history temporally precedes philosophy in Dilthey's life's work, these two spheres of his intellectual activity cannot be understood in isolation from one another. Dilthey was gripped by philosophical interests and intentions from the very start. In a diary entry of 1859 he declared: 'It would not be worthwhile to be a historian if this were not likewise a way to comprehend the world' (*Der junge Dilthey*, 81). More specifically, he was convinced that philosophical reflection would and could be fruitful only if it was rooted in the experience of having undertaken actual scientific investigations:* one of his criticisms of the positivists was that they tried to deal with the problem of the foundation of the *Geisteswissenschaften* '... without the intimate sense of historical reality which one forms only by working with this reality in concrete research over a period of years ...' (*Einleitung*, 23). This conviction gives us an insight into what seems to have been Dilthey's plan for his own life. In a revealing passage in an essay of 1865 on the theologian Ferdinand Christian Baur, he wrote:

It is noteworthy that the boldest critical works are the result of the greatest maturity, the work of the beginning of old age. So little is there to Schopenhauer's statement that productivity ends with one's thirty-fifth year. Kant, Niebuhr confirm our observation. For real and productive criticism arises out of great masses of studies of various kinds, from which spring the new, fruitful combinations through which some area or other is illuminated (IV, 423–4).

It seems likely that Dilthey deliberately postponed his more narrowly philosophical labours until his later years,† hoping that his experience as a practi-

---

* In 1856 Dilthey wrote to his brother Karl: 'Reflection is only fruitful when it rests on the special investigation of some sphere of reality or other, whether it be antiquity or history or nature or even religion' (*Der junge Dilthey*, 36).
† The major work of Dilthey's early period (i.e., the *Einleitung*) was not published until 1883, when he was 50 years old. The period of the later philosophy, which is our special concern in this study, begins around 1900, when Dilthey was 67 years old.

tioner of the *Geisteswissenschaften* would eventually bear fruit in the form of philosophical insights.

The union of philosophical and historical interests is characteristic of Dilthey's personality as well as of his work.* Later in his life he began a sketch of his own philosophy by observing that he had come to philosophy from history.[3] The full significance of this union of philosophy and history can be understood only in the light of Dilthey's belief that there are two kinds of philosophers: 'There are only two classes of philosophical investigators: those who can participate at the same time in the advances of the mathematical-physical sciences, and those who can participate in the advances of the historical and political sciences.'[4] Dilthey, of course, had chosen to be the latter kind of philosopher. Only by participating in the work of the *Geisteswissenschaften* (as he was later to call them) could he earn the right to make philosophical claims about them.

This doctrine of the two kinds of philosophers reveals two early limitations of Dilthey's outlook. First, it indicates that he regarded philosophy as somehow dependent on science and its results, or at least closely linked with it. (Although Dilthey never arrived at a fixed and finished doctrine of what philosophy is, he did go beyond this view of philosophy in later years.) Second, it shows us that he had renounced all hopes of making a significant contribution to our comprehension of nature. His own observations about natural science and knowledge of nature are of interest and importance mainly for what they imply about his outlook on the *Geisteswissenschaften*.

Having established that Dilthey initially approached history more as a historian than as a philosopher, we can now ask what – if anything – characterized his early outlook on history. In general, it can be said that there was nothing exceptional about his outlook, for it was in tune with that of other admirers of historical science during that era. The achievements of the early nineteenth-century historians whom Dilthey held in such high regard[5] had convinced him that history is possible as a science and that it has an important role to play in human life. The eloquent tribute which he paid to history in a book review article of 1862 makes this clear. Fully conscious of the traditional thesis of the superiority of poetry to history, Dilthey begins this article, in which he combats the natural scientific approach to history, by observing:

To tell of the deeds of men and to hear them told is a peculiar need of the human spirit which can be satisfied neither by art nor by science, since neither one is content

---

* In a letter to his father in 1861, Dilthey wrote: '... it is a great joy to me that you see, just as I do, that the combination of the philosophical and the historical is the focal point of my existence and of my studies' (*Der junge Dilthey*, 166).

to present the facts simply, just as they happened. Art casts a veil over naked reality, which is to make it more beautiful and to transfigure it; science seeks an abiding law in the succession of appearances (XVI, 100).

Although history is not superior to poetry, it certainly has become its equal.

The somewhat idyllic picture of history which Dilthey paints here suggests that he had not yet become aware of the full range of thorny problems involved in historical knowledge. His early standpoint on the question of laws in history supports this suspicion. The book review article mentioned above is a discussion of the work of the influential English historian Thomas Buckle. Dilthey contrasted his own glowing picture of history and its importance with the outlook of Buckle, who wanted to turn history into an exact science. According to Dilthey, Buckle maintained that the historical realm is governed by the law of necessity. Dilthey did not take issue with Buckle's contention; he maintained only that Buckle had gone too far in his efforts to apply his approach to the study of history. Dilthey's own position at that time was: 'In the realm of nature as in that of the spirit, everything happens in accordance with fixed laws ...' (p. 102). Five years later, in his inaugural lecture at Basel, he declared: '... the task is to gain knowledge of the laws that govern social, intellectual and moral phenomena. This knowledge of laws is the source of all of man's power, even over against cultural (*geistig*) phenomena.'[6] Dilthey was later to abandon this position;[7] in later years he regularly emphasized the *dissimilarities* between the procedures of the natural sciences and those of the *Geisteswissenschaften*.

Also characteristic of Dilthey's initial approach to history is a rather pragmatic and flexible attitude towards the question of methodology. If his concern with history were focused exclusively on epistemological and methodological considerations, we could hardly expect him to manifest such an attitude. Yet, in an important essay of 1875 entitled 'Ueber das Studium der Geschichte der Wissenschaften vom Menschen, der Gesellschaft und dem Staat,' which was a forerunner of the *Einleitung*, he declared: 'I have little confidence in any effort to determine in advance for all branches of history – even in the most general way – the method by which the actual findings of the historian are to be explained. The best way to find out whether a knife is sharp is to use it. The fruitfulness of a method can only be established by making discoveries by means of it.'[8] What this means, Dilthey declared in an unpublished manuscript in which he also used the example of the knife, is that theory follows praxis.[9] This would seem to indicate, then, that at the outset of Dilthey's career, philosophical questions of methodology were not uppermost in his mind. But by the time he wrote the *Einleitung*, this too had changed.[10]

The early Dilthey, then, was optimistic and confident about the possibility of historical knowledge. Much had already been accomplished, and much more would be achieved in the years ahead. Dilthey was hopeful especially about the prospects of intellectual history or cultural history, the kind of history he loved most and often wrote himself. In the essay of 1875 he declared:

It is my hope that when the history of cultural (*geistig*) movements and of the intellectual progress of mankind – which, furthermore, has the extraordinary advantage that its components (i.e., books) present themselves to us in a reliable and veracious way, since we can be deceived about beliefs and purposes, whereas cultural (*geistig*) productions must present themselves as they are, no illusions being possible here – that when this history will have taken possession of all of its natural aids and tools, no other branch of history will be comparable to it in scientific rigour. Then the unreasonable aversion, indeed, the disdain of many historians of elevated politics for the study of the history of the highest expressions of the human spirit, which disdain can be explained only by their ignorance of these sciences, will disappear (v, 41).

It was primarily this kind or branch of history that was to attract Dilthey's attention in later years.

DILTHEY AS A THEORIST OF HISTORY

Much of the current interest in Dilthey is based on a misconception: he is viewed as primarily an epistemologist of historical knowledge.* For various

---

* Howard Tuttle, for example, regards the question how historical knowledge is possible as the key to Dilthey's thinking and claims that this question was frequently asked by Dilthey (*Wilhelm Dilthey's Philosophy of Historical Understanding*, 6). Yet Dilthey does not pose the question in such terms in the passage Tuttle refers to (*Fortsetzung*, 254) or in any of his other works. In another passage he does ask: 'How is history possible?' (p. 261), but he then continues in a vein that makes it clear that he views this problem in broader terms than Tuttle does, that is to say, not in exclusively epistemological terms: 'In posing this question we presuppose a concept of history. We saw that this concept depends on the concept of life.' Tuttle's error is probably the result of an overestimation of the importance of Dilthey's phrase 'critique of historical reason' (which will be dealt with later). His interpretation is plausible if we assume that Dilthey was trying to extend Kant's conception of knowledge and science into the domain of the *Geisteswissenschaften*, but it finds little support in the texts. Dilthey does recognize a 'problem of historical knowledge' (p. 278), but in the same work in which we find this phrase he writes: 'This is the problem of history: Where one self is separate from other selves, where there is only the operation of forces on one another, how can a subject that acts and is acted upon like a self arise from these individuals?' (p. 262). Unfortunately, Angèle Kremer-Marietti reasons, this picture of Dilthey is inadequate. Two of these reasons will be dealt with here.

First, the unity of Dilthey's lifework cannot be understood if we regard him first and foremost as a philosopher of history. The phrase that Dilthey himself frequently used to sum up his intellectual labours is 'philosophy of life'; the collection of essays which he hoped to publish at the end of his life under the title 'Die geistige Welt' was to be an 'introduction to the philosophy of life.' In Chapter 4 I shall take up the question what Dilthey did and did not mean by the phrase 'philosophy of life.' A key component of this 'philosophy of life' was Dilthey's theory of art and literature. Although his thinking on art and aesthetics has often been neglected or overlooked by students of his philosophy, his treatises on music, poetry, literary criticism, and aesthetics make up a substantial proportion of his published writings. Dilthey's writings, most of which are now available in 24 published volumes, can be divided into three major categories: (1) historical studies, (2) systematic philosophical or psychological studies,* and (3) studies on art and aesthetics.† The philosophy of life which he struggled to express during the last decade of his life represents an effort to unify these three fields of investigation. Because Dilthey tried to bring these areas together, any treatment of his work that ignores his views on art and aesthetics is not faithful to his thought.

A second reason for refusing to characterize Dilthey simply as a 'philosopher of history' is that he himself rejected what he called philosophy of history.[11] To Dilthey the term 'philosophy of history,' which had gained currency largely through Voltaire and Hegel, meant an unscientific synthesis of scientific knowledge, somewhat like the philosophy of nature of the German idealists. In the 1875 essay he wrote: 'Philosophy of history as understood up to now is a delusory image, like philosophy of nature; from a summary overview of the material already dealt with by historians and arranged in a creative way into groups, we will derive – however many psychological, logical and metaphysical elements may be added – only ill-defined half-truths' (v, 47). Philosophy of history is really an attempt to combine the work of several

---

makes heavy use of Tuttle's study in *Wilhelm Dilthey et l'anthropologie historique* (see pp. 64–88), claiming that Dilthey's fundamental question is whether history is possible (p. 85).

* Dilthey did not make a sharp distinction between philosophical and psychological questions. His two treatises on psychology are not to be considered psychology in the modern sense.

† A fourth and smaller category that could be mentioned is pedagogy, but Dilthey's writings on this subject do not play an important role in this study.

separate sciences and must therefore be rejected on methodological grounds. In the *Einleitung* Dilthey complained:

This procedure seeks to unite the ideas already formulated by the historians. But the thinker who takes the historical world as his object must be in direct contact with the immediate raw material of history and must be master of all its methods. He must subject himself to the same law of diligent work with the raw material to which the historian is subject (p. 92).

Although Dilthey's close friend and philosophical associate Count Yorck did not reject the idea of philosophy of history and even suggested to him that he relent somewhat in his opposition to it,[12] Dilthey stood firm. He never wrote a philosophy of history. His view of history must be reconstructed from observations made in a number of different works on different topics.

In the twentieth century, the term 'philosophy of history' has gradually lost the meaning which Dilthey associated with it. Exactly what it does mean today is far from clear. E.H. Carr declares: '... I shall use it to mean, if I use it at all, our answer to the question, What is History?'[13] In recent decades, a distinction between 'critical' and 'speculative' philosophy of history has come to the fore. The latter is identified mainly with the old meaning of the term 'philosophy of history,' the one Dilthey attacked: any metaphysical or theological interpretation of the historical process counts as speculative philosophy of history. But critical philosophy of history limits its interest and scope to historical knowledge or science. More specifically, it represents an epistemological and methodological reflection on the kind of knowledge which historical science claims to give us.

This distinction between two kinds of philosophy of history is sometimes used to support the claim that Dilthey is to be regarded as a philosopher of history. Proponents of this approach argue that while Dilthey rejected speculative philosophy of history, he himself wrote critical philosophy of history, although he did not call it by this name. This conception of Dilthey is not entirely without foundation, but it is misleading and inaccurate nevertheless. Although much of what Dilthey wrote about history focuses on historical *knowledge* and therefore might be called 'critical philosophy of history,' he never abandoned his concern with historical *reality* and the historical process itself. To sum up Dilthey's work as a 'critical philosophy of history' is to overlook a great deal of it.

The tendency to regard Dilthey as a 'critical philosopher of history' has been bolstered somewhat by his use of the phrase 'critique of historical reason': Raymond Aron, for example, has written a book entitled *La philoso-*

phie critique de l'histoire which includes a long chapter on Dilthey under the title 'La critique de la raison historique.'[14] On this interpretation of Dilthey, the terms 'critique' and 'critical' derive their force from Kant, and Dilthey is then to be read as a latter-day Kantian. The 'critical' intent is accordingly regarded as the unifying element in Dilthey's work. H.A. Hodges, writing in this vein, declares: 'The philosophical work of Wilhelm Dilthey all hinges on his attempt to write a *Kritik der historischen Vernunft.*'[15] But this view of Dilthey is also mistaken, for at least two important reasons.

First, although Dilthey used the term 'critique of historical reason' in his writings a number of times over a period of decades, he did not attach any one fixed meaning to it. In 1859, when he was still strongly under Kant's influence, he spoke in a diary entry of a 'new critique of reason' (*Der junge Dilthey*, 80). As Aron suggests, Dilthey's early conception of a critique of historical reason could better be called a historical critique of reason.[16] Over the years, however, Dilthey came to identify the phrase 'critique of historical reason' with the goals of his *Einleitung in die Geisteswissenschaften*[17] – although he refrained from using the phrase as the title of the book, which is a significant fact that should not be forgotten in this context. In the *Einleitung* itself, the phrase is identified with the task of providing an epistemological foundation for the *Geisteswissenschaften*, and 'historical reason' is equated with the 'capacity (*Vermögen*) of man to know himself and to know the society and history which he has created' (p. 116). Dilthey later realized that his early hopes with regard to history and the *Geisteswissenschaften* had been somewhat too grandiose: 'Only visionaries (*Phantasten*) dream of laying a new foundation for historical science,' he wrote.[18] The phrase 'critique of historical reason' was therefore redefined in more general terms. In 1903 Dilthey declared: 'I undertook to investigate the nature of and condition for historical consciousness – a critique of historical reason.'[19] In another passage in the writings of his later period he again emphasized the parallel between his own 'critique' and Kant's critique, although he admitted that the task still awaited completion.[20] That Dilthey made regular use of the phrase 'critique of historical reason' is understandable, for it is indeed a striking phrase. The important point that we must take note of is that he failed to give this phrase the univocal meaning that would justify our using it as a summary characterization of his work.*

The second reason why Dilthey's work cannot be summed up as a 'critique of historical reason' is that this characterization would place too much

---

* Even Hodges, who emphasizes the parallels between Dilthey and Kant, is eventually forced to admit that what Dilthey meant by a 'critique of historical reason' is simply a critique of the *Geisteswissenschaften* (see *The Philosophy of Wilhelm Dilthey*, 341).

emphasis on his affinities with Kant.[21] The question of Dilthey and Kant is complicated by Kant's enormous stature and influence in the world of German philosophy, which meant, among other things, that Kant could not be repudiated outright. But a repudiation of Kant would not have been Dilthey's intention at the outset of his career. He himself called for a return to Kant, and he testified willingly to Kant's influence on his thinking early in his life.[22] But as the years went by and Dilthey's own thinking developed, the gap between them grew, as a point by point comparison would demonstrate.[23] The fundamental Kantian notion of a formal a priori element in our knowledge was simply rejected by Dilthey. The *differences* between Dilthey and Kant are far more important than the similarities. Only if the term 'Kantian' is emptied of most of its meaning can it be applied to Dilthey.[24] It might even be argued that Dilthey can better be regarded as the *Bacon* of the *Geisteswissenschaften* than as a second Kant.[25]

This discussion has left us without a tidy formula for summing up Dilthey's philosophical labours – or even his observations on history. He was not simply a 'philosopher of history' or a 'critical philosopher of history,' and he did not seriously attempt to write a 'critique of historical reason' that would complete the work left undone by Kant. If we need a phrase to characterize Dilthey as a historical thinker, it would be best to call him simply a 'theorist of history.' This somewhat vague, colourless term has the advantage of not identifying Dilthey with any tradition to which he does not belong. And since it leaves the term 'history' ambiguous, it does not restrict the scope of his reflections to historical knowledge or to the historical process. Dilthey was intensely interested in both of these, and in the historical character of human existence as well.

MEANING IN HISTORY

The well-entrenched distinction between critical and speculative philosophy of history is also dangerous in one other respect. Proponents of this distinction usually maintain that the critical philosopher of history concerns himself with the process of establishing what the facts are, whereas the speculative philosopher of history is interested primarily in an interpretation of the whole or in the 'meaning of history.' If Dilthey were regarded as a critical philosopher of history, we would then have to conclude that he did not concern himself with the question of 'meaning' in history, but limited his interest and attention to historical knowledge or science.

I have already argued that to characterize Dilthey as a critical philosopher of history is to fail to do justice to his thought. I now propose to pursue this matter further, this time in relation to the venerable problem of meaning in history. (I do not believe that a hard and fast distinction can be made between 'the meaning of history' and 'meaning in history,' but I will use the latter, somewhat broader phrase, since it is more in line with Dilthey's own thinking.) This will require distinguishing some different senses in which history can be said to have (a) meaning.

Those who insist on regarding Dilthey simply as an epistemologist of historical knowledge might conceivably appeal to certain passages in the *Einleitung* of 1883 in support of their contention that he rejected the question of 'meaning' in history. There we read: 'There is no more a ... final and simple word of history that expresses its true meaning than nature has such a word to reveal,' and also that '... every formula in which we express the meaning of history is only a reflex of our own animated inwardness ...'[26] These declarations, of course, form part of Dilthey's argument against 'philosophy of history,' and thus he never took them back. But in the major work written during the last years of his life, *Der Aufbau der geschichtlichen Welt in den Geisteswissenschaften* (1910), as well as in its unfinished continuation, Dilthey spoke repeatedly of 'meaning' in history. More specifically, he spoke of the 'meaning of history grounded in life itself' (*Aufbau*, 170) and of the 'manifest meaning of history' (p. 172). The historical world is fully pervaded by meaning: 'Wherever life enters the past and comes to be understood, there is history. And where history is, there is meaning in its manifold character' (*Fortsetzung*, 255). Meaning is closely bound up with 'understanding': 'That which cannot be understood cannot have meaning or value. A tree can never have a meaning' (p. 259). Thus, far from ignoring meaning, Dilthey devotes a good deal of attention to it.

We turn now to the different senses in which one could speak of 'meaning' in history. Because of the ambiguity of the term 'history,' the first distinction to be made is between meaning in the historical process and the meaning of historical knowledge. The question of meaning in history is often blurred or confused by the failure to distinguish clearly between these two. I shall begin by considering meaning in the historical process and the historical world.

We could speak first of history as having a 'transcendent meaning.' This is the classic view of history which has been upheld by many of the thinkers usually labelled speculative philosophers of history, and it is also the traditional Christian view. In his book *Christ the Meaning of History*, the theologian Hendrikus Berkhof writes: 'We understand "meaning" in the sense of "goal" and of the movement toward it' (p. 17). God is working behind the scenes in the drama of history, and it is his plan for mankind that determines its course – history is 'Heilsgeschichte.' To say that history has a meaning is simply to say that it is moving towards a goal predetermined by God and that it is helped along by God. The meaning of human historical actions is then assessed in relation to God's redemptive plan. Dilthey, who made no pretence of being a Christian,* rejected this kind of philosophy of history together with its notion of meaning in history.

It has been argued that much modern philosophy of history is a secularized form of the Christian philosophy of history. Thus, corresponding to the transcendent conception of the meaning of history is an immanent conception. W.H. Walsh describes the traditional philosophy of history of the eighteenth and nineteenth centuries as follows: 'Its aim was to attain an understanding of the course of history as a whole; to show that, despite the many anomalies and inconsequences it presented, history could be regarded as forming a unity embodying an overall plan, a plan which, if once we grasped it, would both illuminate the detailed course of events and enable us to view the historical process as, in a special sense, satisfactory to reason.'[27] In other words, human history forms a unified whole, and its meaning must be understood as a total movement in the direction of a particular goal, whether it be the classless society or the ultimate triumph of reason. The goal is predetermined and its eventual realization inevitable. But this notion of meaning in history was also rejected by Dilthey, who could not bring himself to believe in historical inevitability.

Nevertheless, although historical progress thought of as absolute and irreversible strained Dilthey's credibility, he did believe in progress in a relative sense. Patterns manifest themselves in history, and trends that are not immediately apparent can be discerned. In a passage reminiscent of Hegel's 'cunning of reason,' Dilthey declared:

States and sovereigns pursue their goals. In this they are limited by the horizon of their times. They act for themselves, and not for the whole or for history. But the meaning of what they do within the context of history first becomes visible to later

---

* Although Dilthey allowed Christianity an important place in the history of the Western mind, he himself abandoned the faith of his childhood after his father's death in 1867. His letters to his father reveal something of the struggle that went on within him. In a letter of 1860, he spoke of 'my complete and passionate love for genuine Christianity' (*Der junge Dilthey*, 128; see also 23, 144, 152). Although he was first a student of theology, it was not long before he wanted to switch to philosophy. The problem was how to justify this switch to his father (see *Briefe an Scholz*, 457). In 1891, when both of his parents were dead, he wrote to Count Yorck, who was a devout Lutheran: 'I am no Christian in any specific sense, as you know ...' (*Briefwechsel*, 125).

ages; it goes far beyond the goals that they had set for themselves. There is nothing mystical about this; we do not need to bring in Providence here, any more than a goal which history itself pursues. In the more encompassing context of the advance of time, we are able to see the effects of purposive actions in such a way that they then appear as parts of a context which may perhaps later enter into an even more encompassing context. What we see is always only a limited relation between historical parts and the whole formed by history up to the present.[28]

The historian focuses on trends and patterns in his study of history, and these become the great themes of written history. The theme which Dilthey himself emphasized as he wrote various chapters in his unfinished history of the Western mind was the realization of the autonomy or sovereignty of the human spirit. This autonomy reached its highest realization in philosophy. The 'worth of man,' he proclaimed, '... expresses itself as ethical law, as consciousness of right, as consciousness of freedom, and in philosophy it elevates itself to the conscious autonomy of the spirit.'[29] The autonomy of reason was one of the fundamental characteristics of the Enlightenment,[30] and Dilthey therefore defended this era against the attacks of the romantics. He shared the generally optimistic outlook of the Enlightenment, and thus he believed that this overriding historical trend would continue, although he did not rule out the possibility of decline.

We see, then, that Dilthey did believe in meaning in history in the limited sense of individual patterns or of a relative progress that might be reversed. Just as the historian could make use of 'themes' in writing the history of a nation or an epoch, the biographer could use them in tracing the movement of an individual life. (Dilthey regarded biography as an important historical science.) Indeed, a figure selected for biographical study would be chosen only if his life were dominated by such themes, i.e., by a movement towards goals and aims. Dilthey himself wrote a highly acclaimed intellectual biography of Schleiermacher, in which he tells us that Schleiermacher's lifework was 'to reconcile religion with the freedom of science and the beauty of life' (XIII–1, 32).

Up to this point we have spoken of meaning in history as the meaning of overall or partial trends and courses of events. But on most occasions when Dilthey speaks of meaning in the historical world, this is not what he has in mind. The basic and all-pervasive meaning of which he speaks again and again is a 'significance inherent in life itself.'[31] For Dilthey, something does not acquire meaning only because of its place in a larger whole or process of development. 'Every life has a meaning of its own,' he declared (*Fortsetzung*, 199). The historical world is full of meaning because it is full of expressions of the spirit, of external manifestations of life. 'Every expression of life has a meaning insofar as it expresses something as a sign, insofar as it, as an expression, points to something related to life. Life itself does not mean anything else.'* Meaning in the historical world is not only a movement from whole to part but also a movement from part to whole: 'Like the letters of a word, life and history have a meaning' (*Fortsetzung*, 291).

We have established, then, that Dilthey regards the historical process and the historical world as pervaded by meaning or significance. Now we turn to historical knowledge or science. Does the quest for historical knowledge have any 'meaning'? Or is history perhaps 'bunk,' as Henry Ford maintained? The much disputed question whether the study of the past is a waste of time first needs closer definition. If such study is to be anything more than a hobby pursued only by the curious, it must be useful in some sense. One respect in which it might be useful is in teaching us 'lessons.' But the claim that we learn lessons from history is dubious, for the very development that is characteristic of the historical process often renders putative lessons obsolete. Perhaps the only lesson to be learned from history is that it is the realm of change and that we must therefore be exceedingly wary of any and all 'lessons' which it is alleged to teach us.

But the question whether historical knowledge or science is meaningful, whether there is any point in studying history, whether history has any value for us today, can also be approached from a different angle. One might argue that history teaches us about man and about life in a more general sense, that it shows us what man is capable of, that it provides access to past worlds and realms of experience that might otherwise remain forever outside our ken. This, in any event, was Dilthey's position on the question how historical knowledge is significant and important for us today. Central to human existence, in his view, is the life of the mind (understood not as a closed consciousness but as the focal point of our experience). A man's mind, according to Dilthey, is enriched not only by what he experiences directly but also by what he lives through at second hand, by what he re-experiences through the enjoyment of art works and the reading of narrative history. Man broadens

---

* *Fortsetzung*, 234. In Dilthey's philosophy of life, there is nothing more basic than life that could confer meaning on life. This is one of the points where Heinrich Rickert, his philosophical rival, differs sharply with him: 'We can never stop inquiring into the "meaning" of our life,' Rickert writes, and then adds: '... and this meaning can be ascertained only on the basis of values that are valid' (*Die Philosophie des Lebens*, 169). He also writes: 'It remains a meaningless phrase that the *meaning* of life is life itself' (p. 130). Nevertheless, Rickert himself advocates a 'genuine philosophy of life' (pp. 106, 156; see also pp. x, xii, 171–95), although he admits that his own philosophy is really a 'philosophy of values' (*Die Probleme der Geschichtsphilosophie*, pp. vii–viii).

and enlarges his experience through art and history and thereby elevates his own existence. In other words, history helps to make us more complete persons by opening up certain possibilities that simply have not been developed in our own lives. Dilthey makes this clear in a lengthy and very revealing passage about the world of Martin Luther. Although Dilthey had been raised in a Reformed parsonage, he soon abandoned the Christian faith. He regarded himself as a manifestation of a post-metaphysical and post-Christian consciousness. Yet Christianity, as an important historical phenomenon, was still of great interest to him. In the passage on Luther, he writes:

The course of every person's life is a process of continuous determination in which the possibilities inherent in him are narrowed down. The crystallization of his nature always determines his further development ... But understanding lays open for him a wide range of possibilities that are not present in the determination of his actual life. For me as for most people today, the possibility of experiencing (*erleben*) religious states of mind in my personal existence is sharply circumscribed. However, when I go through the letters and writings of Luther, the accounts of his contemporaries, the records of the religious conferences and councils, and the reports of his official contacts, I encounter a religious phenomenon of such eruptive power, of such energy, in which the issue is one of life or death, that it lies beyond the experiential possibilities of a person of our time. But I can re-live (*nacherleben*) all of this ... And thereby this process opens up for us a religious world in Luther and in his contemporaries in the early Reformation that enlarges our horizon by including possibilities that are available to us only in this way. Thus man, who is determined from within, can experience many other existences in imagination. Although he is limited by his circumstances, foreign beauties of the world and regions of life that he could never reach himself are laid open to him. To put it in general terms, man, bound and determined by the reality of life, is made free not only by art – which has often been pointed out – but also by the understanding of things historical (*Fortsetzung*, 215–16).

The choice of Luther as an example is significant, for Dilthey was well aware of the vast differences in character and temperament between himself and the great German Reformer. Thereby he emphasized the importance and value of the process of (historical) understanding.

But historical knowledge was not valuable and meaningful to Dilthey only because of what it reveals about particular persons and epochs: 'The answer to all final questions about the value of history is ultimately that it is in history that man comes to know himself' (*Fortsetzung*, 250). Thus historical knowledge or science has an ultimately philosophical significance: it enables us to respond to the ancient imperative 'Know thyself.'

2

The Autonomy of the *Geisteswissenschaften*

Dilthey's defence of history as a legitimate and significant branch of scientific inquiry led him far afield. In time it drew him into the nineteenth-century debate about the two kinds of sciences. He defended the autonomy of the historical sciences vis-à-vis the natural sciences, but only as part of his general argument for the autonomy of the *Geisteswissenschaften* as a whole. Unless Dilthey was willing to see history and the *Geisteswissenschaften* conform closely to the natural sciences and their method (Buckle's approach), he would have to make a frontal assault on what Heinrich Rickert called 'methodological naturalism.' Since a surrender to natural science as criterion was out of the question for Dilthey, much of his earlier work was devoted to drawing the boundaries between the two kinds of sciences. To grasp Dilthey's approach to historical understanding, then, we must examine his views on the autonomy of the *Geisteswissenschaften*.

GENERALIZING AND INDIVIDUALIZING SCIENCES

Schopenhauer had argued that history singles out the individual and particular as its object and therefore cannot be a science, since science studies the universal and unchanging. The importance of this criticism is that it strikes at the very heart of nineteenth-century history in Germany. The rise and growth of the 'sense of the individual' is the central theme of Friedrich Meinecke's *Entstehung des Historismus*, which sketches the background of nineteenth-century German historical thinking. To Meinecke, proper history was inconceivable without a loving concern for and interest in the singular, the unique, the individual, and it was Goethe's preoccupation with the individual, both in nature and in the historical world, that won him such a prominent place in this book.

Dilthey shared Meinecke's belief in the importance of the individual or of 'individuality' – to use the term which they both favoured – in the historical sciences. He quoted Wilhelm von Humboldt's statement that the mystery of all being is to be sought in individuality (*Ideen*, 227), and he himself wrote: 'The mystery of the world, expressed in positive terms, is individuality.'[1] Thus the significance of individuality is not restricted to the realm of history or the *Geisteswissenschaften*. Yet Dilthey did affirm that it is in history that the unique (*Einmalige*) and the singular have a special place. Grasping the unique is not a means to an end but the end itself, he maintained, '... for the need on which it rests is ineradicable and is given with that which is highest in our nature. Consequently, the historian's focus is fixed with a natural preference on the extraordinary' (*Einleitung*, 91). The task, therefore, was to overthrow the narrow, natural scientific ideal of science and to show that a science of the individual is possible. Dilthey was not alone in this conviction. Prominent among the various nineteenth-century thinkers who wrestled with this problem was the historian of philosophy Wilhelm Windelband.

In 'Geschichte und Naturwissenschaft,' his famous rectoral address delivered at the University of Strasbourg in 1894, Windelband proposed a new division of the experiential sciences. He mentioned the challenges of Schopenhauer and of the 'so-called philosophy of history of positivism' (*Präludien*, II, 154–5), and he proposed to meet them by dividing the sciences on the basis of modes of knowledge (*Erkenntnisweisen*) rather than on the basis of subject-matter. Thus he rejected the division into natural sciences and *Geisteswissenschaften*, arguing that the basic types of sciences can better be delimited on the basis of their differing methods. The real opposition is not between nature and 'Geist' but between laws and events.

Thus we may say that the experiential sciences seek in the knowledge of reality either the general, in the form of laws of nature, or the particular, in the historically determined formation; some of these sciences observe the forms that always remain the same, and others observe the unique content of actual occurrence as determined in itself. The former are sciences of laws, and the latter are sciences of events; the former teach what always is, the latter what once was. If we may be permitted to coin new artificial terms, scientific thought is *nomothetic* in the former case and *idiographic* in the latter. If we confine ourselves to the accustomed terminology, we could speak further in this sense of the opposition between natural scientific disciplines and historical disciplines ... (p. 145).

Although Windelband had spoken of history as a 'science of events,' it was the idea of history as an 'idiographic science' that was uppermost in his mind: the final goal of history is '... to work out the true shape of the past in living clarity on the basis of the mass of material ...' (p. 151). Historical science, in short, is a depiction of individual and unique reality.

Windelband's conception of historical science was expanded and refined by his protégé Heinrich Rickert. The latter also rejected the division into natural sciences and *Geisteswissenschaften* as proposed by Dilthey. One of the defects of this division is the place it awards to psychology, which is really a natural science, according to Windelband and Rickert. Like Windelband, Rickert proposed only to divide the empirical sciences; his remarks have no bearing on mathematics or any other formal or a priori science.

Reality as such does not offer any basis for a division into two types of sciences, according to Rickert. 'In reality there are ... only individual objects and no general objects at all; there is only the unique and nothing that really repeats itself.'[2] The element of universality or generality is introduced by the scientist by means of concepts, which are used in all empirical sciences. The primary principle of division is between two methods: generalizing and individualizing. (Rickert declined to use Windelband's terms 'nomothetic' and 'idiographic' on the grounds that the latter term tends to make us overlook the use of concepts in historical science, thereby furthering the confusion between art and history.)[3] Reality can be grasped by either of these two basic methods, the two basic 'Wirklichkeitsauffassungen': '... any object whatever can be grasped in a generalizing way or in an individualizing way ...'[4] Thus the reality with which the historian deals is not purely cultural or purely mental or purely physical; Rickert characterizes it as 'psycho-physical.' Nevertheless, it is possible to distinguish between nature and history, but only in relation to a knowing subject: empirical reality '... becomes nature when we look at it in relation to what is general, and it becomes history when we look at it in relation to what is particular and individual.'[5] History, in short, is '*unique occurrence* (*einmaliges Geschehen*) in its particularity and individuality,'[6] while nature is 'mental-physical *total-reality* conceived of in a value-indifferent and generalizing way.'[7]

In addition to this formal principle for dividing the sciences, Rickert also proposed a secondary, material division, that is, a division on the basis of subject-matter or content. He distinguished formally between natural scientific and historical methods and materially between nature and culture. The realm of culture is the realm of meaning, and meaning is in turn derived from relation to values. Thus *value* is a fundamental concept in Rickert's conception of historical knowledge. He characterizes the realm of values by means of the contrast between reality and validity: 'In the case of values, which we examine in and for themselves, we cannot ask whether they are *real* (*wirklich*) but only whether they are *valid* (*ob sie gelten*).'[8] To clarify this statement, we must point to Rickert's key distinction between practical valuation (*Wertung*) and theoretical relation to values (*Wertbeziehung*). The person involved in theorizing or science takes a different stance or attitude towards reality than the person engaged in praxis; although the work of the former may involve relating objects and events to values, it always remains value-free, that is, it requires no valuation. Hence Rickert affirms: 'There is *no* science which, *as science*, tells man what he *ought* to want or do.'[9] More specifically, '... history is *not a valuational* science but a *value-relating* science.'[10] This means that '... values are taken into consideration in history only insofar as they are *in fact* affirmed by subjects, thus insofar as certain objects are *in fact* characterized as good.'[11] History only tells us what is, and this, of course, includes what values have been affirmed and are valid – at least for some.

The values which guide the historian in selecting his material and in deciding on the importance of objects and events are called 'general cultural values.' These values – and not the values that the historian as a person happens to affirm – are determinative in historical research; it is on the basis of these values that the historian determines what is essential and what is irrelevant.

The introduction of the question of values really amounts to a second division of the sciences, a division between value-indifferent natural sciences and value-related cultural sciences. This division does not coincide completely with the division between generalizing and individualizing sciences, for both the natural sciences and the cultural sciences can and do make use of both of these methods. Thus Rickert admits that he has really developed a four-way division of the sciences.[12] The value-indifferent natural sciences include physics as a generalizing science and geology as an individualizing science. And within the value-related cultural sciences we could distinguish between generalizing sciences (e.g., sociology and economics) and individualizing sciences (i.e., the historical sciences). The proper definition of the historical sciences, then, is 'individualizing cultural sciences.' Their goal is the representation of the individual and unique within the sphere of culture, not in the sense of copying (*Abbilden*) but in the sense of reconstruction (*Umbilden*).[13]

Rickert's bold logic of historical science, which meets Schopenhauer's challenge by rejecting the Greek tradition of *epistémé* or science as knowledge of the universal,* was based in large part on an appeal to what historians

---

* Rickert declared: 'For a logic that seeks not to control the sciences but to understand them, there can be no doubt that Aristotle's view, which all of modern logic and even some historians have accepted, namely, that the concepts used by science have no place

in fact do as they go about their work. And it seems undeniable that something like Rickert's 'relation to values' is an essential part of the historian's procedure. But his ideas won little acceptance in philosophical circles; Raymond Aron, writing shortly after Rickert's death, pronounced his thought dead.[14]

DILTHEY ON THE TWO KINDS OF SCIENCES

The declaration of independence issued by Dilthey on behalf of the *Geisteswissenschaften* must not be understood as an attack on the natural sciences, for Dilthey held these sciences in high regard and was well aware of the important role they have played in human life.[15] Yet he had little firsthand knowledge of the natural sciences,[16] and his observations about them do not manifest a profound understanding of them. The important point, however, is that he did not harbour the hostility to these sciences that one sometimes encounters in twentieth-century philosophers.

As we have already noted, Dilthey's interest was focused on the body of sciences that he came to call the 'Geisteswissenschaften.' There is some evidence that he contemplated a formal or critical approach to these sciences early in his career, when he proposed a division between 'sciences of the external world' and 'sciences of *Geist*.'[17] (This rather obvious division – in that era, at least – may well have been inspired by Hegel's *Encyclopaedia*.) But by the time he wrote the *Einleitung*, Dilthey seems to have abandoned this approach. In the preface to this work he expressed his desire to provide a philosophical foundation for what the historical school had achieved,[18] but apparently such a grounding did not require a reformation of these sciences. Their unity and the interrelations between them were not to be established in any a priori manner by a philosopher; they were rather the result of a gradual formative process. In the 1875 essay Dilthey was not yet certain whether these sciences could or did form a system,[19] but he had resolved this question in the affirmative by 1883 when the *Einleitung* was published. Comparing these sciences to the system formed by the natural sciences, he declared: '... their internal coherence (*Zusammenhang*) has developed in a different way and must now be examined in the form which it has assumed through its historical growth' (p. 24). Paying attention to the historical origin and growth of these sciences meant emphasizing their ultimately practical intent: science, for Dilthey, does and should serve life. Thus he denounced

---

for anything *special* and *individual*, is completely false' (*Kulturwissenschaft und Naturwissenschaft*, 54). On Schopenhauer, see *Kulturwissenschaft*, 55n; *Die Grenzen der naturwissenschaftlichen Begriffsbildung*, 2, 188, 221.

'the false separation of the theoretical sciences and the practical sciences' (p. 225), and later he declared that the goal of the *Geisteswissenschaften* is not only knowledge but 'the guidance of individual and historical life' (*Individualität*, 251). In short, the Dilthey of the *Einleitung* accepted the sciences as they are, that is, as they have grown up in response to human needs. Commenting on the *Einleitung* some decades later, he observed: 'It was based on the fact of the *Geisteswissenschaften*, particularly as this fact lay before us in the form of the internal coherence (*Zusammenhang*) of these sciences created by the historical school, and it attempted to lay an epistemological foundation for these sciences' (*Aufbau*, 117).

Dilthey's uncritical acceptance of the *Geisteswissenschaften* in the *Einleitung* accounts for the largely descriptive character of this unfinished work. No one clear solution to the problem of the delimitation of the *Geisteswissenschaften* emerges, although a number of interesting points and suggestions are made, many of them reflecting the actual differences between the two bodies of sciences in his time. Dilthey did not limit the *Geisteswissenschaften* to any one goal, such as studying the individual and unique. These sciences do have a particular interest in the singular and unique, but they also note similarities and regularities. Ultimately, they lead to rules and value judgments (see *Einleitung*, 26–7). The *Geisteswissenschaften* are somehow based on the natural sciences, or on the facts of the natural sciences: 'Facts of the mental realm form the upper boundary of facts of nature, and the latter represent the lower conditions for the life of the mind' (p. 17). This would seem to suggest a hierarchy of the sciences *à la* Comte, but as early as 1875 Dilthey had firmly rejected Comte's hierarchy of the sciences and the place it gives to the sciences of man.[20]

A careful reading which takes the continuity of Dilthey's thought into account forces us to the conclusion that he thought in terms of a basic split between the two kinds of sciences rather than of a hierarchy including all the sciences. Such a conception of the sciences requires a basis for making a clear distinction between the two types of sciences. At least three different ways of making such a distinction have been suggested. First, it could be argued that the natural sciences and the *Geisteswissenschaften* differ in subject-matter or content: the former deal with nature, and the latter with culture or the realm of the mind. Second, it could be maintained that the two kinds of sciences are based on different modes of experience or knowledge or perception. Finally, the difference between them might only result from the attitude or approach of the cognitive subject. As we have seen, Rickert relied mainly on the third of these possibilities: the historical sciences are individualizing sciences, while the natural sciences use a generalizing method.

He made a further distinction between the subject-matter of the two types of sciences, but the latter distinction was also rooted in the attitude of the cognitive subject: one and the same object, he admitted, could be viewed in relation to values (the cultural scientific standpoint) or in isolation from them (the natural scientific standpoint).

In the *Einleitung*, Dilthey focused on subject-matter as fundamental to making the distinction between the two kinds of sciences: 'mental facts' (*geistige Tatsachen*), i.e., facts about the mental realm, form the reality which the *Geisteswissenschaften* seek to comprehend (p. 5). This term, unfortunately, is somewhat ambiguous, for mental facts in another sense (i.e., as facts of consciousness) form the material on which all the sciences are based – all science is 'experiential science' (*Erfahrungswissenschaft*, p. xvii) and must take the 'facts of consciousness' as point of departure. It is characteristic of science that it abstracts parts of reality for closer examination: 'Theory is always analysis and abstraction,' Dilthey declared.[21] Science focuses on 'partial contents' (*Teilinhalte*), that is, on parts that together make up a fuller reality than any one science can grasp.[22] The *Einleitung*, we learn from the subtitle, is an attempt to provide a foundation for the study of society and history, and the sciences which it 'introduces' restrict themselves to this double sphere. 'Each individual science is constituted only by the device of isolating a partial content of historical-social reality' (*Einleitung*, 27–8). Although there are only individual *Geisteswissenschaften*, this double sphere which Dilthey calls social-historical reality is what defines and delimits these sciences as a group.

However, this way of drawing the distinction between the two kinds of sciences leaves some difficult questions unanswered. The natural sciences, one might object, also study the objects and events that make up the social-historical world. Are we then to conclude that the natural sciences do or can study all of reality, while the *Geisteswissenschaften* limit themselves to the social and historical? In that case, the distinction would collapse, for the *Geisteswissenschaften* would then form a sub-division (parallel to the biological sciences, for example) under the general heading of natural science. If the *Geisteswissenschaften* are to be limited in subject-matter, the natural sciences must somehow be similarly restricted. But Dilthey apparently did not know how to formulate such a restriction.

The inadequacy of this solution on the basis of subject-matter soon led Dilthey to search for another solution, which could either supplement or replace the first one. Unlike Windelband and Rickert, he did not try to account for the differences between the two kinds of sciences on the basis of the attitude or approach of the cognitive subject. He turned instead to the idea of two kinds of experience as the basis for the two kinds of sciences. This revised conception already came to expression in the *Einleitung*, but the idea of dividing the sciences on the basis of their subject-matter succeeded in maintaining the upper hand. It was only in the two psychological treatises of the 1890s (*Ideen* and *Individualität*) that the new conception became dominant.

In these treatises Dilthey again affirmed the interest of the *Geisteswissenschaften* in the singular and unique,[23] but he still remained far from the views of Windelband and Rickert,[24] as the latter carefully pointed out. Dilthey now declared psychology to be the basis of the *Geisteswissenschaften*, whereas his two neo-Kantian rivals maintained that psychology is one of the natural sciences. Psychology is fundamental for Dilthey because the difference between the two types of sciences is rooted in a difference within the realm of experience; more specifically, it is rooted in two different modes of givenness, i.e., *inner* and *outer experience*. Corresponding to these two types of experience are two types of perception: inner and outer. This is a difficult doctrine, because Dilthey was not entirely consistent in his use of these terms, and also because he sometimes used other terms to refer to this difference within the realm of experience.

By 'outer perception' Dilthey usually means sensory perception. Inner perception is what many traditional philosophers have called 'apperception' (a term that Dilthey himself did not use in this context);[25] it is an awareness of a mental content. The contents of which we are aware in inner perception or inner experience, to use the more embracing term,[26] are ultimately derived from outer perception, although they may appear in inner experience as remembered, as imagined, or in some other mode of consciousness. Inner experience includes not only presentation but also desire and feeling. In short, inner perception is a reflective awareness of sensations first given in outer perception. Out of this material, the rich world of inner experience is built up.

The question that suggests itself at this point is: what is the relation between inner experience and what Dilthey calls 'Erlebnis'? Is the contrast between inner and outer experience perhaps the contrast between 'Erlebnis' and 'Erfahrung'? The answer to this question is again complicated by Dilthey's failure to stick to a consistent terminology. In his earlier writings he often used 'Erlebnis' and 'Erfahrung' synonymously,[27] as many German writers do. But as the word 'Erlebnis' grew in his favour, in part because of its roots in the word 'life' (*Leben*), he began to use it in a more restricted way. Soon we find him using it in a way that suggests a contrast between 'Erleben,' which involves the entire mind, and mere sensory awareness.* For Dilthey, an 'Erlebnis' in the strict sense always involves the subject or self in a way that a mere sensation does not. The 'Erlebnis' is both objective and subjective, and therefore it cannot be regarded as a mere mental content but must be seen instead as a unity of the content and its apprehension: 'In the *Erlebnis*, the awareness and the content of which I am aware are one.'[28] Thus we may take it that 'Erleben' and inner experience are the same thing.[†] This helps to explain why the latter term does not appear as often as one might expect in the later writings.

There is a difference, then, between inner experience or 'Erleben' and outer experience. This difference becomes the foundation for the distinction between the two kinds of sciences. Dilthey writes:

Thus our knowledge of the mental realm is everywhere directly or indirectly grounded in inner experience. Naturally, the validity of this distinction between a physical fact and a mental (*geistig*) fact, which presents itself in experience, is in no way affected by the fact that these two systems of contents are to be met with in the same object, i.e., man, just as the distinction between mathematics and chemistry is in no way affected by the fact that the systems of contents developed in these two sciences are contained in the same natural substances. Man is no more split by the separate development of the two former systems of contents than natural substances are split by the separation between the mathematical, physical and chemical sciences (*Individualität*, 254).

Here the significance of 'Erleben' for the *Geisteswissenschaften* begins to emerge, as does the doctrine of 'understanding,' which at this stage represents the apprehending of an 'Erlebnis.' The opposition between explanation and understanding is rooted in the two modes of experience proper to the two kinds of sciences.

---

* 'In the lived experience (*Erlebnis*), *all* the *mental* processes work together. Coherence is given in the lived experience itself, while the senses only give us a multiplicity of particulars' (*Ideen*, 172; see also *Weltanschauung*, 117).

† These two terms are used synonymously in *Einleitung*, 136. In an essay of 1871, Dilthey speaks of Schleiermacher as 'the profound investigator of inner *Erfahrung*' ('Zum Andenken an Friedrich Ueberweg,' xv, 157). If he had written this essay 20 or 30 years later, he would no doubt have substituted the word 'Erlebnis': compare the language he uses in his remarks on Schleiermacher in the unfinished essay of 1911 on the problem of religion (vi, 295ff). He also writes: 'Inner experience (*Erfahrung*) and understanding are two basic processes in which the world of the spirit and history is given' ('Uebersicht meines Systems,' viii, 183). See also Dilthey's use of the term 'inner experience' in *Aufbau*, Zusätze, vii, 326.

Now the *Geisteswissenschaften* are distinguished from the natural sciences first of all by the fact that the latter have as their object facts that enter consciousness from without, as phenomena, and as given singly, whereas the facts of the former sciences enter consciousness in an originary way from within, as a reality and as a living coherence (*Zusammenhang*). From this it follows that the coherence of nature presented by the natural sciences is achieved only through inferences that add to the given by way of a combination of hypotheses. For the *Geisteswissenschaften*, by contrast, it follows that the coherence of mental life, as something originally given, is everywhere their basis. We explain nature, but we understand mental life (*Ideen*, 143–4).

The opposition between explanation and understanding is further explicated by Dilthey as follows: 'We explain by means of purely intellectual processes, but we understand through the co-operation of all of our mental powers (*Gemütskräfte*) in apprehension' (p. 172). That the co-operation of all the mental powers is necessary for the cognitive operations on which the *Geisteswissenschaften* rest is a constant theme in Dilthey. In the *Einleitung* he had written: 'The power (*Vermögen*) of apprehension operative in the *Geisteswissenschaften* is the whole man ...' (p. 38).

This difference between the two types of sciences also leads to different kinds of results. As Dilthey was well aware, science cannot remain content with grasping individual facts, objects, and events; it must seek structures, connections, and interrelations. At one point he declared that all science is causal knowledge,[29] but it is clear from the context that he was using the term 'causal' in a weak sense, that is, as meaning connection and condition. Both types of sciences are interested in causes in this weak sense, but they arrive at them by different means. In the natural sciences, 'explanation' and 'construction' are necessary to arrive at connections and structures. Dilthey explained:

We know natural objects from without, via the senses. However much we may break them up or divide them, we do not thereby arrive at their ultimate constituents. Such elements are added in thought, in a supplementing of experience. Nor do the senses – looking at their work in a purely physiological way – ever give us the unity of the object. This unity, too, exists for us only by virtue of a synthesis of sensory stimuli which takes place within us (*Ideen*, 169).

To account for the givens of outer experience, we must posit unities and connections, and thereby we arrive at the structure and 'Zusammenhang'*

---

* This always difficult German term, which seems to have been Dilthey's favourite word, has a bewildering variety of meanings in his writings: context, connection, interrelation, interdependence, coherence, structure, system, and so forth. Since it has no English equivalent, it will be left untranslated in some contexts below.

of the natural world. Natural science requires 'hypotheses' and 'supplement-ing inferences' (*ergänzende Schlüsse*). In the *Geisteswissenschaften*, however, structures and connections are immediately given, for inner experience is pervaded by coherence and interconnectedness. Nature is the 'appearance and garment of something beyond comprehension,'[30] but mental life (*Seelen-leben*) is exactly what it appears to be. It is not the less real manifestation of something more real.

What the fundamental distinction between psychological knowledge and knowledge of nature consists in is that internal coherence (*Zusammenhang*) is given in a primary way in mental life, and this is also the first and fundamental distinguishing feature of the *Geisteswissenschaften*. Because there is only coexistence and succession in the realm of outer appearance, the thought of an internal coherence (*Zusammenhang*) could not arise if it were not given in our own inwardly cohering unity (*zusammen-hängende Einheitlichkeit*).[31]

The conclusion of this train of thought is that the opposition between the physical and the mental (*Geistige*) falls within perception itself, as Dilthey put it in a discussion of Schleiermacher.[32] This represents his final view on the difference between the two kinds of sciences; in the *Aufbau* (1910), we find him simply repeating a statement on this question from one of the psychological treatises.[33] Although his thinking on the historical sciences underwent some fundamental changes during the last decade of his life, he did not devote much further attention to the question of the relation be-tween the two kinds of sciences, probably because the point had been largely conceded by then. (The labours of Windelband and Rickert no doubt contri-buted to this in large measure.) If Dilthey had given this problem a fresh treatment during the post-1900 years, he might well have been forced to formulate a new solution.

The opposition between the methods of the two kinds of sciences, as understood by Dilthey, can best be summed up in the terms 'explanation' and 'description.' Dilthey complained that the psychology of his day, which was oriented towards the natural sciences, was explanatory and constructive. He proposed to replace it with a descriptive and analytical psychology, which would then serve as the foundation for the individual *Geisteswissenschaften*. We have already noted Dilthey's contrast between explanation and under-standing. Thus, if understanding is viewed as fundamental to the method of the *Geisteswissenschaften*, it must focus on inner experience or 'Erleben'; more specifically, it must apprehend the structures and connections immedi-ately given in inner experience, thereby preparing the way for the various descriptive sciences. Dilthey continued to speak this language during the post-1900 years: the realm of the *Geisteswissenschaften* was the realm of 'Erleben' and understanding,[34] but these two were then linked by an intermediary, i.e., expression.

INDIVIDUALITY IN THE 'GEISTESWISSENSCHAFTEN'

Dilthey's preoccupation with what is individual, with individuality, places him squarely in the German historical tradition as sketched by Friedrich Meinecke in *Die Entstehung des Historismus*. Meinecke, who saw his own historical thinking as the culmination of this tradition, declared: 'Every individuality is a totality and is only understandable as such' (p. 299). As we shall see, Dilthey would agree with this statement – and with much of what Meinecke tried to establish in this study of the rise of the historicist outlook. Indeed, Dilthey's studies on the rise and growth of historical consciousness contributed a good deal to Meinecke's understanding of these matters, as the latter freely admitted.[35]

Dilthey's affinities with the historical school become much clearer when he is contrasted with Windelband and Rickert, who stand outside the historicist tradition as sketched and defined by Meinecke.* Windelband and Rickert were indeed concerned with the individual (in the sense of the unique), but their notion of individuality is not that of Meinecke and Dilthey. (This is one more reason why it is important not to lump Dilthey together with Windelband and Rickert as three representatives of one point of view.) The individuality in which the two neo-Kantians were interested is the result of an attitude or approach adopted by the cognitive subject; the historian, they maintained, examines the same realm (i.e., empirical reality) as the natural scientist, but he focuses his attention on the unique and singular, deliberately disregarding the general or common. Dilthey recognized no such distinction in attitude, although he did admit that the *Geisteswissenschaften* take a particular interest in uniqueness. An individuality, in Dilthey's view, is not constituted as an object for theoretical investigation by some scientist's focusing on certain aspects of reality and ignoring others; rather, it is given as something individual. Dilthey spoke of individuality as a 'riddle,'[36] and seemed to regard it as something ineffable. On the other hand, he did affirm

---

* Not only did Rickert attack historicism in general, he was especially contemptuous of the idea of historicism as a worldview (see *Die Probleme der Geschichtsphilosophie*, 12, 129–30, 132; *Die Grenzen der naturwissenschaftlichen Begriffsbildung*, 8, 697). Yet it was particularly the historicist general outlook or worldview that Meinecke valued so highly.

that the basic differences between individualities are quantitative rather than qualitative.[37] Thus he did not conceive of individuality as absolute uniqueness, for the individuality of an object or thing arises not from the parts or elements of which it is composed but rather from the arrangement and structure formed by the parts and elements. Unfortunately, Dilthey's statements on individuality do not form a harmonious whole, for he wrote no ontology in which apparent discrepancies would be resolved.

Throughout his entire career, Dilthey worked with the idea of 'individualities' as the subject-matter of the *Geisteswissenschaften*. This is one of the reasons for his abiding interest in Schleiermacher, who also devoted a good deal of attention to the notion of individuality. In his biography of Schleiermacher, he declared that the idea of individuality was the 'central point of Schleiermacher's inner life' (XIII–1, 382). Since Dilthey no doubt hoped to learn something from the historical figures whom he selected for study – he devoted the bulk of his attention to Schleiermacher and Hegel – it would be safe to assume that Schleiermacher interested him particularly because of this central doctrine. But there is a second reason for his long preoccupation with Schleiermacher, a preoccupation which accounts for four volumes of his *Gesammelte Schriften*, and it, too, is relevant to the question of individuality. As we have seen in Chapter 1, Dilthey believed that a philosopher who proposed to write a philosophy of the *Geisteswissenschaften* should first 'learn the trade' by engaging in the work of these sciences. If the *Geisteswissenschaften* focus on individualities as their subject-matter, Dilthey would then have to undertake a study of individualities. But the problem which the *Geisteswissenschaften* face is: what counts as an individuality and what does not? Dilthey was able to avoid this problem temporarily by choosing as the object of his research an undisputed individuality, i.e., the human being. In other words, he chose to gain firsthand experience in the *Geisteswissenschaften* by writing biography – hence his much acclaimed biography of Schleiermacher and also his many shorter biographical studies.

The individual human being, then, is the most basic and concrete individuality with which the *Geisteswissenschaften* deal. Biography, the 'presentation of the individual psycho-physical life-unity,' is therefore a very significant science: 'The position of biography within general historical science corresponds to that of anthropology within the theoretical sciences of historical-social reality' (*Einleitung*, 33). Because of the interaction between the human individual and the world in which he lives, the science of biography becomes a means of access to the larger structures, connections, and 'Zusammenhänge' that make up the social-historical world. Of his life of Schleiermacher Dilthey wrote: 'I now wanted to investigate how entirely scattered elements of culture are shaped in the workshop of an important individual mind of this sort into a whole that in turn has an effect upon life.'[38] Thus Dilthey's strong interest in biography is not the result of any conviction that history is the biography of great men or that the decisions and actions of great men are determinative in the historical process. The reason for it is rather that biography acquaints us with the most basic type of individuality: the human individual, Dilthey was convinced, is the 'fundamental fact' (*Urtatsache*) or 'basic unit' (*Grundkörper*) or 'primordial cell' (*Urzelle*) of history.[39]

The *Geisteswissenschaften*, which always focus on individualities as their subject-matter, can either generalize on the basis of an examination of a number of similar individualities or concentrate on a single individuality by probing its structure, analysing its components, and exploring its relations to other individualities. The cognitive operations basic to the *Geisteswissenschaften* are oriented towards individualities. Dilthey writes: 'Understanding always has something individual as its object' (*Fortsetzung*, 212). But he also tells us: 'We understand only *Zusammenhang*. *Zusammenhang* and understanding correspond to one another' (p. 257). This gives us a significant indication of what Dilthey means by 'individuality': only an object or event with a 'Zusammenhang,' with an inner coherence and structure, qualifies as an individuality and thus as an object of understanding. Not every part or element that can be abstracted in thought from the whole of reality is an individuality. Dilthey further elucidates the nature of the object of the *Geisteswissenschaften* when he says of these sciences: 'As far as they extend, we have to do with a totality, with *Zusammenhang*' (p. 203). The object of the *Geisteswissenschaften* is a totality not in that it is all-embracing but in that it is understandable – to a certain extent, at least – in itself; that is to say, it is a self-contained intelligible structure. The individualities on which the *Geisteswissenschaften* focus, then, are structures that qualify as totalities because they represent a certain completeness in themselves.

But Dilthey's conception of the social-historical world is not as monadic as this doctrine of individuality might suggest at first glance. Individualities conceived of as 'Zusammenhänge' enter into relations with one another and even become part of one another: Dilthey speaks of 'Einzelzusammenhänge' which form parts of larger, more comprehensive 'Zusammenhänge.' The self-contained individuality that forms the object of one *Geisteswissenschaft* may in turn form a subordinate part of the 'Zusammenhang' of a more embracing individuality studied by some other *Geisteswissenschaft*. In more concrete terms, man is studied not only by biography and anthropology but by the entire range of *Geisteswissenschaften*, from different points of view and in relation to different structures and coherences. To each *Geisteswissen-schaft* corresponds a type of individuality: 'Through a process of analysis and abstraction, the *individual Geisteswissenschaften* isolate *individual purposive Zusammenhänge* from human-historical reality' (*Individualität*, 273).

The methodological problem which the *Geisteswissenschaften* face is that of determining what counts as an individuality and thus as a possible object of theoretical investigation. This problem takes on as many particular forms as there are (possible) *Geisteswissenschaften*. I shall examine it here in relation to a kind of history that Dilthey himself loved to write, namely, intellectual history. The intellectual history of nineteenth-century Germany, for example, is not simply the sum of the intellectual biographies of all nineteenth-century German thinkers: it is about something more encompassing. But what is this more encompassing whole? Is science not limited to making statements about concrete individuals, e.g., human beings?

Historians before Dilthey had often handled this problem by speaking of the 'spirit' of a people or of an age (*Volksgeist, Volksseele, Zeitgeist*). One could then make general statements about the German people in the nineteenth century in such a way that what is true of the German 'Volksgeist' need not be true of every individual German thinker. An intellectual history of nineteenth-century Germany would focus on an individuality called 'the German mind.' Intellectual history, which need not include an exhaustive account of all intellectual activity, would then be first and foremost a history of the 'Zeitgeist' or 'Gemeingeist.'

The 'Volksgeist' and its associates have long been regarded with great suspicion by empirically minded historians. Dilthey himself, as an opponent of traditional metaphysics, was afraid that the use of such a concept would lead to a metaphysical hypostatization; he pointed out that the '... spirit of a people (*Volksseele*) lacks the unity of self-consciousness and of action that we express in the concept of mind (*Seele*)' (*Einleitung*, 31). Yet his own writings often included references to superindividual spirits or minds.[40] Like many another historian, he found it virtually impossible to do without this useful concept. Hence he tried to defend it by giving it a non-metaphysical definition: he spoke of 'the *unity* in a period and a people which we call the *historical spirit* of an age' (*Poetik*, 230). He also used the notion of a 'life-horizon' to give this concept a meaning:

In this sense we speak of the spirit of an age, of the middle ages or of the Enlightenment. This implies at the same time that each such epoch is bound by a *life-horizon*, by which I mean the limitation in which the people of an age live in relation to their thoughts, feelings and desires. Within this horizon there exists a relationship of life,

The autonomy of the *Geisteswissenschaften* 39

lived relations, personal experience, and the formation of thought which confines and binds the individual in a limited sphere of modifications of apprehension, formation of values, and setting of goals (*Aufbau*, 177–8).

But such definitions are of little help. Intellectual history requires an individuality in the sense of a structure and totality as its theoretical object, and Dilthey seemed unable to account for such an individuality. Thus, in practice he wrote the history of the German mind as a series of separate chapters on separate individuals.

The problem of the role of the superindividual spirit or mind in intellectual history serves only as an example here. Analogous objections could be raised about various other concepts used in the *Geisteswissenschaften*. But our particular concern in this study is historical science. The 'problem of history,' according to Dilthey, is the following: '... if one self is separate from other selves and there is only the operation of forces on one another, how can a subject that acts and is acted upon like a self arise from these individuals?' (*Fortsetzung*, 262). In other words, what is the relation of the basic, concrete individualities (i.e., human beings) to the more embracing wholes and totalities in which the *Geisteswissenschaften* are also interested? This, according to Raymond Aron, is the 'mystery' of history in Dilthey's eyes.[41] Therefore, Dilthey devoted his last major work to the structure and construction of the historical world which the *Geisteswissenschaften* study. (This work, like so many of his other projects, was never completed, although the first part was published.)

3

Beyond Psychology

It was not until Dilthey finally got psychology out of his system that he was able to develop a new and more fruitful conception of understanding and its significance for human life. The preoccupation with psychology at a certain stage in his career can easily be misunderstood: it did not mean a change in goals or orientation. Psychology was a rising discipline in his time, and it should not surprise us that Dilthey looked in its direction as he tried to devise a new method or approach. Yet the focus of his attention was still history and the *Geisteswissenschaften*.

'GEIST' AND THE 'GEISTESWISSENSCHAFTEN'

Dilthey's reflection on the *Geisteswissenschaften* can be properly understood only if we bear in mind that it is closely bound up with what he identified as his most basic philosophical concern – grasping 'life.' The governing impulse in his philosophy, he wrote near the end of his life, was the effort to understand life out of itself. He then added: 'I yearned to penetrate ever more deeply into the historical world in order to catch a glimpse of its soul, as it were, and the philosophical impulse to find the entryway to this reality, to ground the validity of this reality and to make our objective knowledge of it certain, this urge was to me only the other side of my desire to penetrate ever more deeply into the historical world.'[1] This desire to get at the very mind and experience of the past also pervaded Dilthey's vision of the historical sciences: 'We seek the mind (*Seele*); this is the final goal at which we have arrived after the long development of historiography' (*Fortsetzung*, 282).

The sciences of 'Geist,' of which history is one,[2] seek to penetrate to the realm of 'mental life' (*Seelenleben*), and they do so by way of 'Geist.' 'Everywhere in the realm of the spirit (*in allem Geistigen*) we find *Zusammen-*

hang ...', Dilthey declared (*Fortsetzung*, 195), thereby linking this realm of the spirit with understanding, for as we saw earlier (p. 37), we understand only 'Zusammenhang.' The question that must be raised at this juncture is that of the relation between mental life or the stream of human experience and the realm of 'Geist.' Dilthey's thinking on this point underwent an important change, as we shall see.

We should note first of all that Dilthey was reluctant to adopt the term 'Geisteswissenschaften.' It occurs in various forms in his earliest writings,[3] and it had been used by other thinkers before him,* but Dilthey himself still refused to endorse it in the 1875 essay, in which he spoke instead of 'sciences of man, society, history, and the state.' By 1883, however, he had overcome his hesitation about the term 'Geisteswissenschaften':

I join in the linguistic convention of those thinkers who speak of this other half of the *globus intellectualis* as the *Geisteswissenschaften*. This characterization has now become common and generally understood, and to this the wide distribution of John Stuart Mill's *Logic* has contributed more than a little. Thus, compared with all the other unsuitable names between which we must choose, it seems to be the least unsuitable.[4]

Dilthey here makes a celebrated error, which should give us some indication of what he meant at this point by the term 'Geisteswissenschaften.' Mill had used the term 'moral sciences' in his *Logic*, but the German translator had often rendered this term as 'Geisteswissenschaften.'† Thus Dilthey, who knew English, must have assumed that Mill had used some English term that could be regarded as a simple equivalent of 'Geisteswissenschaften,' probably 'mental sciences.'[5] In any event, Dilthey did regard the *Geisteswissenschaften* as sciences based on mental facts (*geistige Tatsachen*), and this

---

* On early uses of this term, see Erich Rothacker, *Logik und Systematik der Geisteswissenschaften*, 2–16. Hegel's followers had used the term occasionally, usually in the singular. The physiologist Helmholtz had used it in 1862, and the Dutch philosopher Allard Pierson had spoken of 'geestelijke wetenschappen' in 1858 (see Kamerbeek, *Wilhelm Dilthey en Allard Pierson*, 8n, 10).

† Dilthey read Mill in the Schiel translation of 1849 (second edition, 1862), which he cites in the 1875 essay (see v, 55n). Schiel had translated the title of Book vi of Mill's *Logic* as 'Von der Logik der Geisteswissenschaften oder moralischen Wissenschaften' (English: 'On the Logic of the Moral Sciences'), and in the text he often used 'Geisteswissenschaften' where Mill used 'moral sciences.' As it happens, Dilthey himself was not entirely satisfied with the Schiel translation, which he criticized in 1874 when a new, authorized translation of Mill's works by Gomperz was published (see 'Die "Gesammelte Werke" John Stuart Mills,' xvi, 456–7).

would explain his error about Mill and his approval of the term 'Geisteswissenschaften.' At this stage in his thinking, these sciences were indeed mental or perhaps psychical sciences, that is, sciences based on mental or psychical (as opposed to physical) phenomena. Mental facts in this restricted sense – and not simply as 'facts of consciousness' – form the 'most important content' of the *Geisteswissenschaften* (*Individualität*, 249–50) in Dilthey's earlier works, and the adjective 'geistig' was often used as synonymous with 'seelisch' or 'psychisch.'[6]

It was this meaning of the term 'Geisteswissenschaften' (i.e., sciences of the mental or psychical sphere) that was uppermost in Heinrich Rickert's mind when he refused to adopt the term. The word 'Geist,' he argued, is normally used to denote the psychical sphere in opposition to the physical sphere. Since the realm of culture goes beyond the psychical sphere in its inclusion of 'meanings' and 'irreal sense-bearing formations' (*irreale Sinngebilde*), the cultural sciences cannot be regarded as sciences of 'Geist.' Yet, in later publications and editions Rickert admitted that the word 'Geist' was changing in meaning and was now used by some writers in much the same way that he himself used the term 'culture.' But he maintained that there was still too much confusion surrounding the term 'Geisteswissenschaften,' since the old meaning of the word 'Geist' had by no means vanished. Therefore he continued to refuse to speak of 'Geisteswissenschaften.'[7]

Dilthey was aware of this shift in the meaning of the term 'Geist'; in fact he had helped to bring it about. One of the most important differences between his earlier and later philosophical positions concerns this very point. During the post-1900 years, Dilthey no longer thought of the realm of 'Geist' primarily as the private psychical sphere of experiences; he conceived of it rather as a public, common world of meanings and of objects which are to be regarded as expressions or objectifications of life and the mind. In other words, he no longer identified 'Geist' with mental life but thought of it instead in terms of what he called 'objective spirit.' The *Geisteswissenschaften* were still sciences of 'Geist' – therefore no change of name was necessary – but the latter term had taken on a different meaning. These sciences were still oriented ultimately towards mental life and human experience – 'We seek the mind' – but by way of an intermediate realm of expressions and objectified life. Thus Dilthey no longer spoke of the *Geisteswissenschaften* as focusing on 'mental facts' (*geistige Tatsachen*) but wrote instead that they seek to grasp 'the world of the spirit' (*die geistige Welt*) (*Aufbau*, 156). Mankind, understood as 'human-social-historical reality,' now became the 'fact (*Tatsache*) of the *Geisteswissenschaften*,'[8] and the 'understanding' of 'the world of the spirit' – rather than the direct apprehension of the psychical sphere – became the basis for the historical sciences (*Fortsetzung*, 212–13).

During the post-1900 years, Dilthey still felt the necessity of justifying his use of the term 'Geisteswissenschaften,' but in doing so he no longer appealed to Mill. He admitted that the term is not entirely satisfactory and explained what meaning he attached to the word 'Geist': 'It is the same meaning in which Montesquieu spoke of the spirit of laws, Hegel of objective spirit,* or Ihering of the spirit of Roman law' (*Aufbau*, 86). The *Geisteswissenschaften*, then, are sciences of (objective) spirit, or perhaps of culture.[9] Summing up his new concept of the *Geisteswissenschaften*, Dilthey wrote:

Here the concept of the *Geisteswissenschaften* is completed. Its range extends as far as that of understanding, and understanding has now found a unified object in the objectification of life. Thus the concept of *Geisteswissenschaft* is determined, according to the range of phenomena that fall under it, by the objectification of life in the external world. The spirit understands only that which it has created. Nature, the object of natural science, embraces the reality which is produced independently of the operation of the spirit. Everything on which man has actively set his stamp forms the object of the *Geisteswissenschaften*.

And the expression 'Geisteswissenschaft' also receives its justification at this point. Earlier there was talk of the spirit of laws, of right, of constitutions. Now we can say that *everything in which the spirit has objectified itself* falls within the sphere of the *Geisteswissenschaften* (*Aufbau*, 148).

In this passage, as well as in some others, Dilthey comes close to making metaphysical affirmations. The 'Geist' of which he speaks here is more than objective. This 'Geist' *understands*, and the object of its attention in understanding is what it has *created* – not simply what it finds before itself. Thus 'Geist' in Dilthey's new sense embraces subjective spirit in the sense of mind as well as objective spirit in the sense of culture. By speaking simply – and perhaps somewhat abruptly – of 'Geist,' Dilthey brings culture and the mind into a close relation and thereby lays a foundation for the possibility of our knowledge of the cultural realm and the historical world, for he breaks

---

* Elsewhere Dilthey qualifies this by stating that his concept of objective spirit is by no means identical with that of Hegel. Artistic, religious, and philosophical expressions form part of the realm of objective spirit for Dilthey, but not for Hegel (see *Aufbau*, 148ff). The similarity in terminology should not cause us to overlook the important differences between Dilthey and Hegel in this area.

through the barrier between the mind and the outer, public world presented to the senses. The knowledge of the *Geisteswissenschaften* – which is reached by way of understanding – then becomes a kind of re-discovery, or perhaps even a self-discovery. Just how this is to be interpreted depends on the metaphysical status given to 'Geist,' and on this point Dilthey was not specific. The relation between the mind of the empirical individual and the 'Geist' which understands what it has created was not made clear.

The movement in Dilthey's thinking on the *Geisteswissenschaften*, then, is away from the identification of 'Geist' with mental life or the psychical sphere, for 'Geist' now includes the cultural realm as well. The former remains Dilthey's ultimate object, and the cultural realm now becomes a new, public means of access to it. Because of this basic shift, the term 'Geisteswissenschaften' cannot be translated into English by any one term: at least two terms would be necessary. Unfortunately, most English and French discussions of Dilthey do propose and use some equivalent for the term 'Geisteswissenschaften.'* This furthers the confusion about this body of sciences in two ways. First, it encourages us to overlook the question whether there is indeed such a unified body of sciences for which the English language should have a generic name. (The traditional division into two types of sciences has been replaced in most quarters by a division into three or more fundamentally different types of sciences.) Second, it ignores the important shift in the meaning of the terms 'Geist' and 'Geisteswissenschaften.' The German word 'Geisteswissenschaften' is sufficiently broad and flexible to cover both conceptions of these sciences, although Dilthey would have done well to dispel the confusion by adopting a new term in the post-1900 writings; but I know of no English term that can do the same. Therefore, I have chosen to leave the term 'Geisteswissenschaften,' which by now is fairly well known in the English-speaking world, untranslated.

THE FUNDAMENTAL SHIFT IN DILTHEY'S THINKING

That there were a number of changes in Dilthey's thinking should come as no surprise in view of the fact that his active intellectual career spanned half a century. Yet the significance of those changes has all too often been overlooked. The major reason for this, in all likelihood, is that Dilthey himself admitted to no fundamental shifts in his thinking. Of course, he could not deny that there had been changes of some sort, but he consistently refused

---

* Some of the (English) candidates are: human sciences, moral sciences, sciences of man, cultural sciences, humanities, social sciences.

to affirm their significance. Although Dilthey avoided dealing explicitly with the question of the development of his own thought, he did manifest his attitude towards it when he faced the prospect of issuing new printings or editions of his works.

We have already seen that the *Einleitung in die Geisteswissenschaften* (1883), the first of Dilthey's major philosophical works, contained views that he later abandoned or seriously modified. Yet it was and remained a highly important work which had made a considerable impact in its time. Some years later, when the book had long been out of print, Dilthey was invited to prepare a new edition. This, of course, gave him the opportunity to make the minor corrections, changes, and additions that such books usually require, but it also forced him to face the awkward question of his own development. He apparently sensed that if he was to begin making changes, he would eventually have to rewrite the entire book. In a preface written for the second edition (which never appeared), he explained that Book I, the systematic part of the *Einleitung*, was unchanged, for '... it did not seem advisable to me to blot out the tone of the period from which the entire enterprise stems. Thus here I only propose to turn aside a few misunderstandings that have manifested themselves in discussions of this volume, admitting that I myself have helped to create them by using overly strong expressions.'[10] Dilthey manifested a similar ambivalent attitude towards the question of his own development when he struggled with the problem of revising the *Poetik* (1887), his major treatise on literature. He was aware that his thinking had changed considerably during the two decades that had passed since the publication of this treatise, but he hoped to preserve as much of the original material as possible, in part because he realized that he was too old to undertake the arduous labours of an entirely new study. Thus he proposed to retain parts of the original version '... in an abbreviated form that conserves that which was already properly formulated then ...'[11]

The problem posed by Dilthey's development is furthered by the mode of publication of his *Gesammelte Schriften*. The editors have rightly avoided the question of development and have grouped the material by topic in most volumes and chronologically within some volumes and sections. Near the end of his life, Dilthey himself played an important role in preparing two of the volumes for publication. His intention was to bring together various of his essays and treatises with some new material written specifically for the projected volume, which was then to be published under the title 'Die geistige Welt.' He wrote an interesting and important preface for this volume, which was finally published (after a delay of some years) as Volumes V and VI of the *Gesammelte Schriften*. He opened the preface by observing: 'The essays that are collected here in accordance with the wishes of younger friends and with their help are reprinted unchanged. The effort to adapt them to my present standpoint would rob them of the unity of conception and the tone of earlier years' (v, 3). This two-volume collection includes writings from 1864 to 1911. Thus, major changes would have been necessary if all was to be brought into line with the standpoint adopted by Dilthey after 1900. That he was reluctant to undertake such revisions is understandable, as is his refusal to repudiate his earlier works. (Dilthey was by no means the first philosopher to maintain that his later standpoint was somehow expressed or reflected – albeit inadequately – in his earlier works.) Yet his tendency to deny the importance of the differences between his earlier and later works has spawned a great deal of confusion among interpreters of his thought.

Unfortunately, although the secondary literature on Dilthey is rather extensive, the question of the development of his thought has been largely ignored. Many of the studies speak of an earlier and a later period, but without spelling out carefully what is at issue in the transition from the one to the other. I have found only two studies that support my own conclusion that Dilthey's thinking must be divided into a minimum of three periods.[12] Although the question of development is not my primary concern in this study, it cannot be avoided entirely, for many of the criticisms made of Dilthey's thought are misdirected because they apply only to positions which he eventually gave up. (Indeed, Dilthey himself would have agreed with some of the criticisms.) General criticism of Dilthey which does not limit its scope to a particular publication is in order only after his final position has been sketched and distinguished from his earlier positions. The failure to take the final position into account is the fatal weakness of many of the studies of Dilthey now in circulation. Some of these studies do little more than summarize the major writings of one of the periods of Dilthey's thought, while the more confusing of them draw indiscriminately on all three periods.[13]

The confusion as to what Dilthey did and did not maintain is also due in part to the tendency to identify Dilthey with his 'school,' that is, with students of his who were active long after his death and who paid tribute to his influence on their thinking. Some of these students took their point of departure in the thought of Dilthey's second period, and others in the third. (Eduard Spranger, perhaps the best known of them, incorporated elements from both the second and the third periods in his own thinking.) Lumping together the views of Dilthey's students and then attributing them all to Dilthey himself will only add to the confusion about his thought. Unless we focus on Dilthey's own writings and recognize the fundamental shift that is clearly reflected in them, the doctrine of understanding, which came to its fullest expression only in the writings of the post-1900 years, will remain obscure and mystifying.

The fundamental shift in Dilthey's thinking is important not only because it explains much of the confusion that pervades the Dilthey literature but also because it led to a revision and enlargement of the doctrine of understanding, which in turn contributed substantially to Dilthey's final outlook on historical knowledge. I alluded to this shift earlier when I noted that Dilthey transferred the attention of the *Geisteswissenschaften* from the realm of inner experience to an outer, public world, and that the realm of 'Geist' gains a certain autonomy vis-à-vis the psychical sphere in Dilthey's later writings. This shift must now be related to Dilthey's basic philosophical intentions. As we have seen, both philosophy and the *Geisteswissenschaften* seek to penetrate the world of mental life and human experience – 'We seek the mind.' They do so first of all through our experiencing (*Erleben*) of our inner states. But, by way of inner experience, we also gain access to the mental states of others. Through the power of imagination and on the basis of what is given to us outwardly in sensory perception, we re-live (*nacherleben*) the experience of others by interpreting their outward manifestations in accordance with the principle of analogy. We are aware of the connections and correlations between our own inner and outer states, and we make use of this awareness in the re-living of the experiences of others. At this stage in Dilthey's thinking, understanding is simply 'Nacherleben,' a re-living of experience, and it culminates in an imaginative transposition (*Hineinverstezen*) in which we try to develop a sense of the situation and life of the other, not first of all by making it our own but by identifying what we feel and experience with the other. This cognitive operation, which plays an important role in non-scientific life, is what makes possible the knowledge which the *Geisteswissenschaften* give us.

Our effort to gain knowledge of man, then, requires an observation of inner states as we live (*erleben*) our own experiences and re-live (*nacherleben*) those of others. Insofar as this effort represents a scientific method, it is bound to introspection or self-observation. Thus the *Geisteswissenschaften*, in some of Dilthey's earlier writings, are dependent on the method of introspection, although their work is by no means limited to the observation of our inner states. The major shift in Dilthey's thinking is that he called into question and finally rejected the method of introspection or self-observation. Unfortunately, his reasons for doing so are far from clear: nowhere does he explicitly discuss his philosophical conversion. There were probably a number of factors that played a role in this change in his thinking. The most important of them seems to have been his own suspicion about the very notion of introspection.*

Dilthey pointed out that any attempt to fix our attention on inner states disturbs and alters those states (*Fortsetzung*, 194–5). Introspection can never do justice to the restless movement of mental life: 'In introspection, which is directed toward our own experience, we cannot grasp the forward march of the psychical process, for every fixation arrests that on which it focuses and gives it a certain duration' (p. 231). Nor is it conceivable that the observation of inner states could ever be a pure, non-interpretive apprehension: 'Observation itself is conditioned by the questions which I pose.'[14] Furthermore, the 'Erlebnis,' as an inseparable unity of content and apprehension, does not lend itself readily to a reflective analysis. These arguments are significant not so much for their intrinsic merits but because they paved the way for a more fruitful conception of the world of the mind or spirit, and thereby for a new approach to the question of man's knowledge of himself. The conclusion reached by Dilthey, which he repeated in various forms in his later writings, was: 'Man knows himself only in history, never through introspection.'[15] Man's knowledge of himself was now to be gained by way of an 'intermediary' or 'detour' (*Umweg*).†

Nietzsche may have played a role in bringing about the shift in Dilthey's thinking. There are a number of references to Nietzsche in the later writings, and in some of these passages Dilthey associates him with the ill-fated method of introspection. We read: 'In vain did Nietzsche seek his original nature, his a-historical essence, in solitary self-observation. He peeled off one skin after another. And what was left? Still only something historically conditioned: the features of the Renaissance man of power.'[16] By abandoning introspection, Dilthey could also answer Nietzsche's challenge to the science of history by enhancing the importance of history as the arena of man's self-disclosure. 'We do not grasp human nature through introspection,' wrote Dilthey. 'That was Nietzsche's colossal mistake. Hence he was also unable to grasp the meaning of history' (*Fortsetzung*, 250). The en-

---

* Dilthey only began to use the term 'introspection' regularly *after* he had rejected the method of introspection. This, too, may have encouraged his readers to overlook the fact that his criticism of introspection applies to his own earlier position.

† After criticizing introspection as a basis for scientific knowledge of man, Dilthey writes: 'Therefore only a different method can take us further, a method that involves an intermediate stage' (Notes towards a revision of the *Poetik*, VI, 318). In the *Aufbau* he writes: '... only his actions, his fixed expressions of life and their effects on others teach man about himself; thus man gets to know himself only via the detour of understanding' (p. 87).

counter with Nietzsche's writings seems at least to have confirmed Dilthey in his movement in the direction of an increasingly dynamic conception of man and of human life. But the challenge posed by Nietzsche was only one of a number of factors that brought about the fundamental shift in Dilthey's thinking.[17] His own doctrine of the historicality of consciousness (which will be dealt with later) also had the effect of undermining the idea of 'Nacherleben' and self-observation as basic to the method of the *Geisteswissenschaften*.

Because Dilthey's recognition of the inadequacy of introspection or self-observation brought in its wake the new features of his post-1900 thinking, it must be characterized as the most important shift in his thought. First of all, by insisting that understanding proceeds by way of the 'detour' of expression, Dilthey opened the door to the recognition of a new realm of spirit or culture. He spoke of this realm repeatedly as 'the world of the spirit' (*die geistige Welt*) and remarked as early as 1898 that it is given to us only by way of the physical world.[18] Thus he broke free of the closed outlook that recognized only physical and psychical reality. He soon attributed a certain autonomy to the realm of expression and transferred the primary attention of the *Geisteswissenschaften* from the psychical sphere to this public realm. This in turn requires recognizing that understanding has a double object. In the earlier writings understanding was conceived of as 'Nacherleben,' as an apprehension of the lived experiences of others as we live them afterwards. Now understanding becomes first and foremost a grasping of expressions, both as meanings and as objectifications of experience. In other words, understanding now has a direct or primary object (the outward expression given to us via the senses) and an indirect or secondary object (the mental life or experiences which the expression renders public). The former object is primary because we get at the secondary object only by means of it. Of course, we may also ignore the secondary object and consider the primary object in itself. This enlargement of the doctrine of understanding had important consequences for history and the *Geisteswissenschaften*, for it gave those sciences a public object or focus of theoretical attention that was accessible in principle to all.

THE QUESTION OF PSYCHOLOGY

We noted earlier that Dilthey played a prominent role in some of the philosophical debates of his time, and that his thought as a whole is sometimes wrongly identified with his position in one of these controversies. The discussion about the relation of the *Geisteswissenschaften* to the natural sciences is one such debate. The discussion about the need for a new psychology to supplement or perhaps replace the prevailing psychology of that time, which was oriented towards the natural sciences, is another. Dilthey, who proposed and outlined a new 'descriptive and analytical psychology' during the 1890s, became a somewhat controversial figure through his role in this debate. As a result, his statements about psychology have played too large a part in subsequent treatments and evaluations of his thinking. Dilthey's proposed descriptive psychology forms an important new departure in his thought, but it did not dominate his thinking on history and the *Geisteswissenschaften* during the post-1900 years. The most important disagreement between students of Dilthey's later philosophy revolves around the question whether he ever abandoned the 'psychological approach' to the *Geisteswissenschaften*. I hope to show that although he never abandoned his interest in psychology and continued to speak of 'descriptive psychology,' he did cease to regard such a psychology as fundamental to the *Geisteswissenschaften*.

Dilthey's observations on psychology may well constitute the weakest link in his thinking. As a young professor, he said that he found psychology 'the most difficult of all philosophical lecture courses.' He spoke of it at that time as a 'heavy burden' (*schwere Stein*) and admitted that his lectures on the subject were by no means the best.[19] Yet, he insisted on dealing with psychology in some form or other, even in his earliest publications, in which he spoke of 'Realpsychologie,' 'Individualpsychologie,' 'Einzelpsychologie,' 'induktive Psychologie,' 'empirische Psychologie,' and even 'deskriptive Psychologie.'[20] In the *Einleitung* Dilthey declared that psychology has as its object 'psychical unities' or 'psycho-physical life-unities' and that it is to provide us with knowledge of the universal characteristics of man (pp. 29, 32). He did speak of it there as a 'fundamental (*grundlegend*) science' which should limit itself to a descriptive method (p. 32), but he also observed that its domain does not include all the facts with which the *Geisteswissenschaften* are concerned (pp. 29–30). Because psychology focuses on the human individual, it is only a single, limited *Geisteswissenschaft*: 'Thus the object of psychology is always only the individual, which is separated from the living fabric (*Zusammenhang*) of historical-social reality; and via a process of abstraction, psychology is supposed to present the universal properties which individual psychical entities develop within this fabric' (p. 30). As a science of the individual, psychology really amounts to anthropology.[21] Because Dilthey at this point still chose to delimit the *Geisteswissenschaften* vis-à-vis the natural sciences by way of subject-matter rather than on the basis of different modes of experience or perception, he also defined psychology by reference to its subject-matter. It was only when he struck upon the idea of dividing the sciences on the basis of two types of experience that he began to view the new 'descriptive psychology' as an underlying fundamental science on which all of the *Geisteswissenschaften* would then be based.

One might wonder why Dilthey considered psychology so important. Could the epistemological side of his program not have been carried out without dealing with 'psychological' considerations? Part of the answer to this question is that epistemology and psychology were not separated as strictly then as they are today. Philosophy and psychology were often joined in academic journals and professorships in the late nineteenth century.* But at least two other factors played an important role in Dilthey's preoccupation with psychology. One was his aversion to intellectualism, which manifested itself in his constant demand that the 'whole man' somehow be involved in the cognitive operations on which the *Geisteswissenschaften* are based: 'The power of apprehension operative in the *Geisteswissenschaften* is the whole man ...' (*Einleitung*, 38). What did he mean by the 'whole man'? He meant man as a 'creature of will, feeling and presentation' (*wollend fühlend vorstellendes Wesen*).[22] Dilthey was opposed to all one-sided conceptions of the life of the mind, and he hoped to overcome them by insisting that all three of the traditional mental functions (i.e., presentation, feeling, and will) be involved in the operations of the *Geisteswissenschaften*. This emphasis is one of the constant features of Dilthey's thought throughout his career. He always viewed the *Geisteswissenschaften* as related to will, valuation, and practical intentions, and he emphasized the co-operation of all three mental powers in understanding: 'We explain by means of purely intellectual processes, but we understand through the co-operation of all of our mental powers in apprehension.'[23] In this regard, the *Geisteswissenschaften* mirror life itself: 'In every full moment of life, the totality of our mental powers is operative' (*Individualität*, 276). By stressing the importance of psychology, Dilthey was able to emphasize all three mental functions. Thus his 'psychological' emphasis must be understood in the light of his desire to combat intellectualism and any epistemology that underestimates the significance of feeling and will in our relations with the world. While talking about 'psychology,' of course, Dilthey was generally making points of an epistemological nature. Yet, because he apparently feared a relapse into intellectualism, he preferred to call his observations 'psychology' rather than 'epistemology.'

* There is a striking example of this in the history of the Johns Hopkins University, which was founded in 1876 as the first university in the USA devoted to teaching and research on a graduate level. Josiah Royce, William James, Charles Sanders Peirce, and John Dewey were all associated in some way with the new university and were all (informal) candidates for the chair of philosophy. But the appointment – after some delay – went to G. Stanley Hall, who is remembered chiefly for his contribution to child psychology.

A second factor underlying Dilthey's deep interest in what he called 'psychology' was his commitment to probing and exploring 'life,' i.e., man and his world. Poetry and art were allied with philosophy and science in this endeavour. One of the reasons why Dilthey valued poetry so highly was that it gives us knowledge of man: 'Poetry presents the eternally valid, the ever human ...'[24] He regarded art in general as a valuable organ for understanding life and the world[25] and declared at the end of his life that the great poets (Shakespeare, Cervantes, Goethe) had taught him to understand the world.[26] He thought particularly highly of Shakespeare, whom he hailed as the greatest poet produced by mankind:[27] 'Shakespeare is a great poet because of his deep knowledge of the human heart and his refined psychology.'[28] Although art and poetry had led the way in gaining knowledge of man, it was now time for scientists (i.e., psychologists) to consolidate this knowledge and pre-scientific psychology by constructing a new psychology that would focus on contents and structures. (Dilthey was already interested in reforming psychology before he made it the basis for the *Geisteswissenschaften*.) Thus psychology, philosophy, and religion were to co-operate in building up our knowledge of man.*

It was this outlook on psychology that came to expression in Dilthey's *Einleitung*. But this work, like so many of his other projects, was not completed as planned. In 1883 Dilthey published Volume I, comprising Book I (an introduction to the introduction) and Book II (dealing with the history of metaphysics in relation to the *Geisteswissenschaften*). In the preface he promised that he would continue his discussion of the historical background in Book III and would devote Books IV and V to the epistemological foundation of the *Geisteswissenschaften*. Various studies towards Book III were written and eventually published separately,[29] but Books IV and V, which were to form the real substance of the *Einleitung*, were never completed. Insofar as the published first volume outlined the task at hand, it was a highly significant work, yet it remained, as Ortega y Gasset remarks, 'solely a beginning and not an adequate exposition of Dilthey's thought.'[30] Dilthey himself was

---

* This was one of the points on which Rickert, who viewed psychology as a natural science, sharply disagreed with Dilthey: 'We speak not only of historians but also of poets and artists as "psychologists," for we rightly assume that they must be "students of mankind" to carry out their tasks. Yet the "psychology" of which artists are capable has nothing more in common with the conceptual science of mental life than the name: no one would advise a poet to study scientific psychology in order to learn to write better poetry' (*Kulturwissenschaft und Naturwissenschaft*, 62; see also *Die Grenzen der naturwissenschaftlichen Begriffsbildung*, 154, 485ff).

well aware that the *Einleitung* fell far short of what he had hoped to achieve, for it was not only incomplete but also somewhat obscure in certain respects: '... I must write the second volume in a much more simple and comprehensible way,' he confessed to his friend Count Yorck (*Briefwechsel,* 42). Because of these factors, those who write about the *Einleitung* are often at a loss to state precisely what it was that Dilthey achieved in this work. Georges Gusdorf, in his own introduction to the human sciences, observes that it was Dilthey's special achievement to have understood fully – better than Auguste Comte or John Stuart Mill – that the new wine cannot be poured into old wineskins, and he adds that Dilthey's effort was somewhat premature.[31]

The new wine of the *Geisteswissenschaften* was certainly in need of new wineskins, but Dilthey had not succeeded in providing them. His major publications of the 1890s, the two psychological treatises, continued in the line of the *Einleitung* by working towards the same goal, but they approached it from a different angle. Their publication amounted to a fresh start and must thus be viewed as representing an implicit abandonment of Dilthey's plans for completing the *Einleitung.* In *Ideen über eine beschreibende und zergliedernde Psychologie* (1894), Dilthey bases the difference between the natural sciences and the *Geisteswissenschaften* on two different types of experience (i.e., inner and outer experience) and proclaims psychology the basic science on which the other *Geisteswissenschaften* are based. His efforts to provide an epistemological foundation for the *Geisteswissenschaften* had been hindered by the inadequacy of the psychology of his time. This 'psychology without a psyche' (*Seelenlehre ohne Seele*), as he called it (p. 159), would have to be replaced by a new psychology (to be provided by Dilthey himself), which he characterized as a 'descriptive and analytical psychology.' The point of his contrast between 'explanatory and constructive psychology,' on the one hand, and 'descriptive and analytical psychology,' on the other, is that the former is a psychology of elements while the latter is a psychology of structures.[32] Since mental life is not a play of atomic elements joined together in accordance with 'laws of association' but rather a unified whole pervaded by coherence and structure,[33] the sciences that deal with mental facts as given in inner experience must be based on a psychology that accepts structures as givens and proceeds to describe and analyse them.

In the final analysis, the contrast between the two psychologies must be understood as a contrast between two epistemologies. Dilthey hoped to overcome 'methodological naturalism' by showing that its epistemology (i.e., its explanatory psychological conception of mental life and knowing processes) cannot account for all of our experience and knowledge. It must be supplemented by a new psychology, which then assumes the function of an epistemology of *geisteswissenschaftlich* knowledge. The new psychology focuses on aspects and features of mental life that have simply been overlooked by explanatory psychology. Its commitment to exploring all that is given in the life of the mind requires a willingness to use a number of different methods: 'Psychology must seek to make up for the shortcomings of its various particular tools and aids. Thus it combines the perception and observation of ourselves with the apprehension of others, comparative procedures, experiment, and the study of anomalous phenomena. It seeks access to mental life through many doors' (*Ideen*, 199). But the basis for its procedure is the scientific observation of inner states.

Dilthey sketched the new psychology and contrasted it with explanatory psychology only as a preliminary step towards the execution of the task with which he was primarily concerned, namely, laying a foundation for the *Geisteswissenschaften*. The question of the relation between the two psychologies was not fully answered. Dilthey rejected the claim of the explanatory psychology of his day to the title of psychology as such, but he did not reject all the procedures used by the explanatory psychologists. His hope was to salvage what he could of this science and to make it part of the new psychology which he had outlined.

Dilthey's comments on the psychology of his day quickly provoked the psychologists to wrath. The most important critique came from his friend Hermann Ebbinghaus. In a sharply critical review article that attacked Dilthey both in substance and by its tone, Ebbinghaus charged that Dilthey had grossly misrepresented psychology as practised at that time. Moreover, much of what Dilthey proposed in the way of a new psychology was already being done by psychologists. Ebbinghaus simply did not acknowledge the great gap between explanatory psychology and the new psychology proposed by Dilthey. Dilthey's entire argument, he complained, was based on misunderstandings. Furthermore, it was poorly thought out and executed:

It is obvious from the outset that he attempts too much. Instead of taking a single difficult problem in its breadth and depth and showing to the satisfaction of everyone, through the most painstaking descriptions and penetrating analyses, that his procedure can here achieve the clarity that has heretofore been sought in vain, he embraces the entire framework of his science at once. Thereby we get a great deal of framework but, unfortunately, little content.[34]

Dilthey, understandably, was very upset by Ebbinghaus's attack.* He quickly began work on a reply, but never published it.[35] He did, however, publish a second psychological treatise (*Ueber vergleichende Psychologie: Beiträge zum Studium der Individualität*), in which he carried further the line of thought begun in *Ideen*. But sometime between 1896 and 1900 he began to have serious doubts about the new psychology as a basis for the *Geisteswissenschaften*. His 1900 essay on 'Die Entstehung der Hermeneutik' is the first solid indication of the emergence of a new position. Dilthey's critics, led by Ebbinghaus, probably played a role in his philosophical conversion, but Dilthey was apparently too proud to acknowledge this. Thus the excessively sharp tone of Ebbinghaus's criticism may have contributed to the blurring of the differences between Dilthey's pre-1900 and post-1900 thinking (i.e., by forcing Dilthey to pretend that he really had not changed his mind about the earlier position that was so fiercely attacked).

In the writings of the post-1900 years, Dilthey did not abandon psychology entirely, nor did he 'lose interest' in it, as one commentator puts it.[36] Psychology lost its position as the basic science because mental life was now to be approached by way of its 'objectifications' or 'manifestations': we grasp mental life through the process of 'understanding,' that is, by the apprehension of 'expressions.' Therefore, hermeneutics and philology suddenly became of special interest to Dilthey. Although he still spoke of 'descriptive psychology' and the descriptive method, psychology itself reverted to roughly the same status that it occupied in the *Einleitung*. Dilthey now regarded it as the 'science of life-unities,'† and he identified it as one of the *Geisteswissenschaften*.‡

---

* From Dilthey's correspondence, we learn that he used to go on walks with Ebbinghaus and had exchanged philosophical and scientific ideas with him (see *Briefwechsel*, 38, 46). But after the attack by Ebbinghaus, Dilthey wrote to Yorck: 'I can only say that under no circumstances will I sit down with Ebbinghaus in the same room where I might have to greet him or exchange a few words with him' (p. 210). For the mild-mannered Dilthey, this was highly unusual.

† *Aufbau*, 117. On the same page Dilthey indicates that in a certain sense, the *Aufbau* itself represents a reversion to the outlook of the *Einleitung*. Since the excursion into psychology really represents a *cul-de-sac* in the progression of Dilthey's thought, we should regard the post-1900 writings as a 'Fortsetzung' more of the *Einleitung* than of the *Ideen*.

‡ *Aufbau*, 79; see also *Fortsetzung*, 239–40, and *Philosophie*, 372. The survival of Dilthey's descriptive psychology is not without parallel in the history of philosophy. After Husserl's conversion to transcendental idealism, his earlier psychological explorations of consciousness were given the new, reduced status of 'phenomenological psychology,' but they were not by any means cast aside.

As we noted earlier, the question of Dilthey's post-1900 attitude towards psychology is a matter of considerable contention among students of his thought. Jean-François Suter insists that '... Dilthey, in his hermeneutical theory, remained faithful to the idea of providing a psychological basis for historical knowledge.' He also maintains: 'The idea of founding historical knowledge upon psychology goes back to the very beginning of Dilthey's career. He was preoccupied with this question all his life.' Thus Suter concludes: '... I do not believe that Dilthey ever abandoned the psychological solution.'[37] But in the *Aufbau* of 1910, as we have seen, Dilthey uses the concept of 'Geist' as defined by Ihering when he spoke of the 'spirit of Roman law.' 'The understanding of this *Geist* is not psychological knowledge,' Dilthey writes. 'It means going back to a cultural formation (*geistiges Gebilde*) with a structure and lawfulness of its own' (p. 85). Implicitly criticizing his own earlier position, he also writes: 'Now it is a common error to look to psychology for our knowledge of this inner side of the course of psychical life' (p. 84). Understanding is oriented not only towards the psychical sphere as its ultimate goal but first and foremost towards a public world of meanings and objectifications of life and experience. This development is the so-called 'objective turn' in Dilthey's thinking. O.F. Bollnow expresses this shift by declaring that Dilthey went beyond 'psychologism' in his later period.[38]

The question of Dilthey's new psychology and its relation to his post-1900 thought has been further confused by the widespread practice of attributing a 'geisteswissenschaftliche Psychologie' or a 'verstehende Psychologie' or both to Dilthey.[39] 'Geisteswissenschaftliche Psychologie' is the name chosen by Eduard Spranger, one of Dilthey's students, for his own new psychology, which is by no means identical with that of Dilthey. And although it might seem reasonable to characterize Dilthey's descriptive psychology as 'geisteswissenschaftlich' – for it was intended to serve as a foundation for the *Geisteswissenschaften* – we should refrain from doing so, in order to prevent the identification of Dilthey's psychology with that of Spranger. (Dilthey, in any event, provided more than enough names for his new psychology.) Spranger operates with a distinction between 'Seele' and 'Geist' that was not present in Dilthey's pre-1900 thinking: he incorporates 'Geist' in Dilthey's post-1900 sense into his psychological framework. His thinking represents a path that Dilthey might have followed during the post-1900 years but did not.

The talk of Dilthey's 'verstehende Psychologie' is more dangerous, for it fuses the new psychology with the doctrine of understanding, which was fully developed only during the post-1900 years. It thereby obliterates the distinction between Dilthey's second and third periods and negates the new dimension that appeared in his thinking after 1900. If understanding were a process concerned exclusively with psychical givens and mental life, it would make no sense to speak of an understanding of 'expressions' considered as meanings or of 'objective spirit' as a remnant of the past. 'Verstehende Psychologie' is really the creation of Karl Jaspers, who has cleared up the question of the origin of this conception of psychology. In his 'Philosophical Autobiography,' Jaspers writes: 'Over against the psychology of theoretical explanation, Dilthey had put another, "descriptive and analytical psychology." I adopted this approach, called it a "*verstehende Psychologie*" and worked out the already practiced procedures ...' In another work Jaspers explains that his notion of 'verstehende Psychologie' is by no means identical with Dilthey's descriptive psychology but was influenced by Dilthey as well as by Droysen, Spranger, Weber, Simmel, and Ebbinghaus.[40] The term 'verstehende Psychologie' does not occur in Dilthey's writings.

One final misconception to be dealt with in connection with Dilthey's new psychology is the confusion about the question of Dilthey and phenomenology. We read that Dilthey used 'the method of phenomenology' in some of his writings, and one historian of phenomenology has gone as far as to speak of 'the phenomenology of Dilthey.'[41] Furthermore, Dilthey's name comes up frequently in discussions of the origin and background of the phenomenological movement. The most important point to be made in this context is that in his final period, Dilthey was moving *away from* Husserl's phenomenology rather than towards it. Much could be made of the fact that Dilthey thought highly of Husserl's *Logical Investigations* (1900–1901) and that Husserlian terms appear in some of the writings of the immediate post-1900 years. Yet the resemblances between the two philosophers are superficial.[42] Dilthey, ever the enthusiast, had hoped that the young Husserl (who was also the author of a 'descriptive psychology') would become his ally in the struggle to place the *Geisteswissenschaften* on a firm foundation. But Husserl, of course, went his own way, and after a few years his name no longer appeared so often in Dilthey's writings.

From a phenomenological standpoint, it is mainly the second period in Dilthey's philosophizing, i.e., the thinking expressed in *Ideen*, that is of interest. Husserl himself dealt with this work in his lectures on phenomenological psychology, where he reports: 'At first I was more than a little surprised to hear from *Dilthey* personally that phenomenology – in fact, the descriptive analyses of the second, specifically phenomenological part of the *Logical Investigations* – is in essential harmony with his *Ideen* and is to be regarded as the first step toward a real elaboration of the ideal psychology with a fully mature method that he had in mind.' He praised Dilthey's work as a 'preview' of phenomenology and a 'first step' towards it,* but he was careful to point out the differences between his own thought and that of Dilthey. What the two thinkers had in common, of course, is that both were swimming against the stream and that both had followed the example of Brentano in adopting the name 'descriptive psychology' for their respective examinations of consciousness.[43]

Dilthey was not a phenomenologist in the strict sense, then, but a post-Husserlian phenomenology might conceivably draw inspiration from his work: Ludwig Binswanger, a phenomenological psychiatrist, calls for a synthesis of Dilthey and Husserl.[44] Dilthey himself spoke of a 'phenomenology of metaphysics' or of 'religious consciousness,'[45] and some of his own analyses might be characterized as phenomenological in a loose sense. Furthermore, the method of introspection, which is central to the thought of Dilthey's second period, might well be put to some limited use within a phenomenological context.[46]

THE UNITY AND FRAMEWORK OF DILTHEY'S THOUGHT

Throughout this study and particularly in this chapter, I have emphasized the changes in Dilthey's thinking and argued that it underwent considerable development. This was necessary first of all because Dilthey's doctrine of understanding in the post-1900 period differs in important respects from his pre-1900 conception of understanding. It was also necessary because much of the Dilthey literature goes astray by ignoring the development of his thought. This in turn exposes Dilthey to various unjustified criticisms that apply only to one stage of his thinking. As we have seen, Dilthey himself is in part responsible for this state of affairs, for he remained silent about the turning points in his thinking.

Those who deny any essential development in Dilthey's thinking like to appeal to the 'unity' of his thought and the common elements present throughout as a justification for their approach. In stressing these factors, of course, they stand on solid ground. Studies of a philosopher's 'development' and 'periods' are rightly regarded with suspicion in certain quarters, for many of them place far too much emphasis on the changes and not enough emphasis on the common elements that bind the development together. It is

---

* *Phänomenologische Psychologie*, 34, 35; see also 6–20, 354–60. Husserl apparently read too much agreement into the enthusiasm displayed by Dilthey, who generally preferred to stress what he had in common with other thinkers. This led to misconceptions on Husserl's part about Dilthey's post-1900 thought.

the presence of common elements and persistent themes that makes the question of development interesting and worthwhile. But any attempt to interpret Dilthey's thought *solely* on the basis of its unity and common elements will be tripped up by the basic contradictions between the second and third periods.

Some of those who interpret Dilthey on the basis of the common elements in his thought appeal to a comment made by Clara Misch, Dilthey's daughter, in her preface to *Der junge Dilthey*, a posthumous selection of materials drawn from Dilthey's letters and diaries. Mrs Misch writes that her father had often told her that all of his work was merely the execution of ideas and plans conceived in his youth (p. v). It is not necessary to take issue with this claim on the part of Mrs Misch, for in no way does it contradict the thesis that Dilthey's thought underwent some fundamental changes. Dilthey himself, in a discussion of Rousseau's development, gives us an indication of how the unity of a philosopher's life and work might be understood in relation to the changes in his thought:

The normal life of a historically significant man contains two clearly separate halves: the first is the time in which he becomes aware of his historical task, after having undergone many changes, and the second is then the time of interaction between the world and the efforts that fill his life from then on. Rarely does he undergo a change of direction in the second half of his life comparable to the changes of the first half.[47]

I am convinced that this observation has autobiographical significance, for it sketches the pattern that Dilthey's own life followed. In the first half of his life he gained an orientation in the intellectual and cultural world of his time and explored its problems. This led him to his conception of the many-sided task that was to become his destiny, namely, plumbing the depths of 'life' and – on the basis of an understanding of life – constructing an epistemological foundation for the *Geisteswissenschaften*. The three periods in Dilthey's thinking are all responses to this self-imposed task, and therefore we are fully justified in speaking of the 'unity' of his thought. Insofar as he remained faithful to his own conception of his task, Dilthey could well claim that the shifts in his thinking were only of secondary importance.*

* This is also the emphasis of Rudolf Makkreel in a recently published study entitled *Dilthey: Philosopher of the Human Studies*. Makkreel puts too much stress on the Kantian element in Dilthey (see pp. 3–4, 179, note 19, 245, 247–8). Yet he also points out: 'The whole tenor of Dilthey's philosophy is to challenge Kant's form-content dualism. Dilthey sees form as everywhere implicit in content' (p. 126). Makkreel opposes the 'common tendency to divorce Dilthey's early psychological from his later hermeneutic and historical

The unity of Dilthey's thought must be sought first and foremost in relation to what he called 'life.' He insisted on calling his own thought a 'philosophy of life,'[48] and the collection of essays and treatises that eventually became Volumes V and VI of the Gesammelte Schriften was to be an 'introduction to the philosophy of life.' Dilthey was convinced that grasping 'life' was the need of the hour. Shortly before his death he wrote: 'The philosophical thought of the present hungers and thirsts for life.'[49] The governing impulse in his philosophy, he declared, was to understand life out of itself, and he used the same phrase to characterize the task of poetry.[50] In one of his unpublished manuscripts, he formulated his intent as follows: 'To reveal life as it is, that is what we strive for. To describe life, that is our goal.'[51] Since life encompasses both subject and object, both the reality to be grasped and the self that apprehends it, Dilthey declared of the Geisteswissenschaften: 'Life here apprehends life ...' (Aufbau, 136). Philosophy, the Geisteswissenschaften, art, and religion are all bound together by the ultimate goal of exploring the inexhaustible depths of life. Dilthey regarded life and the world as a 'riddle,' and he viewed philosophy as an eternal pursuit because the riddle is never solved. To think philosophically is to confront the riddle, to stare at 'the countenance of life, with its laughing mouth and sad eyes.'[52]

Dilthey was certainly justified in characterizing his philosophy as a 'philosophy of life,' for the two major streams of thought that together make up the bulk of his work (i.e., the writings on art and on the Geisteswissenschaften) find their place within this framework. They complement one another by approaching the same goal from different angles. We have already dealt at some length with Dilthey's philosophy of the Geisteswissenschaften and have seen that his efforts to provide a philosophical foundation for these sciences went through at least three phases, corresponding respectively to the Einleitung of 1883, the Ideen of 1894, and the Aufbau of 1910. At the same time that Dilthey was working on his historical and psychological studies towards a philosophy of the Geisteswissenschaften, he also wrote numerous essays and

---

writings,' the 'temptation to contrast an early position to a later, more fashionable standpoint' (pp. ix, 14). Yet, on the all-important issue of psychology, Makkreel admits: 'Generally, in his late writings, the status of psychology is made ambiguous at best, and its contributions to historical knowledge appear to be minimized or even excluded' (p. 294). In Dilthey's later writings we find 'an obvious element of self-criticism' (p. 295). The difference between Makkreel's interpretation and mine concerns exactly that point: my thesis is that Dilthey deliberately dropped a certain line of thought at one point in his career and picked up themes and ideas with which he had worked before his infatuation with psychology. Makkreel argues instead for the 'essential continuity' of Dilthey's writings (p. ix).

treatises on art and poetry. The most important of these works is *Die Einbil-dungskraft des Dichters: Bausteine für eine Poetik* (1887). Also significant for our purposes are the numerous essays on 'Dichtung,' a category that includes the lyrical poetry of Goethe, the comedies and tragedies of Shakespeare, the novels of Charles Dickens, and much more. The philosopher of life must give considerable attention to art and literature because art, as Dilthey put it, is an organ for understanding life and the world: 'Art tries to express what life is' (*Individualität*, 280).

It is unfortunate that Dilthey's philosophy of art and his philosophy of the *Geisteswissenschaften* are usually dealt with separately, for the former seems to have had a considerable influence on the latter. Dilthey's thinking on art is somewhat more unified than his thinking on the *Geisteswissenschaften*, and it does not manifest fundamental shifts comparable to those discussed earlier in this chapter. The outlook of his writings on aesthetics, literary criticism, and the history of literature, most of which were composed before 1900, reflects – at least implicitly – his post-1900 position. The reason why the connection between the two streams in Dilthey's thought is so important is that he apparently applied what he had learned in his intensive study of artistic expression to the shaping of his post-1900 position on the *Geisteswissenschaften*. This accounts in part for the 'aesthetic' quality of Dilthey's final outlook on history and the *Geisteswissenschaften*.[53] The cycle of experience (*Erlebnis*), expression, and understanding, which is fundamental to his post-1900 conception of the *Geisteswissenschaften*, was revealed to him through his study of artistic expression and aesthetic experience (which includes both the enjoyment of art works and our aesthetic encounters with the world of nature and culture). The aesthetic experience, he realized, has a significant effect on human consciousness, on subsequent perception, and thereby on later artistic expression. This influence which Dilthey's study of art exercised on his conception of the Geisteswissenschaften represents a fulfilment of his hope that his work as a practitioner of the *Geisteswissenschaften* (in this case, literary history) would eventually bear fruit in the form of new insights to be applied throughout the *Geisteswissenschaften*.*

---

* As early as 1887, Dilthey stated that the study of literature could have an important bearing on the study of history: 'Because poetry offers the methodological advantage of manifesting with exceptional clarity the mental processes through which historical products were brought forth, I have recently been drawing on it as I dealt with the problems of historical mental life' (1887 Antrittsrede, v, 11). Also: 'The philosophical view of history was developed among us in connection with literary history. Perhaps poetics has a similar significance for the systematic study of historical expressions of life' (*Poetik*, 109).

These two streams in Dilthey's thought come together in his doctrine of understanding. In the post-1900 years, as we have seen, understanding is not a 'psychological' process involving only inner experience; it can better be thought of as akin to aesthetic processes, for it involves feeling and takes its point of departure in sensory givens that bear a meaning (i.e., expressions of life and the mind). Therefore, Dilthey emphasizes that in the cognitive operations of the *Geisteswissenschaften* (of which understanding is the most important), the 'totality of our mental powers' must be harnessed, for the human world which we seek to understand is more than merely intellectual. The same emphasis is present in Dilthey's thinking on art: the poet '... draws on the totality of his powers' (*Philosophie*, 396). All of our mental powers co-operate in the forming of expressions: ' ...a poem or an epistle of Paul contains more than knowledge.'[54] Because artistic expression and aesthetic experience draw on the 'whole man,' they lead not merely to intellectual enrichment but to an 'elevation' and 'enlargement' of our existence.[55] In his final period, Dilthey claimed a similar existential significance for historical understanding, as the key passage about Luther quoted earlier makes clear.* Thus, to regard Dilthey's 'understanding' merely as a scientific technique or device based on a new 'psychological' approach to consciousness is to misrepresent it. Understanding, as we shall see, arises out of non-scientific life and has been transposed from that sphere for use in history and the *Geisteswissenschaften*. Therefore it is important not to lose sight of the connection between understanding and aesthetic experience, for it is in the realm of artistic creation and enjoyment that the process of expression and understanding assumes its most awesome form.

Our discovery of the roots of Dilthey's doctrine of understanding in his studies of art and poetry† is a manifestation of the unity of his thought in a second respect: very few genuinely new elements entered his thinking during the crucial last three decades of his career. It was all there at the start, as it were. A number of his most notable ideas were inherited from lesser known thinkers before him, e.g., J.G. Droysen, whose lectures on historical science

---

* See p. 23. Dilthey had already realized the existential significance of understanding in the *Einleitung*: 'When we join in living through something past by employing the art of historical imagination, we are taught, just as though life itself were our teacher; indeed, our being is expanded, and psychical powers stronger than our own elevate our existence' (p. 91).

† Dilthey's study of his beloved Goethe seems to have played a special role in his development of the notion of understanding and its relation to expression and lived experience. Therefore the essay 'Goethe und die dichterische Phantasie' (in *Erlebnis*, pp. 124–86) can be read as a useful introduction to Dilthey's thought.

touched briefly on many of the same major points which Dilthey developed during his final period. During the later years of his life, Dilthey made considerable use of ideas with which he had become acquainted decades earlier, although he may have neglected to develop them or even mention them during the intervening years. (This reliance on ideas acquired during his youth was no doubt part of what Dilthey meant when he told his daughter that all his later work was the execution of ideas and plans conceived in his youth.) The post-1900 emphasis on hermeneutics really represents a revival of interest in a science about which Dilthey had already written more than once years before,[56] and the introduction of the cycle of experience, expression, and understanding can be seen as a new formulation of the relation between lived experience and poetry which Dilthey had recognized long ago as operative in the aesthetic sphere. It seems that it took him quite some time to realize the implications of the set of ideas that he had acquired early in his life. His quest for a new psychology, which really represents a *cul-de-sac* in his career, apparently stood in his way.

Dilthey's fundamental and overarching philosophical concern, that is, the effort to grasp 'life,' is the most important unifying factor in his work. But towards the end of his career, he was forced to face the fact that he had not accomplished as much as he had hoped in this regard. Although he sometimes spoke of 'life' in much the same way that various other philosophers have spoken of 'being,' he did not write anything resembling an ontology. Dilthey conceived of 'life' in increasingly more dynamic terms, and at the end of his life he proclaimed: 'We have no knowledge of any bearer (*Träger*) of life that can be experienced. Such a thing would be transcendent to life itself ... We have knowledge only ... of events (*Geschehen*) and have no right to posit a bearer of the same, for this would represent a transfer of the concept of substance to the world of lived experience.'[57] Therefore, he always dealt with particular manifestations of life, no one of which is identical with life as such. Perhaps towards the end of his life, this professed enemy of metaphysical speculation was willing to accept this as an inescapable limitation. He and his followers continued to explore life 'in motion,' in its individual human manifestations, and this has finally led to the charge that Dilthey and company abandoned philosophy.[58]

Because life was to be grasped 'in motion,' as it moved through the cycle of experience, expression, and understanding, Dilthey's thought became a philosophy of expression, or perhaps of culture – if the term 'culture' is not too static to be used here. Most of the philosophical production of the post-1900 years really amounts to a survey of the major modes of expression, i.e., art, religion, and philosophy. A philosophy of art emerged from Dilthey's years of reflection on literature. From Schleiermacher he borrowed a philosophy of religion, and he also valued highly the contribution to our understanding of religious expression made by William James in *The Varieties of Religious Experience*.[59] It remained for Dilthey himself in his later years to write a philosophy of philosophy, on the basis of his theory of worldviews.

Insofar as the cycle of experience, expression, and understanding represents an entirely human process that cannot be traced back to a transcendent deity or accounted for in terms of an all-embracing world order, Dilthey's thought could perhaps be regarded as an anthropology – albeit a historical anthropology depicting what man has become rather than a systematic anthropology revealing his essence. Dilthey himself did not explicitly identify his work as an anthropology or a philosophy of man,[60] but he certainly left such an impression behind him in the philosophical world.[61] Yet, although his concern was with man, it was to history that he turned more and more for answers to the basic philosophical questions: 'History is to teach us what life is,' he wrote (*Fortsetzung*, 262). Nevertheless, the relation of the individual manifestation of life to life itself continued to puzzle and intrigue him to the day of his death.

TYPES OF 'GEISTESWISSENSCHAFTEN'

As we saw earlier, one of the changes in Dilthey's thinking over the years was a realization that his initial philosophical goals were somewhat too ambitious and grandiose. His 'philosophy of life' remained partial and incomplete, and the projected grounding of all of the *Geisteswissenschaften* eluded him. One reason why the latter goal proved so elusive is that there is so much diversity within the *Geisteswissenschaften*. This 'other half of the *globus intellectualis*,' as Dilthey called it (*Einleitung*, 5), included all the sciences that are not natural sciences. But his discussions of the *Geisteswissenschaften* made it clear that although he had a strong interest in some of these sciences, he had relatively little interest in others. Later in his life, realizing that he would not be able to live up to his promise to provide a foundation for all of the *Geisteswissenschaften*, he began to concentrate more explicitly on certain of these sciences. Within this limited sphere he was somewhat more successful: indeed, he can be credited with showing how an epistemological foundation – but not a complete methodology – for a certain group of *Geisteswissenschaften* could be constructed.

Dilthey's success in this regard suggests that there are various types of *Geisteswissenschaften* and that the question of an epistemological foundation must be dealt with separately for each basic type. In the Dilthey literature, a certain amount of attention has been given to this question of dividing the *Geisteswissenschaften*. Two or three basic types are usually distinguished, in accordance either with the divisions of the sciences popular today or with distinctions made by Dilthey in the *Einleitung*.[62] One such division is that between social and cultural sciences, which coincides roughly with the opposition between generalizing and individualizing *Geisteswissenschaften*. There is a certain amount of justification in Dilthey's writings for making such a division. In the *Einleitung* he admitted that some of the *Geisteswissenschaften* deal with large groups of facts and move in the direction of 'general theories' (p. 113). In the same work he wrote: 'The position of biography within general historical science corresponds to that of anthropology within the theoretical sciences of historical-social reality' (p. 33). This contrast between descriptive individualizing sciences and systematic generalizing sciences is also present in the post-1900 writings, where we find Dilthey again speaking of 'systematic' *Geisteswissenschaften*[63] and distinguishing between two classes of sciences, namely, 'the study of history up to the current state of society and the systematic *Geisteswissenschaften*.' These two groups of *Geisteswissenschaften* together deal with the same 'fact' (i.e., mankind) and thus form a whole (*Aufbau*, 81). We might then speak of the descriptive individualizing *Geisteswissenschaften* as historical sciences and thereby solve the problem of the relation between history and the *Geisteswissenschaften*. But although such an outlook on history is reflected to some degree in Dilthey's writings,[64] it does not do justice to his thinking on the historical sciences, for history, he tells us, is 'the most complicated problem of the *Geisteswissenschaften*' (*Einleitung*, 380).

A consideration of the question how the *Geisteswissenschaften* are to be divided into types cannot afford to ignore the development of Dilthey's thinking on these sciences. One plausible way to divide sciences into types or groups is on the basis of their subject-matter. In the post-1900 years, as we have seen, the material with which the *Geisteswissenschaften* work is no longer inner experience and the facts given by means of it but the domain of expressions or manifestations of life (*Lebensäusserungen*). If expressions can be divided into basic types or classes, this might pave the way for distinguishing basic types of *Geisteswissenschaften*. Dilthey offers a broad definition of the category of expression, a definition which suggests an important division within it: 'By "manifestation of life" (*Lebensäusserung*), I mean here not only the expressions that (intend to) mean or signify something but likewise those which, without intending to do so, make something in the mind understandable for us' (*Fortsetzung*, 205). He then goes on to distinguish three types of expressions: thought-contents (e.g., concepts and judgments), expressive actions, and expressions of experiences (*Erlebnisse*).

The first of these types is of no special interest to Dilthey. He observes: 'Here understanding is directed toward the mere thought-content, which remains identical in any context ...' (p. 206). A judgment, for example, has no essential relation to the person who affirms it: 'Thus the judgment is the same in the person who expresses it as in the person who understands it: it is carried unchanged from the possession of the one who utters it to the possession of the one who understands it' (p. 205). Expressions of this type are not revelatory of man, and thus they are not dealt with by the *Geisteswissenschaften*. The second type of expression, i.e., expressive actions, represents the sphere of special interest to the social and behavioural sciences. We understand actions, gestures, and anything that human beings do in relation to purposes and goals, despite the fact that many of these actions were not intended to mean or reveal anything. Such a notion of understanding plays an important role in certain of the social sciences, and Dilthey made a small contribution to it. But his contribution is only a beginning and does not represent a philosophy of the social sciences. Dilthey's real interest was the third type of expression. The expression of an experience is something sacred to Dilthey; meanings, values, and perspectives born within human consciousness are made public, but in such a way that they become more than mere reflections of consciousness. In fact, the expression contains *more* than the experience, for it draws on depths and dimensions of mental life of which we are not fully aware. Like the thought-content, it can be adequately grasped when we disregard its author – otherwise an anonymous poem would mean nothing to us, which is obviously not the case – yet it is revealing of man and his experience in a potentially universal sense.

The distinction between expressive actions and expressions of experience can be made the basis for an implicit distinction between types of *Geisteswissenschaften*. The behavioural sciences, which uncover meaning in all that we do – and even in what we refrain from doing – form one class, to which Dilthey's contribution was minimal. Dilthey was interested primarily in the *Geisteswissenschaften* that focus on deliberate expressions of meaning, and his later philosophy can be seen in part as an attempt to provide a foundation for the sciences that study the realm of objectified mind or objective spirit. If we disregard his rather curious objections to the terms 'culture' and 'cultural science,'[65] we could characterize this class of *Geisteswissenschaften* as 'cultural sciences.' In this context, culture is to be understood not simply as something fixed and finished to be displayed in a museum but as a process of expression and communication by way of public manifestations, a process that includes art, the sciences, philosophy, and religion. In short, the cultural sciences have as their object the entire intellectual world or world of the spirit.

Within the domain of the cultural sciences, we could conceivably apply the opposition between systematic generalizing sciences and descriptive or historical individualizing sciences. Dilthey, however, tended to view the cultural sciences mainly from the historical standpoint, although he did not by any means equate the cultural sciences with the historical sciences. It is within the sphere of the historical-cultural sciences that his particular contribution is to be sought. This has been recognized by various writers who emphasize Dilthey's contribution to 'Geistesgeschichte.' Dilthey himself did not use this term,[66] but the idea of such a historical science is indeed reflected in his work. In fact, he looked upon this science, which is broader than intellectual history or history of ideas and can best be called 'cultural history,'[67] as especially privileged, as we see from a sentence in the introduction to his biography of Schleiermacher: 'The history of cultural (*geistig*) movements has the advantage of working with material that is veracious. One can be deceitful about his intentions, but not about the content of his own inner life that is expressed in his works.'[68] This idea dating from the first period of his thinking was developed more explicitly during the post-1900 years. The cultural sciences, he then argued, can make great headway because their subject-matter (i.e., expressions of experiences) can be understood in terms of itself. These expressions are simply what they are, and therefore they cannot lead us astray. That which is meant in them is not to be regarded as part of the ever-flowing psychical stream of some individual consciousness. Dilthey illustrated this by means of his favourite example, literature:

Before me lies the work of a poet. It consists of letters; it has been set by typesetters and printed by machines. But literary history and poetics are concerned only with the relation of this perceivable system of words to that which is expressed through it. And the decisive point, now, is this: the latter consists not of inner processes within the poet but of a fabric of meaning (*Zusammenhang*) created within him but separable from him ... Thus the object with which literary history or poetics is first of all concerned is completely distinct from any psychical processes in the poet or in his readers (*Aufbau*, 85).

Precisely because the expression of an experience is not to be taken simply as a manifestation of a psychical process, the possibility of deception is excluded in principle. Here the distinction between expressive actions and expressions of experience becomes important.

There is something frightful about the fact that in the struggle of practical interests, any expression can deceive us, and that interpretation is also affected by the changes in our position. But when some great work in the world of the spirit frees itself from its creator, the poet, artist or writer, we enter a realm in which deception ends. No truly great work of art ... can seek to reflect a cultural (*geistig*) content foreign to its author – indeed, it does not seek to say anything whatever about its author. Veracious in itself, it stands before us fixed, visible, abiding; thereby a secure, rule-directed (*kunstmässig*) understanding of it becomes possible (*Fortsetzung*, 207).

It is this realization that enables us to place the historical study of expressions of experiences on a firm foundation. We can overcome skepticism about historical knowledge, Dilthey argued, simply because the difficult question of motives, the question what went on within the dark corners of the historical individual's mind, can be disregarded: 'Historical skepticism can only be overcome if historical method need not concern itself with establishing motives. Historical skepticism will only be overcome when the understanding of cultural formations (*geistige Gebilde*) takes the place of psychological subtlety. These formations lie before us as outward objectifications and can thus be made the object of rule-directed understanding.' (p. 260).

This conception of history as a cultural science enables Dilthey to answer two of the traditional objections to historical science. First, it meets the methodological need for a fixed object. The fact that expressions of experiences are public and open to inspection by any historian makes a degree of objectivity possible. Second, it disposes of the second objection to historical science raised in Chapter 1 (pp. 9–10), namely, that history purports to deal with non-existent (i.e., past) objects. Cultural history deals with presently existing subject-matter, i.e., the realm of expression and objective spirit insofar as it has been preserved. 'In this objective spirit,' Dilthey writes, 'the past is abidingly and constantly present for us.'[69]

However, this hopeful outlook on history is marred by one important question: what is the relation of cultural history to history in general, to history as written by political historians, military historians, social historians, and so on? Dilthey certainly did not equate cultural history with history as such; he recognized that much of what can and should be called history falls outside his concept of cultural history. The real concern of the historian, he argued in an essay of 1889, is the person behind the words and deeds:

Books are forces in a derived sense; we seek the persons that stand behind them. In real life we always become aware first of persons who act and write. These always appear to us as the major concern; once they have faded into the darkness, leaving only deeds and words behind them, it becomes the task of historiography to make these operative powers visible again.[70]

The historical world includes both the realm of objective spirit and individual human beings. 'Objective spirit and the power of the individual together determine the world of the spirit,' wrote Dilthey. 'History rests on the understanding of both of them' (*Fortsetzung*, 213). Therefore Dilthey's founding of the cultural sciences is at best a partial answer to the epistemological problem of history. He never achieved a unified conception of the historical process and our knowledge of it.

4

A Philosophy of Life

Once we get beyond Dilthey's preoccupation with psychology and his effort to draw a careful line between distinct and different types of sciences, his major philosophical concern comes clearly into focus – the effort to grasp 'life.' This favourite term is no cliché for Dilthey. 'Life' is his chief object of interest as a philosopher; it is our common humanity, our very being, in an all-embracing sense. Therefore, his statements on 'life' must be explored as background to his doctrine of expression and understanding.

LIFE AND THE MIND

We have already noted that Dilthey called his own thinking a 'philosophy of life' (*Lebensphilosophie*), and that his emphasis on the importance of 'life' for philosophy is one of the constant features of his thought. Unfortunately, the significance of this insistence on Dilthey's part has often been overlooked: commentators on Dilthey have tended to regard the emphasis on life as a mere manifestation of a transitory philosophical fashion* that could safely be ignored in summarizing the substance of his thought.[1] The very term 'philosophy of life' is puzzling: Heidegger complains that it is about as helpful as speaking of a 'botany of plants.'[2] Since the term is far from specific, it has been applied to such diverse thinkers as Nietzsche, Bergson,

---

* Rickert complained in 1922 that the term 'life,' '... for some time now, has been used with increasing frequency and plays a great role not only for journalists but also for scientific philosophers. "Life" (*Leben*) and "vivid" (*lebendig*) are beloved words, and no view is so quickly hailed as modern as the view that it is philosophy's task to provide a theory of life on the basis of lived experiences, a theory that flesh-and-blood people can truly make use of as they give shape to their lives in a full and living way' (*Die Philosophie des Lebens*, 4).

Georg Simmel, Max Scheler, Heidegger, Jaspers, William James, Ortega y Gasset, Ludwig Klages, and, of course, Dilthey himself.

Talk of a 'philosophy of life' often occurs within a polemical context. This might lead one to suppose that the question of philosophy and life is a question not of substance or principle but rather of emphasis: Dilthey, who was a steadfast opponent of intellectualism, argued that '... intellectualism always calls forth a reaction from the vigour of life, which feels its strength in incomparable immediacy ...'[3] Yet for Dilthey, the opposition between intellectualistic thought and a philosophy rooted in life represented a conflict about basic principles: philosophies of life have appeared at various points in history to do battle with intellectualistic philosophies.[4] The apparent 'disappearance' of philosophy of life before World War II might conceivably be regarded as evidence that the emphasis on 'life' was actually a reaction to philosophical one-sidedness. But philosophy of life did not really disappear or go out of style; Herman Nohl, one of Dilthey's students, observed in 1935: 'Philosophy of life today appears in elevated form as *existential philosophy*.'[5] Although the term 'life' has largely been replaced by 'Dasein' and 'Existenz,' many of the philosophical concerns and emphases underlying philosophy of life are still operative in the philosophical world today. As we shall see later, the connection between philosophy of life and existential philosophy is important for understanding Dilthey's conception of history.

That Dilthey was serious about founding his philosophy on 'life' is clear from his frequently repeated claim that life is the fundamental given behind which thought cannot penetrate. In an epistemological essay of 1892 he declared:

Life itself, as something lived, behind which I cannot penetrate, contains cohering structures (*Zusammenhänge*) which are then explicated in all experience and thinking. And here, now, is the decisive point for the entire possibility of knowledge. Only because the entire structure that appears in forms, principles and categories is contained in life and experience, only because it can be demonstrated analytically in life and experience, do we have knowledge of reality.[6]

The conditions making knowledge possible, then, are somehow contained in life: 'The fundamental presuppositions for knowledge are given in life, and thinking cannot get behind them.'[7] In these earlier formulations, Dilthey means 'life' in the sense of consciousness. In *Ideen* he writes: 'We cannot construct an internal coherence (*Zusammenhang*) apart from that which is given to us ... Consciousness cannot get behind itself.'[8] Dilthey's early view of philosophy is that it is based on facts of consciousness: 'Only in inner experience, in the facts of consciousness, have I found a firm anchor for my thinking ...,' he wrote in the preface to the *Einleitung* (p. xvii). In an early unpublished manuscript he declared: 'Philosophy analyses, but produces nothing ... Since it dissects, analyses, it can only point out particulars and sum up what is there, what it finds among the facts of consciousness.'[9] Any inquiry into the ground of life or the transcendental conditions for life and consciousness is ruled out.

We find similar affirmations in the writings of the post-1900 years, but now a new element is added. 'Experience' (*Erleben*), Dilthey writes, is 'unfathomable' (*unergründlich*), and thought cannot get behind it (*Fortsetzung*, 224). We also read: 'Now life is the fundamental fact (*Grundtatsache*) that must form the point of departure for philosophy. It is that which is known from within; it is that behind which we cannot penetrate. Life cannot be brought before the tribunal of reason' (p. 261). The new element here is that life is known from within. In his preface to Volume V, Dilthey had declared that the governing impulse in his philosophy was to understand life out of itself (p. 4). In another version of this preface he wrote that the governing impulse was '... to confine myself, in the spirit of the great Enlightenment, to empirical (*erfahrbar*) reality as the one world of our knowledge' (V, 418). These two statements do not contradict one another: the former should be seen as more explicit than the latter. In his earliest statements on the philosophical significance of 'life,' Dilthey had spoken of conditions making knowledge possible, and we now see what those conditions are. It is because we are equipped in advance with an implicit comprehension of life that we are able to understand life – to some degree, at least – wherever it manifests itself. Therefore, we could speak of 'life' as an a priori making our knowledge of social-historical reality possible. It is not a formal and universal invariant a priori of which we become aware through transcendental analysis; it is simply that which gives meaning and sense to our knowledge and comprehension of others and of the world of the spirit. It was this insight that Dilthey was to apply to history: '... the first condition for the possibility of historical science is that I myself am a historical being, that the one who investigates history is also the one who makes history.'[10] More specifically, such an a priori is the basis for the possibility of understanding: 'The spirit understands only that which it has created' (*Aufbau*, 148). What this means is that '... understanding is a rediscovery of the I in the Thou; the spirit rediscovers itself at ever higher levels of coherence ...' (*Fortsetzung*, 191).

At this point the interesting parallels between Dilthey and Ortega y Gasset become manifest. Ortega, who liked to point to the resemblance, was fully aware of the centrality and significance of Dilthey's idea of 'life.' In his essay 'History as a System,' he hailed Dilthey as 'the writer to whom we owe more than to anyone else concerning the idea of life' (p. 216). Unfortunately, Ortega writes, Dilthey was not able to develop his discovery fully and clearly;* this honour was left to Ortega himself, who spoke of life as the 'basic reality' (p. 165) and of knowledge as an 'internal function of life' (p. 181). Life (understood as human life) is '... something not merely singular, but unique. Life is the life of each one of us' (p. 206). Therefore, we say of man not that he *is* but that he *lives.*[11] Ortega's concept of life includes the same historical turn as that of Dilthey: 'Man is what has happened to him, what he has done' (p. 216). Thus he concludes: 'Man, in a word, has no nature; what he has is ... history.'[12]

Like Ortega, Dilthey did not conceive of life in biological terms: 'I limit the meaning of the expression "life" in the *Geisteswissenschaften* to the human world; it is determined here by the sphere to which it is applied and is not open to misunderstanding.'[13] The 'life' on which philosophy is to be based is 'the life lived by man' (*das von den Menschen gelebte Leben*);[14] it is 'the life of each one of us,' to use Ortega's phrase. Thus 'life,' in Dilthey's later years, is much more than what is directly given in consciousness. In an unfinished manuscript of 1911 he wrote: 'Life is the dynamic interaction (*Wirkungszusammenhang*) that exists between the self and its surroundings.'[15] Life is neither wholly subject nor wholly object but encompasses both. Because it must be sought in the interaction between self and milieu, it is revealed to us in moods.

* 'The great new Idea in which man is beginning to abide is the Idea of life. Dilthey was among its first discoverers, but he still moved on that unknown ground with all the toil and trouble that falls to the lot of the pioneer. This study will make it clear that, strictly speaking, Dilthey never knew that he had arrived at a new continent, and he never succeeded in taking possession of the land on which he trod. For fifty years he stretched out his hands in untiring effort to catch that fleeting vision of the Idea that had flashed upon him in his early youth. In vain. The Idea, which at first appearance had seemed so easy to lay hands on, proved more and more elusive to any attempt at capture by clear concepts' ('A Chapter from the History of Ideas,' 132). Ortega claims that his own thought is neither identical with that of Dilthey nor a continuation of it: it is parallel to Dilthey's thought. 'Parallels do not touch each other, because they start at different points ... They *tackle the problem on different levels,* one more advanced and plenary than the other. With respect to the problem of life, *living reason* marks a higher level than *historical reason* at which Dilthey came to a halt' (pp. 141-2). Dilthey was a 'stammering genius' (p. 166) who 'stopped midway' in 'the pursuit of his own idea,' i.e., the idea of life (p. 140). Ortega was a student in Berlin in 1906 while Dilthey was an emeritus professor there, but they did not meet. Ortega writes that he did not 'become acquainted' with Dilthey's work until 1929 (see pp. 136-40).

Nothing is more fleeting, more fragile or more changeable than man's mood vis-à-vis the totality (*Zusammenhang*) of things in which he finds himself or than the ideas about the inner coherence (*Zusammenhang*) of life and the world that arise within him. Sometimes life casts deep shadows across our soul, sometimes it imparts life and joy to it ... Our sense of life (*Gefühl des Lebens*) changes like light and shadow moving across a landscape.[16]

Philosophy is to bring what is contained and manifested in life to explicit awareness. Thus Dilthey wrote to Count Yorck: 'Philosophy is an action which elevates life, that is, the subject in its relations as something living, to consciousness and thinks it through to its end' (*Briefwechsel*, 247 – italics omitted). It represents an understanding and interpretation of life out of itself.

At this point we must pause to see what lies behind this talk of 'life.' Why must philosophy be a philosophy of 'life,' and how does 'life' make knowledge possible? The point that Dilthey sought to bring out through the use of such language was that there is a relation present from the outset between the subjective and the objective, between the thinker and what is thought. This point could not be made as well if 'being' were adopted as the fundamental term, for 'being' stands over against thought and does not appear to include thought. Dilthey spoke of 'life' instead because this term clearly suggests the unity of thought and its content or object, of activity and what is acted upon. The choice of the term 'life' does not, then, reflect the widespread interest in biological matters that is typical of the late nineteenth century. Dilthey, in fact, manifested no special interest in biology and did not use the term 'life' in a biological sense.

In Dilthey's earlier writings, the concept of life already included both the subjective and objective aspects, but 'life' was nevertheless described in somewhat narrow terms. When he spoke of 'life,' he meant consciousness or the mind, which embraces both mental activity (the subjective side) and mental contents or facts of consciousness (the objective side). The insistence on developing a philosophy of *life* then meant that the process of thought and the content of thought are originally given in an intimate relation: the problem is not how these two are to be brought together. But in his later philosophical reflection, Dilthey broke through the barrier between the mind as a self-enclosed entity and the outer, public world which must somehow be reflected or represented within consciousness. This in turn paved the way for a broader conception of 'life.' On the subjective side, life now came to embrace the whole range of human activities dominated by thought, feeling, and will. On the objective side, life included all that man is in contact with insofar as it is actually in relation to him. As we have seen, Dilthey described life as the 'dynamic interaction' (*Wirkungszusammenhang*) between the self (not simply the mind as an isolated entity) and its surroundings (not simply the mind's contents). Here the unity between the subjective and the objective is developed further than in the earlier writings, for the subject is now a self situated in a world to which it relates through a variety of intentional processes.

Given this conception of life, the idea of philosophy as a philosophy of life follows naturally. If philosophy is about the concrete world – as Dilthey steadfastly believed – and not about a world behind this world or about abstractions underlying our experience, then it must trace some of the paths followed by the living self in its relations with the other. The material for philosophy is neither the self nor the other but both, together with the bond between them. And this bond is nothing other than life itself. It is the profound phenomenon before which we stand continually in awe. It is also what we know in a most intimate and familiar manner, although our knowledge of it does not yet approach the clarity and generality which philosophical reflection and analysis can bestow. Reaching this clarity and generality is the task of the philosopher. Thus philosophy is not a meditation on God or an analysis of the most general of all concepts but an observation and interpretation of the process of life itself on the basis of the implicit comprehension of life which a man enjoys in virtue of the fact that he is a living being. The decisive point is that the philosopher who thinks is also a person who *lives*, who responds on various levels to the world around him and affects it through his expressions, feelings, and actions.

At this juncture, the connection between Dilthey's reflection on literature and his post-1900 philosophical position again comes into view. We have seen that Dilthey relinquished the conception of philosophy as an analysis of facts of consciousness in favour of the view that philosophy must explicate life on the basis of the implicit comprehension of life that grows in each one of us from the moment of our birth. The 'life of each one of us' is that something 'known from within' which philosophy adopts as its starting point. This is what Dilthey means when he declares that philosophy must seek to understand life out of itself. But in his important essay on Goethe, Dilthey had already assigned to poetry the task of understanding life out of itself. In the same essay he spoke of an 'interpretation (*Auslegung*) of existence out of itself' (*Erlebnis*, 162), of a 'completely universal interpretation of life itself' (p. 164), and of Goethe's 'unfettered interpretation (*unbefangene Auslegung*) of life out of itself' (p. 172). 'Life and its interpretation' is the very foundation of Goethe's poetry.[17] In his essay on the poet Hölderlin,

Dilthey spoke of an 'interpretation (*Deutung*) of life out of itself' (*Erlebnis*, 273), and in his essay on the types of worldviews we read that the poetic task is 'to make life again understandable out of itself' (VIII, 93). In the post-1900 years, this poetic task then becomes the task of philosophy. In *Das Wesen der Philosophie* (1907), Dilthey declares that modern philosophy of life seeks to construct an 'interpretation of life' (*Lebensdeutung*) on the basis of our experience of life and then adds: '... life is to be interpreted out of itself – this is the great idea that unites these philosophers with the world's wisdom and with poetry' (pp. 370–1).

Because philosophical activity, which is in effect life reflecting on itself, begins with an implicit understanding that precedes reflection, its method is essentially circular. In a letter to Count Yorck, Dilthey wrote: 'Philosophy has no presuppositionless, universally valid beginning. Its beginning is caught in a circle.'[18] Here we encounter a first form of the hermeneutical circle, which is not to be avoided within the framework of Dilthey's philosophy of life. Life is many-sided, Dilthey pointed out,[19] but my own life is one-sided.[20] How is one-sidedness to be avoided in my understanding and interpretation of life? The answer, of course, is that it cannot be avoided entirely: the plurality of worldviews and philosophical outlooks is inescapable. Life is too rich and manifold to be adequately grasped in any one conception. But excessive one-sidedness can certainly be avoided. In the process of understanding others and understanding the social-historical world, I deepen my self-understanding and thereby enlarge my basis for understanding. More specifically, I come to understand myself more fully by deepening my understanding of the human world in which I live. My understanding of life and the world is necessarily limited, for it is tied to the fundamental a priori that is my life and range of experience. I understand others in terms of my own life, that is, in terms of the common humanity with which I am acquainted only through my own life. But I am always free to broaden my basis for understanding by broadening my life to include as wide a range of experience and knowledge as possible. Of course, a presuppositionless understanding of life and the world will not be attained thereby, for philosophical comprehension always moves from the already known to the not yet known. There is no absolute beginning, for I always implicitly presuppose a history; that is to say, I begin with what I have, what I have become.

My life, then, as the totality of my experience (i.e., all that I have lived through and 'understood') plays an important role in my philosophical reflection. It also affects subsequent experience, as many thinkers have pointed out. Therefore, the mind must be conceived in such a way that the cumulative effect of previous experiences is somehow brought to bear on our conscious acts. Dilthey approaches this complicated problem by speaking of the mind as a 'developed mental system' (*erworbene seelische Zusammenhang*). This system, which we might better speak of as 'develop*ing*,' is acquired and built up over a period of time and includes the effects of all that we have lived through and 'understood.' Thus Dilthey sees the mind neither as a stream of conscious states nor as a system of invariant, transcendental conditions for experience. The life of the mind does include a stream of experiences, and there are indeed factors that condition our experience. The essential point, however, is that these factors develop and change in time.

Every individual act of consciousness, Dilthey declares, is conditioned by this developing mental system (*Ideen*, 177). This idea plays an important role especially in his theory of poetic imagination and artistic creation. Dilthey insisted that one and the same image or presentation never appears twice in mental life: 'In a stream of mental life conceivable to us, the same presentation no more reappears in one consciousness than it occurs in a second consciousness as precisely the same. No more than the new spring again makes the old leaves on the trees visible to me are the presentations of a past day re-awakened today, perhaps only in a somewhat more obscure and unclear form.'[21] Metamorphosis governs all of mental life, including memory: '... in memory itself we discover a side through which it is related to the power of imagination; metamorphosis governs the entire life of images in the mind.'[22] A remembered presentation, Dilthey explains, is built up from a certain inner point of view.[23] Thus the developing mental system is not bound to unchangeable 'mental atoms.'

By the metamorphosis of individual presentations, I mean that the individual presentation or image is not a constant atom of mental life but a process that occurs under changing conditions ... Thus presentations are not altered only from without, in their relations, as it were, while they themselves remain stable; rather, they are agents and processes ... that undergo changes. The developed system of mental life (*erworbene Zusammenhang des Seelenlebens*) operates as a regulating apparatus in relation to this metamorphosis (*Briefwechsel*, 58).

Because the developing mental system grows and changes through time, consciousness itself must be regarded as historical. 'In the developed mental system,' writes Dilthey, 'the past is victorious ...' (*Ideen*, 217–18).

My life, as the totality of my experience, remains with me in the developing mental system that governs and conditions all of my conscious acts. Dilthey did not, however, work out this idea in any detail. In his lectures on ethics he declared: 'We know nothing of any mental substance. We have knowledge only of processes and their interaction' (x, 47). Yet he had admitted that there is something beyond conscious processes by which the latter are somehow affected. The developing mental system, he wrote, is 'operative without being distinctly conscious' (*Ideen*, 190). Thus this system, which includes rules of action, values, and the effects of countless experiences, both remembered and unremembered, could well be regarded as an unconscious or subconscious sector of the mind that can be explored and known only by way of indirect methods. Psychologists in Dilthey's time were already working with the idea of the subconscious,[24] although Dilthey himself was inclined to be suspicious of the notion of unconscious elements in mental life.[25] Yet such an idea was already implied in his doctrine of the developing mental system. Therefore, we finally find him embracing the idea of unconscious factors at work in the life of the mind: he wrote that '... the small sphere of consciousness rises out of inaccessible depths like an island.' Introspection, which could at best focus only on the island itself, would then be inadequate as a means of gaining knowledge of mental life. Hence Dilthey immediately added: 'But the expression draws on these depths' (*Fortsetzung*, 220). The depths of mental life, then, can be explored adequately only by way of the method of expression and understanding.

DILTHEY'S REJECTION OF METAPHYSICS

For many students of Dilthey's thought, the question of Dilthey and metaphysics poses no special problem. Dilthey, they claim, was a professed enemy of metaphysics in all its forms: he regarded metaphysics as a closed chapter in the history of the Western mind.[26] They point out – rightly – that Dilthey accepted Kant's critique of metaphysics: 'This standpoint of a critique of our knowledge of reality itself first puts an end to metaphysics,' he wrote.[27] And in an inaugural address delivered to the Prussian Academy of Sciences in 1887, Dilthey declared: '... the systems of the metaphysicians have collapsed ...'[28]

Some of the commentators who emphasize this side of Dilthey's thinking have concluded that he was an empiricist with one foot, at least, in the British philosophical tradition. In an article on Dilthey we read: 'Dilthey was basically an empiricist ...'[29] H.A. Hodges, the author of two books on Dilthey, claims: 'Dilthey himself would have no dealings with metaphysics, whether in the ancient or in the post-Kantian form. His attitude on this point was clear from the start and never wavered.' Hodges concludes: 'Dilthey's philosophy does not belong to the idealist family at all. It belongs rather to the progeny of Locke and Hume, to the family of the British empiricists.'[30]

The claim that Dilthey was an empiricist is mistaken, although he did share with the classic empiricists the conviction that our knowledge is somehow limited to the givens of experience. The issue, of course, is the nature of experience. Dilthey was well aware that his own position on this question was far removed from that of the British empiricists. His insistence on the metamorphosis of images and presentations is contrary to Hume's theory of consciousness; indeed, he formulated this doctrine in direct opposition to the empiricist position, as is apparent from the quotation on p. 77 above. Furthermore, he charged that empiricism distorts and mutilates experience by reducing it to atomic sensations and presentations.[31] He regarded John Stuart Mill as the logical outcome of the extremes of empiricism,[32] and he left no doubt that he was not a follower of Mill. Dilthey was well aware that the term 'empiricism' had become indissolubly linked with the philosophical outlook of Locke and Hume, and accordingly he made no attempt to appropriate it for his own philosophy of experience. As he saw it, empiricism in the historical sense was something to be combated. This he proposed to do by way of a book to be entitled 'An Essay on Philosophy of Experience and Reality in Opposition to Empiricism and Speculation.' The motto of the book was to be 'an empirical approach but not empiricism' (*Empirie und nicht Empirismus*).[33] This project was a forerunner of the *Einleitung*, in which the 'standpoint of experience, of an unfettered empirical approach (*unbefangene Empirie*) in opposition even to empiricism' (p. 81), was affirmed. Thus Dilthey can hardly be characterized as an empiricist.

Dilthey's lifelong preoccupation with Schleiermacher and his later interest in Hegel are also indications that his outlook on metaphysics is hardly that of the British empiricists. Friedrich Meinecke saw Dilthey as part of a movement towards a 'new metaphysical idealism' and reported that '... Dilthey was regarded as the man who had still been able to catch a glimpse of the last rays of the sunset of the old idealism and to absorb them into his own soul ...'[34] Other writers have spoken of a 'metaphysics of experience' (*Erlebnismetaphysik*) or a 'metaphysics of becoming' in connection with Dilthey,[35] and one even hails him as a misunderstood metaphysician of a new kind.[36] Georg Misch, Dilthey's son-in-law, points out that Dilthey tended to use metaphysical language in speaking of 'life.'[37] Thus it appears that Dilthey's outlook on metaphysics is comprised of more than a simple rejection.

To shed some light on this matter, we must first determine what Dilthey meant by the term 'metaphysics.' In Book II of the *Einleitung*, which contains his most extensive discussion of metaphysics, he observes that he uses the term in the Aristotelian sense (p. 133) and credits Kant with clarifying the concept of metaphysics:

Via the secure insights of the critical philosophy, we derive from the Aristotelian definition of the concept of metaphysics one distinguishing characteristic which is likewise beyond dispute. Kant rightly emphasized this characteristic. All metaphysics goes beyond experience. It supplements that which is given in experience by means of an objective and universal inner coherence (*Zusammenhang*), which is created only in the processing of experience in accordance with the conditions of consciousness (pp. 130–1 – italics omitted).

In a later manuscript, Dilthey notes that the cosmic, objective type of metaphysics was eventually replaced by a metaphysics of subjectivity and adds that the latter is just as unacceptable as the former.[38] Within his outline of the history of metaphysics, he distinguishes between an old and a new metaphysics. The old metaphysics had sought to provide the foundation for the various sciences and for all of our knowledge of reality. This pretence was destroyed by the rise of modern science. Metaphysics then assumed the task of gathering the results of the sciences and shaping them into a total outlook on life and the world.

According to the views of the metaphysicians, science only produces the individual words – and the rules for combining them – which are first shaped into a poem by the metaphysician. But a poem has no claim to universally valid truth. In approximately the same era, one could hear Schelling proving his philosophy of revelation, Hegel his cosmic reason, Schopenhauer his cosmic will, and the materialists their anarchy of atoms, all on equally good or equally bad grounds.[39]

The very plurality of such systems, which Dilthey speaks of as 'enchanted castles of scientific imagination' (p. 359), makes a mockery of their claims to scientific validity. 'Wherever metaphysics continued to exist,' he wrote, 'it was transformed into a merely private system for its author and for those who were attracted to it because of a similar mental constitution' (p. 358). This state of affairs, he pointed out, inevitably leads to skepticism. Indeed, skepticism is 'inseparable' from metaphysics; it accompanies metaphysics as its very shadow (pp. 125, 407). Metaphysics claims universal validity, but it does not employ a method capable of establishing such validity.[40] Dilthey therefore concluded that metaphysics as a science, as a scientific worldview, is impossible.[41] There is no place for metaphysics in philosophy; it has been replaced by epistemology: 'At the *end of its journey*, then, *metaphysics merges with epistemology*, which takes the cognitive subject as its object. The transformation of the world within the cognitive subject through these modern systems is, as it were, the euthanasia of metaphysics.'[42]

This is not to say, however, that metaphysics is without value. Insofar as a metaphysical system embodies a worldview, a total outlook on life, we can learn something from it, just as we learn from art and religion. Worldviews are more basic than these three forms in which they come to expression, and therefore Dilthey defined metaphysics in terms of worldviews: 'When a worldview is grasped conceptually, grounded, and elevated to universal validity, we call it metaphysics.'[43] Thus we can study a metaphysical system to penetrate its worldview and the lived experience by which this worldview was shaped. Such an approach would constitute a 'phenomenology of metaphysics,' in which we are guided by the principle: 'Each metaphysical system is representative only of the situation from which one soul has viewed the riddle of the world' (*Einleitung*, 406). The true metaphysicians, Dilthey informs us, have lived what they write (p. 358). To study their metaphysical systems is, therefore, to study philosophical experience: 'Every metaphysical genius expresses in concepts one side of reality which has never before been seen as he sees it. This side becomes a part of his metaphysical experience. Seen biographically, this experience consists of a series of experiential processes; however, it becomes philosophical experience because a universal state of affairs is grasped thereby.'[44] This phenomenology of metaphysics amounts to a hermeneutics of metaphysical expression in which a social or ethical truth, for example, may be uncovered via an interpretive process that translates metaphysical symbols and concepts back into inner experience.[45]

At this point, the structure and shape of Dilthey's projected (non-metaphysical) philosophy of life begins to become clear. Fundamental to it is the theory of worldviews, for the worldview is mankind's basic response to the totality of life and the world. The theory of worldviews then serves as the basis for a philosophy of philosophy (i.e., a philosophy of metaphysical expression), a philosophy of artistic expression, and a philosophy of religious expression. Although the 'totality of our mental powers' is involved in each of these forms of expression, one of the mental powers becomes dominant in each. Art is the sphere dominated by feeling. In metaphysics, thought or presentation is uppermost. And religion, according to Dilthey, is bound up with will; it is inseparable from morality and action.[46] Religious expression developed first in the history of mankind, and artistic and metaphysical expression grew up in its shadow, gradually becoming independent of it. These three basic forms of expression have a common task.

The riddle of existence faces all ages of mankind with the same mysterious countenance; we catch sight of its features, but we must guess at the soul behind it. This riddle is always bound up organically with that of the world itself and with the question what I am supposed to do in this world, why I am in it, and how my life in it will end. Where did I come from? Why do I exist? What will become of me? This is the most general of all questions and the one that most concerns me. The answer to this question is sought in common by the poetic genius, the prophet and the thinker.[47]

The three types of expression reflect and depict the totality of reality, each in its own limited way: 'This immeasurable, incomprehensible, unfathomable universe is mirrored in diverse ways in religious seers, in poets, and in philosophers.'[48]

But the task of a philosophy of life is by no means limited to summing up what artists, metaphysicians, and prophets have revealed to us about life as a totality. Philosophy of life must also probe the relation between the totality and the reflection or expression of this totality in the individual human being who responds to it. More specifically, it must investigate the formation of worldviews. In the process, it will formulate a new critique of metaphysics as a science.

Life itself, Dilthey tells us, is the final root of all worldviews (*Weltanschauung*, 78). Our experience of life as a totality is conditioned by various factors, including our previous experience as retained in the developing mental system, our physical position within reality, and the mood of the moment. Every experience of life and every mood is potentially the source of a new worldview. Each worldview, writes Dilthey, '... grasps one side of the reality of things; we are not able to grasp the totality in an objective way.'[49] Thus, although we cannot form a concept of the totality, we do respond to it in some way, for each worldview is the product of an encounter between the totality of life and a particular person in a particular situation in a particular mood at a particular time:

... the worldviews are grounded in the nature of the universe and in the relationship of the finite cognitive mind to it. Thus each worldview expresses one side of the universe within the limits of our thought. To this extent each worldview is true. But each is one-sided. It is not granted us to view these sides together. We can glimpse the pure light of truth only in various broken rays.[50]

It is precisely because it is impossible to grasp the whole, because life is many-sided and endlessly manifold, that each and every metaphysical system is bound to fail. The metaphysician universalizes his own outlook on life and then claims scientific validity for it. His claims are contradicted by other metaphysicians, and there is simply no way to settle the dispute between them. Therefore metaphysics is impossible as a science. But a metaphysical system, like a poem, has a content in the form of a worldview or perspective[51] which is valuable and worthy of our attention. A worldview, as one person's authentic and total response to the totality,[52] reveals something about the totality and about man's existential and experiential possibilities as well. Insofar as philosophy of life is interested in life as a totality, it must approach the totality by studying worldviews and the various types of expressions in which they are embodied. There is simply no other way for the philosopher of life to come to grips with life as a totality. Because of this limitation, his work is never finished but always remains an approximation.

Although Dilthey's writings include numerous attempts to define philosophy, relatively few of them come close to the conception of philosophy sketched above. Unfortunately, the many conflicting characterizations and definitions of philosophy scattered throughout Dilthey's works have served as a seed-bed of confusion. His ponderous pronouncements on 'what philosophy is' or 'the nature of philosophy' or 'the basic idea of my philosophy' all too often leave us mystified. They contain some revealing statements, but perhaps more significant is the fact that he was rarely able to complete them: his unsuccessful effort to write a sketch of his own philosophy for Ueberweg's history of philosophy illustrates this all too well.[53] Dilthey finally declared: 'We must ask history what philosophy is.'[54] Perhaps the best Diltheyan definition of philosophy has been supplied by Ortega: 'In Dilthey's opinion philosophy is an empirical science; it is the last and decisive act in which man *qua* intelligence takes possession of the *whole* reality which is *his* reality, without such abstractions as are, and always were, performed by all other forms of cognition, including traditional philosophy.'[55] Dilthey himself says of philosophy: 'Its function is to elevate to consciousness, to conceptual thought, the unity of our being in its various expressions of life.'[56] His own best definition is probably the following: '... philosophy is the elevation of our totality, from whose darkness all great manifestations of the spirit have proceeded, to a consciousness of its unity and thereby of the interconnectedness (*Zusammenhang*) of all of its expressions.'[57] In the same spirit he spoke of philosophy in later years as the spirit's reflection on itself (*Selbstbesinnung des Geistes*).[58]

No doubt the major factor in Dilthey's caution and indecision in defining philosophy was his fear of lapsing into metaphysics. To avoid this, he tried to define philosophy as much as possible in terms of the (human) subject that lives life. Yet, philosophy is concerned also with the 'interconnectedness' of all of the subject's expressions, which certainly cannot be explained without reference to the totality to which all of these expressions respond. But this totality is left out of the definition – except on occasions when Dilthey speaks of the 'riddle' of life or the world as the object of philosophy.[59] Nevertheless, the idea of the totality is clearly present in Dilthey's conception of philosophy, for he never claimed to be able to account for human experience and the expressions which arise out of it solely in terms of the subject. Thus, to the extent that this 'totality' of life, to which each world-view is a response, represents a metaphysical notion, there is a metaphysical element in Dilthey's thought. And this perhaps explains his tendency to equate philosophy as such, which is a legitimate intellectual pursuit, with metaphysics, which is an illegitimate enterprise: in writings of the post-1900 years, both are described in the same terms, that is, as related to poetry and religion insofar as they attempt to give an answer to the riddle of life, and as related to science insofar as they claim universal validity.[60] Furthermore, it turns out that Dilthey's 'philosophy of philosophy' (which will be dealt with later) is for the most part a treatment of metaphysics.

5

Expression and Understanding

Once we have grasped life as our spiritual food and drink, the source from which we draw constantly, we must turn to the question how it shapes expressions, which are the medium of human interchange. By way of the expression we get at life itself; we absorb something of the lives of others and even our own forgotten past, and thereby we become larger selves. The task, for Dilthey, is to show how understanding, in our daily contacts with others, already gets us beyond the confines of our own individuality. Once this is clear, he can point out its potential for developing a consciousness and outlook that embraces a vast range of human experience and history. To Dilthey, such an expanded self, a self open to life in all its manifestations, is definitely a cultural ideal to strive for in a world of converging societies and histories.

LIVED EXPERIENCE AS THE SOIL OF CULTURE

The connection between life and experience, on the one hand, and the various forms of expression, on the other, is very important in Dilthey's later philosophy: 'Everything produced by man springs from mental life (*Seelenleben*) and its relations to the outer world' (*Philosophie*, 372). The philosopher of life is interested in this connection to the extent that an examination of the forms of expression may reveal something about life as a totality. By going in the direction of the particular, the cultural scientist reverses this procedure. He examines life and the stream of experience as the soil from which particular expressions spring in order to clarify and understand expressions by tracing their roots in experience. From such a study of particular expressions, he can then go on to make and support some general statements about the culture of an age.

Dilthey's contention that the forms of expression are rooted in 'life' really amounts to the claim that they are rooted in lived experience, in 'Erlebnisse.' He writes: 'Poetry is the presentation and expression of life. It expresses experience (*das Erlebnis*) ...'[1] One of the reasons why Dilthey used the terms 'Erleben' and 'Erlebnis' so often is that they contain the term 'life' (*Leben*). In an early diary entry he observed: 'To live means to allow all the forces of the world to affect us in our contemplation and action, to work out all the features of our nature into a unified *Gestalt* – in this way the art work of our existence is born' (*Der junge Dilthey*, 117). Life thought of in this way is the lived experience from which the rich world of expression springs. Thus in some passages in his later writings, Dilthey uses the term 'life' where we would expect him to use 'Erlebnis.'[2]

'Erleben' must be seen not only as *lived* experience but also as *inner* experience, that is to say, as experience conditioned by inner factors. Chief among these, of course, is the developing mental system, which is acquired in time and develops throughout our lives. Because this system influences all of our conscious acts, we must look upon human consciousness as historically conditioned. Dilthey therefore speaks of the 'historical character of mental life,' which is the 'deepest fact of the *Geisteswissenschaften*.'[3] To say that man is a historical being is to say – among other things – that he is 'filled by the entire memory of the human race' (*Fortsetzung*, 277). In other words, the history of mankind conditions my present experience and conscious life: in the developing mental system, the past is victorious (*Ideen*, 217–18). The historicality of present experience entails the historicality of expression, for every expression draws on my experience and is influenced at the same time by the developing mental system, which is also historically conditioned. This then entails that understanding is historically shaped, for its primary object (i.e., the expression) is conditioned by the past, and understanding itself, as a conscious process, is under the influence of the developing mental system. This thoroughgoing historicality of consciousness represents Dilthey's fundamental difference with empiricism, for his theory of consciousness leaves no room for 'mental atoms' or presentations that remain the same through a variety of conscious acts and processes.

As we examine the relations between lived experience and expression, we must keep the aesthetic slant of Dilthey's thought in mind. Count Yorck spoke of aesthetics as Dilthey's 'proper (*eigenthümlich*) domain' (*Briefwechsel*, 149), and Dilthey himself made no secret of his deep love for the arts. Music, he confessed early in his life, was his favourite of all the arts;[4] he viewed it, like the other arts, as a way of giving expression to experience (*Fortsetzung*, 221). Yet despite his great love for music, it was to poetic ex-

pression that he turned his special attention. Poetic imagination and creation – as exemplified by Goethe – was his model for expression in general.
Dilthey steadfastly refused to view art as a peculiar species of human activity
isolated from the basic concerns of life[5] and tended instead to view human
life in terms of art: he liked to speak of the poet as the true man.[6] Because the
only type of expression with which Dilthey dealt at any length is poetic expression, we will have to draw on his writings on literature.

In the writings of the post-1900 years, Dilthey often spoke of the cycle of
experience, expression, and understanding. This might lead us to conclude
that the expression arises out of a single experience, and that the understanding of this expression would then consist in the re-living (*nacherleben*)
of this experience. Dilthey does tell us that every act of understanding is a
re-living,[7] and in some passages he leaves the definite impression that a
single expression springs from a single experience.[8] Rudolf Bultmann thus
observes that for Dilthey, understanding means 'reproducing past psychical
experiences by imagination.'[9] Nevertheless, this impression is mistaken, as
is apparent from the bearing of some of Dilthey's other views on this question.

If each expression arises out of a single experience, we must be able to
identify experiences as separate and individual. But a single experience cannot so easily be isolated from other experiences, for Dilthey's definition of
an experience is fairly elastic: 'An experience (*Erlebnis*) is a unity whose
parts are bound together by a common meaning' (*Fortsetzung*, 234). The idea
of discrete experiences succeeding one another in consciousness is incompatible with Dilthey's view of mental life. He sketched the relations between
conscious processes as follows:

Now these processes follow one another, but not like wagons, one after the other,
each one separated from the one before, like rows of a regiment of soldiers, always
with a space between them ... These processes are squeezed together in such a way
that there is always something present in my consciousness, just as objects that were
ahead of or beside a hiker who moves steadily forward fade away behind him as
others appear ahead of him, while the continuity of the landscape is preserved
throughout (*Ideen*, 201).

We could better speak of a particular expression as arising out of a certain
stream or complex of experiences.

The correlation of an expression with a single experience would be too
easy a solution for Dilthey, for mental life is a 'great riddle' (*Ideen*, 223); it is
'something unfathomable' (*ein Unergründliches*).[10] He compares psychical

life to a plant with its roots deep in the earth;[11] what appears on the surface of consciousness is part of a more encompassing whole. The expression does not reflect the surface only; it sends its roots deep into the earth. It draws on unconscious factors that determine the expression itself: 'It is the deepest mystery of lyrical poetry how the inner mental process, which appears to express only an experience, at the same time expresses the poet's total nature which, unconsciously and in inaccessible depths, determines the experience of the poet.'[12] Thus the expression does not correspond precisely to the underlying experience which occasioned its creation; Dilthey maintains instead that the inner experience is made more complete (*ergänzt*) through the expression.[13] This means that '... expressions of experience contain more than is present in the consciousness of the poet or the artist, and therefore also evoke more' (*Fortsetzung*, 214). Consequently, understanding is not to be viewed as a re-capture or re-creation of a single experience underlying the expression. Understanding goes beyond experience: the poet understands and depicts things that he could not personally experience.[14] By means of the process of understanding, we overcome the limitations of personal experience (*Aufbau*, 141); we are led from the narrowness and subjectivity of personal experience to the universal and the whole (p. 143). Hence Dilthey speaks of a clarification, broadening, and completion of experience through understanding (p. 145). Thus we are not to think of one and the same experience as present throughout the cycle of experience, expression, and understanding.

We have seen that Dilthey sometimes claims that the expression expresses an experience. But he also writes that it expresses 'unfathomable life itself,'[15] that it expresses something mental (*ein Geistiges*),[16] and that it expresses something inward (*ein Inneres*).[17] There is, indeed, a very close relationship between lived experience and the expressions that arise out of it, but this relation does not represent a one-to-one correspondence. Dilthey regarded this relation as so significant that he published a book of essays on various German poets under the title 'Das Erlebnis und die Dichtung.' This book, which has probably been the most widely read of his works throughout the twentieth century, has inspired a good deal of speculation about what an 'Erlebnis' is and what role 'Erlebnisse' play in artistic imagination and creation. Most of this speculation goes far beyond Dilthey's own thinking and does not concern us here. Dilthey himself wrote that 'Erlebnisse' are the 'sources' from which the poetic work is nourished, that lived experience represents the 'basic stratum' (*Grundlage*) and the 'central substance' (*kernhafte Gehalt*) of poetry, and that it provides the poet with his 'material' or 'stuff.'[18]

In his later years, Dilthey began to speak of art more and more as a depiction and representation of life in its meaning or significance, thereby moving even further away from the idea of an exact correspondence between expression and experience. He now spoke of poetry as expressing the 'meaning of life'[19] – a phrase which he left unclarified – and declared: 'The essence of poetry is to express what is experienced, to present the objectification of life in such a way that the event on which the poet focuses is manifested effectively in its meaning for the whole of life.'[20] Understanding, likewise, is not merely a re-creation of experience; it seeks the 'much deeper meaning of expressions of life' (*Fortsetzung*, 234); that is to say, it seeks to penetrate experience as pervaded by a meaning derived – in part, at least – from subconscious or unconscious depths of mental life, e.g., the historically acquired developing mental system.

An expression, then, is not to be regarded as a manifestation of a single event in its author's conscious life. Therefore, the study of expressions is not by any means a form of biography. As we saw earlier (p. 68), great works of art as such say nothing whatever about their creators. The meaning embodied by a work of art – or any expression, for that matter – is not first and foremost a biographical meaning. (This is not to deny that many expressions and art works are in fact biographically revealing.) Dilthey makes this especially clear through certain remarks on Shakespeare and Goethe. He freely admits that Goethe's poetry reveals a good deal about his life: 'Thus the poems of Goethe always lead us back to the great man who speaks to us in them. Each of his works points to the personality that is present in all of them.'[21] But Shakespeare's works do not reveal the man Shakespeare to us: 'These works are as silent about their creator as they are revealing about the way of the world.' Yet in the same essay from which this sentence was taken Dilthey hails Shakespeare as the 'greatest poet produced by the human race.'[22] Thus the fact that Shakespeare's poems and plays do not reveal his life and person to us clearly does not detract from their value and excellence in Dilthey's eyes. Shakespeare has a great deal to teach us – but not about himself. Dilthey makes the same point with reference to Kant and Schleiermacher: 'We can understand the philosophy of Kant fully without concerning ourselves further with his personality and life; Schleiermacher's meaning, his worldview and his works require a biographical presentation if they are to be understood thoroughly.'[23] Schleiermacher, apparently, drew much more directly on his own life and experience than Kant.

The expression, then, embodies a meaning drawn from experience and the depths of mental life. It may be intended to evoke in the beholder some experience which the author of the expression has actually undergone, but not all expressions have this intent. All understanding, certainly, is in some sense a re-living,[24] yet not every experience which we re-live is an immediate, non-reflective experience or conscious process. What I re-live may be a conscious process embodying a meaning arising out of material provided by immediate experience. Furthermore, our re-living does not correspond exactly to the author's conscious process. It usually fails to re-create the author's experience fully, although in some respects it may be more complete and full – Dilthey affirms the possibility of 'Besserverstehen,' that is, of understanding an author better than he understood himself. The ideal and goal of 'Besserverstehen,' he observes, is a necessary consequence of the doctrine that unconscious factors play a role in the formation of expressions.[25]

Dilthey's enthusiastic affirmation of the significance of lived experience for the formation of expressions leads to a somewhat one-sided picture of the process of expression. The emphasis falls too heavily on the material side of expression, on *what* is expressed. There are also formal factors to be considered, for most human expressions conform closely to pre-established forms and patterns, and few break as much new ground as the work of such writers as Goethe and Shakespeare. Dilthey discusses poetic expression at considerable length, but he does not devote enough attention to the role of language as such. He admits that language is historically formed and conditioned,[26] and that each particular language embodies a certain conception of the world.[27] Therefore, the world's highly developed languages are by no means equivalent to one another in terms of what can be expressed: 'Translation is often possible ... only through a rethinking.'[28] Dilthey emphasizes that human inwardness achieves its fullest expression through language,[29] but he almost leaves the impression that conscious processes are translated into expressions without the mediation of forms and structures. This one-sidedness is a manifestation of an 'individualistic' strain in Dilthey's thought: he focused his attention almost exclusively on expressions and cultural creations produced by individual human beings.

UNDERSTANDING AS THE BASIS FOR COMMUNITY

Understanding, for Dilthey, is not first and foremost a specialized scientific method or technique invented by historians or cultural scientists. It is rather a means of contact between human beings that has then been adapted for specialized use in scientific investigation: 'Understanding grows up first of all in the interests of practical life. Here persons are dependent on contact with one another ... The one must know what the other wants. Thus the elementary forms of understanding are the first to arise. They are like letters, whose combination makes higher forms of understanding possible' (*Fortsetzung*, 207). Therefore understanding must first be examined within the social context, that is, as it functions in non-theoretical life.

According to Dilthey, understanding in all its forms presupposes some sort of common element; it moves from what is known to what is not yet known, from '... something already grasped to something else that can be understood through it' (*Fortsetzung*, 234). We grasp the part in the light of the whole: '... in understanding we proceed from the coherence (*Zusammenhang*) of the whole, which is given to us in a living way, in order to make the particular understandable to ourselves through the whole' (*Ideen*, 172). Dilthey speaks of an 'identity (*Selbigkeit*) of the spirit in the I in the Thou, in every subject in a community' (*Fortsetzung*, 191), as a condition making understanding possible.

In his earlier writings especially, Dilthey accounted for this commonness by positing a 'common' (*gemeinsam*) or 'uniform' (*gleichförmig, einheitlich*) human nature.[30] He often spoke of man as a bundle or system of drives.[31] The uniformity of all men and the drives that dominate the lives of all men would then provide a common basis for understanding: I understand the other because he is like me in essential respects and is driven by the same needs and desires. In his later writings, Dilthey still affirmed that human nature is 'always the same' (*immer dasselbe*),[32] but he no longer looked upon a common human nature as the sole ground for the possibility of understanding. The historical side of his thought came more to the fore, and therefore he began to think of man and his nature in terms of realized possibilities: 'Each individual person realizes only one of the possibilities of his development, which could always have taken a different turn at some important stage in the life of the will. Man is only given to us at all under the condition of realized possibilities' (*Fortsetzung*, 279). We have no way of knowing what unrealized possibilities may lie undeveloped in a particular person or even in the entire human race. Thus Dilthey must conclude, in full conformity with his empirical attitude, that man is what he has become; in Ortega's words, man has a history rather than a nature. Dilthey also emphasizes that a particular person is what he is only in relation to his social and cultural surroundings, which entails that a person cannot be properly understood in isolation from the context in which he lives and goes about his work.

In Dilthey's later writings, the common element presupposed in understanding is no longer derived solely from a universal human nature in which all men share; it now takes the form of a historically and culturally developed sphere of 'objective spirit' in which all members of a community participate.

As early as 1883 Dilthey had declared that the '... circumstances (*Tatbestände*) in society are understandable to us from within ...' (*Einleitung*, 36). He developed this idea further during the post-1900 years. Expressions are immediately understandable to those who live in the same social and cultural community, he explained.

Every *single expression of life* in the realm of this objective spirit represents *something common*. Every word, every sentence, every gesture or polite formula, every work of art, and every historical deed is understandable only because those who express themselves in it and those who understand it are connected by having something in common. The individual always experiences, thinks and acts within a sphere of commonality, and only within such a sphere does he understand. Because of this commonality, everything understood bears intrinsic features of familiarity, as it were. We live in this atmosphere; it surrounds us constantly. We are immersed in it. We are at home everywhere in the historical and understood world; we understand the sense and meaning of it all; we are woven into this common sphere ourselves (*Aufbau*, 146–7).

Dilthey even speaks of 'products of the common mind' (*Erzeugnisse des Gemeingeistes*) in connection with this public world (*Ideen*, 180). He does not mean to posit a superindividual mind; his point is that the expression can only have a meaning if it springs from and presupposes something common or shared, for '... everything in which the spirit has objectified itself contains something common to the I and the Thou' (*Fortsetzung*, 208). This common element may be a tradition or a constellation of meaning like a common language: a sentence, Dilthey writes, '... is understandable because of the sphere of agreement (*Gemeinsamkeit*) within a linguistic community with respect to the meanings of words, the forms of inflection and the significance of syntactical arrangements' (p. 209). The process of expression and understanding presupposes this common sphere and at the same time furthers it: 'Mutual understanding safeguards the sphere of commonality that exists between individuals' (*Aufbau*, 141). In other words, the existence of a community makes understanding possible, and the process of expression and understanding in turn binds the members of a community together, thereby keeping the community alive. Without such interchange, the community would disintegrate and eventually die.

Dilthey maintains, then, that the existence of a human community presupposes the process of expression and understanding, but he also claims that this process itself presupposes the existence of such a community. The question how these two claims are to be reconciled, which involves the question how such a community can ever come about, is not dealt with by Dilthey. He bases his thinking on the fact that there *are* communities and that the process of expression and understanding is underway. How it all began is not Dilthey's concern, just as it is not his concern how language was born. Dilthey restricts himself in his philosophical thought to describing and exploring the world as it now exists. He ignores the world's genesis, and thus he accounts neither for the actual historical beginning of the human community nor for its transcendent or transcendental origin or ground. No doubt he feared that dealing with questions of genesis would lead to metaphysical entanglements.

Dilthey's conception of understanding and its roots in human life must not be identified or confused with the many other discussions of understanding to be found in nineteenth- and twentieth-century thinkers. Many of the more recent views of understanding are far removed from Dilthey's. Karel Kuypers observes that the term 'understanding' (*Verstehen*) has been so widely used that it has become more or less of a cliché. He also writes that its popularity is in part a reaction to a one-sided empiricism.[33] The notion of understanding is so prevalent in German thinking that it has been traced (without the term) as far back as Martin Luther.[34] There has even been discussion of applying the concept of understanding in biology.[35] Because the term 'understanding' has been applied to so many different – albeit related – ideas, we must first explain what Dilthey did *not* mean by it.

At the outset we should note that Dilthey makes no appeal to etymology in his explication of the concept of understanding. Philosophy, in any event, is not etymology, although the philosopher is entitled to make use of etymology in his thinking as well as in the presentation of the results of his thought. H.G. Gadamer notes that one of the meanings of the German verb 'verstehen' is '... a "savoir faire," a "pouvoir," a "capacity" to carry out a task on the practical level.'[36] This idea plays an important part in recent discussions of understanding and hermeneutics, but Dilthey himself did not think of understanding in such terms. Related to this outlook on hermeneutics is the conviction that understanding is only possible 'with one eye on the object' (*mit dem Blick auf die Sache*).[37] As the epigraph for his discussion of understanding in the *Geisteswissenschaften*, Gadamer chooses a significant sentence from Luther: 'Qui non intelligit res, non potest ex verbis sensum elicere' (Anyone who does not understand the things cannot elicit the meaning of the words). Thereby he indicates his fundamental disagreement with Dilthey and the entire hermeneutical tradition that had attempted to establish the meaning of a text while ignoring that about which the text speaks. The task, according to Gadamer, is to follow Hegel more than Schleiermacher.[38] Dilthey's inclination to suspend or ignore the question of truth has therefore come in for some criticism in recent hermeneutical discussions. Emerich Coreth maintains: 'The problem of understanding points to the question of truth. All understanding seeks to grasp truth.' He speaks of understanding as a triangle involving the person, the statement or text, and the object of discourse.[39] The emphasis on truth is also fundamental for Gadamer, as the title of his *magnum opus* ('Truth and Method') suggests. The goal of understanding, he argues, is agreement about the object of discourse (*Einverständnis in der Sache*). Anyone who seeks to understand a text must be prepared '... to let the text tell him something.'[40]

The connection between understanding and truth is not part of Dilthey's outlook, in part because he rejects correspondence as the test for truth and regards every authentic expression and every worldview as true – albeit one-sided.[41] The truth, for Dilthey, is to be sought not so much in things as in our human expressions, even though some of our expressions have nothing to do with the world outside us and are pure creations of the imagination. As we have seen (p. 90), the significance of the linguistic dimension of expression – and thereby also of understanding – is largely overlooked by Dilthey, and thus the prospect of a *rapprochement* with Gadamer's hermeneutics must be ruled out. Gadamer emphasizes that understanding is bound to language, for '... to approach the world by way of language ... is the human situation in general.'[42]

In recent existential theology, understanding is sometimes seen as an encounter in which I am changed, in which the text does something to me.[43] In the process, 'Verständnis' becomes 'Einverständnis'; that is to say, 'understanding' leads to 'an understanding' or to agreement. This existential turn is achieved by blurring or dropping the traditional hermeneutical distinction between explication and application. Dilthey does emphasize the existential significance of understanding, as we have seen (p. 62), but he does not go as far as to say that every act of understanding does or should change us. Understanding represents a possibility for profound existential change, but it is also an everyday act through which we apprehend meanings, often in connection with rather trivial purposes. Understanding, for Dilthey, is not an encounter or a mode of existence but a mode of knowledge: 'Understanding falls under the general concept of cognition, whereby we conceive of cognition in the broadest sense as a process in which we strive for universally valid knowledge.'[44]

For existential thinkers, the act of understanding is closely bound up with sympathy and love, and Dilthey is sometimes criticized for not taking this into account. Josef Böckenhoff writes: 'What we miss in his historical explorations – from the standpoint of a philosophy of encounter – is love, which first discloses the other and makes understanding possible.'[45] But one of Dilthey's defenders writes: 'Love is the foundation of understanding, and understanding enables us to love more deeply.'[46] Dilthey himself observed in earlier writings: 'We understand a person only when we sympathize with him, when we feel his emotions within ourselves; we understand only through love.'[47] Furthermore, he spoke of a 'loving understanding of the personal' and a 'loving immersion' in the human world.[48] Yet Böckenhoff's reading of Dilthey is essentially correct, for in his later writings Dilthey did not invariably link understanding with sympathy and love. Understanding can involve 'empathy' (*Einfühlen*), 'sympathy' (*Mitfühlen*), or a mere re-living (*Nachfühlen*), but it is not to be equated with any one of these.* There are acts of understanding that involve feeling in the sense of 'Nachfühlen' but not in the sense of 'Mitfühlen.'

The fact that understanding so often involves sympathy, then, should not lead us to equate it with sympathy (in the sense of sympathetic re-living). But once this is clear, we must also recognize that Dilthey placed great emphasis on the value and importance of sympathetic understanding. In a diary entry of 1859, he wrote: '... man fulfills himself only in the contemplation of all forms of human existence ...' (*Der junge Dilthey*, 88). And in a letter to Count Yorck about the delights of vacationing in Italy, he wrote: 'I regard such intimate knowledge of another nation and its people as one of the highest joys, and for persons like us it means unspeakably more than any kind of enjoyment of nature' (*Briefwechsel*, 117). Dilthey also spoke of the enjoyment he derived from observing important people and imagining their inner states (*Der junge Dilthey*, 79). As a biographer and intellectual historian, he usually chose subjects about whom he could become enthusiastic and with whom he could sympathize. But he did not deny that we can and do understand expressions and persons that do not evoke our sympathy or agreement; we do not understand our enemies as well as we understand our friends, but we do understand them and what they have to say to some degree.

What Dilthey means by understanding has also been somewhat obscured by an inadequate but often quoted definition offered in his 1900 essay on hermeneutics and repeated (with minor variations) in *Zusätze* and notes:

---

* The term 'empathy' represents an English rendering of the German 'Einfühlung' via the Greek 'empatheia.' Its meaning: 'The power of projecting one's personality into, and so fully understanding, the object of contemplation' (*The Shorter Oxford Dictionary*, Oxford: Clarendon Press, 1967). In American English, the word 'empathy' is often given a different meaning, somewhat closer to sympathy.

'What we call understanding, accordingly, is the process whereby we come to know something psychical through signs, which are expressions of it, given to the senses.'[49] This definition is weak first of all because it fails to specify that the psychical process known is a meaning-conferring act. Secondly, it overlooks the connection of understanding with 'Zusammenhang,' that is, with connections, structures, and relational contexts. For Dilthey, understanding always involves some sort of insight into or apprehension of structures or connections, whether implicit or explicit. Thirdly, the definition ignores the role of the awareness of values in understanding. Understanding is not valuation – although Dilthey maintains that there is no understanding without a sense of value (*Wertgefühl*),[50] for understanding involves not only thought but also feeling and will – but it is related to values. This is why we 'understand' the human world, which is pervaded by value, while we do not 'understand' nature.[51] The 'relation to values' (*Wertbeziehung*) which Rickert sees as part of the historian's method (see p. 27 above) is incorporated by Dilthey into understanding on the non-scientific level. The 'general cultural values' that guide the historian's selection of material form the background to our understanding of expressions and purposes. To understand not only the meaning (*Sinn* or *Bedeutung*) of an expression but also its significance (*Bedeutsamkeit*) is to gain insight into its bearing on generally accepted values and its relation to the values accepted by its author. Thus, in understanding the meaning of a particular statement, I may judge it completely immoral from my own point of view (i.e., in conflict with the norms and values which I accept), fully moral from its author's point of view, and only barely tolerable from the point of view of the generally accepted values of society. The fact that I find it repugnant does not prevent me from understanding its meaning as well as its significance, although it is not to be denied that the expressions which I understand most fully are those with which I am in sympathy or agreement. There are degrees of understanding, and the task of understanding is never finished.[52]

There is an interesting parallel, then, between Rickert's conception of historical method and Dilthey's later theory of understanding.[53]. The difference is that Dilthey applies the notion of relation to values or insight into value structures on the non-scientific level as well. Therefore it is a mistake to maintain that Dilthey's understanding is '... a kind of historical imagination through which one is able to project himself into the past and enter the mind of a philosopher or the ethos of a culture.'[54] The notion of imagination is indeed useful for explicating Dilthey's doctrine of understanding, but the operation of imagination must not be restricted to the work of the historian or our efforts to gain knowledge of the past. We also transpose ourselves into the situations of others in everyday life. In this transposition we normally maintain a certain distance or detachment: empathy (*Einfühlen*) is not to be equated with sympathy (*Mitfühlen*). Thus we can better think of understanding in terms of aesthetic detachment (not unlike the neutrality of the historian engaged in 'relation to values') than in terms of ethical commitment. Understanding is this sense was characteristic of Dilthey as a person, for he was both deeply sympathetic and deeply reserved. This comes out clearly in the revealing passage on Luther (see p. 23 above). Dilthey manifests the deepest sympathy for and interest in Luther and the religiosity of his time. Yet this does not lead him to embrace Luther's faith or to commit himself to Luther's vision of the meaning of life and death. Luther's religious experience remains 'beyond the experiential possibilities of a person of our time.' Luther's faith is something to be enjoyed from a distance but not something to be appropriated. Explication does not become application.

6

Hermeneutics and Historical Science

Dilthey's doctrine of understanding and its potential significance for human life would not be complete without an explanation of how understanding works in situations where cultural or temporal distance is an obstacle. If understanding is not to be an arbitrary, essentially mystical communion with the other, it must have a developed hermeneutic – and it does. At this level Dilthey's work begins to benefit the historian. But historical understanding is not an end in itself. Once the educated citizen of the realm of the spirit is equipped with the intellectual sophistication that a historical method can give him, he is able to take more and more of the past and of foreign cultures into himself in his quest for personal growth. He even dares to dream of appropriating the other by understanding him better than he has understood himself.

THE LIMITS OF IMMEDIATE UNDERSTANDING

One of the reasons why it was necessary to deal with the shifts in Dilthey's thinking is that his post-1900 doctrine of understanding, which is our central concern, is by no means an elaboration of the ideas developed in the writings of the decade before. Instead it represents something of a return to conceptions and ideas which he had already worked with *before* he turned to descriptive psychology as the basis for the *Geisteswissenschaften*. This becomes especially clear when we consider the parallels between Dilthey's formulation of the doctrine of understanding and that of Johann Gustav Droysen. In his lectures on historical method, Droysen characterized understanding as follows:

Understanding is the most perfect kind of knowledge that is humanly possible. Therefore it is an immediate, sudden process that takes place without our being conscious of the logical mechanism operative in it. Thus the act of understanding is like an immediate intuition, like a creative act, like a spark of light between two electrophoric bodies, like a receptive act. In understanding, the entire spiritual and sensory (*geistig-sinnlich*) nature of man is fully operative, at the same time giving and taking, producing and receiving. Understanding is the most human act of the human being, and all truly human activity is based on understanding, seeks understanding, finds understanding. Understanding is the most intimate bond between men and the basis of all ethical being.[1]

Dilthey spoke highly of these lectures in an article of 1862,[2] and in the *Aufbau* (1910) he observed that Droysen '... was the first to apply the hermeneutical theory of Schleiermacher and Böckh to methodology' (p. 114). The path that Dilthey was to follow, then, had already been mapped out in part by Droysen and does not represent a continuation of the descriptive psychology of the 1890s. Ernst Cassirer therefore observes that it was in Droysen's lectures that the idea of understanding as found in Dilthey '... was brought into focus ... for the first time and described in all its essentials.'[3]

According to Droysen, understanding is 'immediate,' and the historian must seek to understand documents and sources in the same immediate way that the hearer understands the speaker.[4] Dilthey was in agreement with the latter claim, although he admitted that not all understanding is immediate. He made an important distinction between 'elementary understanding,' which is immediate and non-reflective, and the various higher forms of understanding. The elementary forms of understanding arise 'in the interests of practical life' (*Fortsetzung*, 207), in the most basic forms of communication and contact between human beings. Such understanding represents the grasping of a single expression and does not rest on any inferential process: 'Elementary understanding is not an inference from an effect to a cause' (pp. 207–8). Neither does it represent an interpretation of the expression in the light of our total knowledge of the person: 'In this elementary understanding, accordingly, we do not go back to the entire lived inner coherence (*Zusammenhang*) which forms the abiding subject of expressions of life' (p. 207). We focus on the expression and not on its author.

We have already distinguished between understanding expressions as such and using them to get at the persons and experiences behind them (p. 49 above). We must now formulate this distinction in a more exact way. Hans Freyer points the way by distinguishing between expression and meaning: 'I maintain that complexes of signs *express* something mental (*etwas Seelisches*) and *mean* something objective in the realm of the spirit (*etwas objektiv Geistiges*).'[5] This is like the distinction between meaning as an ideal unity and meaning as a mental process or psychical event, which Husserl used in the *Logical Investigations* and later works to combat psychologism. Dilthey thought highly of the *Logical Investigations*, as we have seen (p. 57), and he, too, began to distinguish between the mental act, which forms part of the life history of some individual, and its content or reference or meaning, which is bound up with that life only contingently and must be regarded as separable from it. In 'Der Strukturzusammenhang des Wissens,' a short study in which Husserl is cited several times, Dilthey affirms that the object meant – and not the act in which it is meant – should be the focus of our attention (VII, 39–40). But the inadequate definition of understanding formulated by Dilthey in the 1900 essay on hermeneutics (see pp. 95–6 above) presents understanding as the apprehension of something 'psychical.' This essay, however, was published *before* the second volume of the *Logical Investigations* which Dilthey found so illuminating. Therefore it appears that Husserl's elucidation of the relation between expression and meaning was decisive for Dilthey's efforts to become clear in his own mind on this matter. After he read Husserl, he no longer spoke of meaning as 'psychical' or 'mental.'[6]

This distinction between expression and meaning fits in well with Dilthey's doctrine of understanding as first formulated by Droysen. In the verbal exchanges that make up a large part of our everyday contacts with our fellow human beings, we do not try to understand the person who addresses us as a whole person, nor do we probe his mental life. If we are inclined to believe and trust him, we ignore what may be going on in his mind and focus our attention solely on the meaning presented. Furthermore, elementary understanding does not require any extensive or intimate knowledge of the speaker. It is rooted in the common sphere of objective spirit, which includes language, customs, traditions, and everything else that falls under the concept of culture. If the speaker and the hearer have all of this in common, they will understand one another immediately, even if they have never met before and take no personal interest whatever in each other. Elementary understanding limits itself to the meaning and ignores the person. Therefore, it is not an endless task, and the principle of 'Besserverstehen' does not apply to it: Dilthey did not claim that we must undertand meanings or expressions better than those who have formulated them, but that it is possible to understand an *author* better than he has understood himself.[7] Thus his version of 'Besserverstehen' rests on the insight that a person's knowledge of himself is sharply limited. 'Besserverstehen' applies only to the higher forms of understanding.

Dilthey seems to distinguish between different kinds of meaning, but his distinctions are not always clearly reflected in his use of the terms 'Sinn,' 'Bedeutung,' and 'Bedeutsamkeit.' Sometimes he uses these terms in separate, contrasting senses, and at other times he uses them interchangeably. Nonetheless, there are distinctions to be made. A part, e.g., a word in a sentence, can be said to have a 'meaning.' This is to be distinguished from the meaning of a whole made up of various parts, each bearing its own meaning. We could perhaps speak of the meaning of the whole as 'sense.'[8] Finally, the meaning of a part can have implications for the sense of a whole, and the sense of a whole – even when it is only partially understood – casts light on the meaning of its constituent parts. Thus we can speak of the 'significance' of a part or of a whole, that is, its bearing on the sense or meaning of the whole or of other parts. Elementary understanding limits itself to the meaning of parts as determined by the background of a whole whose sense (i.e., the common sphere of objective spirit) is agreed upon in advance by the speaker and the hearer. The higher forms of understanding focus more often on the sense of larger wholes and on significance, although they are also used to clarify the meaning of parts.

Because elementary understanding focuses on a single meaning, it is immediate and involves no special difficulties. But this is not to say that it is always free from error. It is subject to mistakes just as well as sensory perception, which is always immediate and non-reflective. When we do make mistakes in elementary understanding, they are usually revealed to us by the incongruity of a certain meaning with other meanings apprehended within the same context or situation. Once this makes us aware that a mistake of some sort has been made, we must reckon with the possibility of deception and then apply the higher forms of understanding to find out what was really meant by the expressions originally accepted at face value. The interpretive techniques which Dilthey speaks of as higher forms of understanding are also rooted in praxis and are no more to be regarded as inventions of scholars than is elementary understanding itself. In the higher forms of understanding, we often go back to the total person with his hopes, fears, ambitions, and life history in our effort to understand the meaning of his expressions. As we have seen, this is unnecessary in elementary understanding.

Schleiermacher, who exercised a great influence on Dilthey's thinking on understanding and hermeneutics, pointed out that we use hermeneutical procedures even in conversation,[9] and he liked to speak of hermeneutics as the art of avoiding misunderstanding. Thus there is a close connection between hermeneutics, interpretation, and the higher forms of understanding.

Whenever and wherever persons do not understand one another, whether because of linguistic barriers, cultural distance, the differences between generations,[10] fundamentally opposed outlooks on life, or attempts at deception, interpretive methods must be applied. The person as a totality must be taken into account. In elementary understanding, the background of the whole and its sense, without which the meaning of single expressions is unrecognizable, is assumed as common to the speaker and hearer, but in the higher forms of understanding, the sense of the whole must first be established by 'going back to the lived inner coherence.'

These interpretive techniques, which are to be found to some degree in every culture and society, are the conditions in life itself making the cultural sciences possible. In a highly closed society, the operation of such interpretive processes will hardly be noticed. In a more open society with an awareness of historical change and of the cultural, social, and linguistic differences between various human communities, they will be recognized and cultivated. It is only in such communities that historical consciousness can arise, for the historical outlook is very closely bound up with interpretive methods and hermeneutical traditions. The historically aware cultural scientist views alien cultures and their expressions not as meaning-less or as non-sense but as bearing a meaning and sense of their own, which can be elicited through the use of interpretive methods and the higher forms of understanding.

DILTHEY'S INTEREST IN HERMENEUTICS

As we saw earlier (p. 63), Dilthey's interest in hermeneutics goes back to the early years of his philosophical career. Yet it was only during the last ten or fifteen years of his life that hermeneutics assumed a special importance for him. During the 1890s, he was preoccupied with the idea of basing the *Geisteswissenschaften* on a direct observation and apprehension of mental states, be they our own experiences or the experiences of others which we 're-live' (*nacherleben*). When this approach ran aground, he turned to the notion of (higher) understanding as developed by theorists of hermeneutics. This understanding, which is not to be equated with reliving, could be broadly defined as an apprehension of the meaning, sense, or significance of texts, gestures, statements, and events presented to us through sensory givens. It is a mode of knowledge founded in perception; that is to say, the object of our attention is first perceived as a physical thing and is then understood as a bearer of meaning or sense. The essential point here is the connection between understanding and meaning: meaning, in the words of Emilio Betti, is not something 'perceivable' (*vernehmbar*) but something 'understandable' (*verstehbar*).[11] Because the cultural sciences focus on realized and expressed meanings and values, and not on physical objects as such, they must be based on a mode of knowledge that goes beyond perception.

Dilthey's interest in hermeneutics was no doubt stimulated in part by his intensive study of Schleiermacher. The latter is a pivotal figure in the history of hermeneutics, as Dilthey emphasized in his essay on this subject. The birth of a general science of hermeneutics (*allgemeine Hermeneutik*) was largely Schleiermacher's doing. Various interpretive techniques and some sophisticated hermeneutical traditions had already been developed by the beginning of the nineteenth century, but the essential unity and identity of the process of understanding and interpretation had not yet been brought properly into view. This was to be the contribution of Schleiermacher, who had one foot planted in each of the two major hermeneutical traditions – the philological, which concerned itself with texts from the Greco-Roman world, and the theological, which explicated the Scriptures. These two traditions had long developed independently because of the distinction between sacred and profane hermeneutics. Schleiermacher now undercut this distinction by denying that the inspiration of the texts comprising the Old and New Testaments is of an essentially different nature from the 'inspiration' animating other important texts that have retained their power over men throughout the centuries. These two traditions could then interact, which opened up the possibility of developing a general theory of understanding and interpretation.

Schleiermacher's thinking on hermeneutics, which includes much more than the suggestion of interaction between these two traditions, underwent an interesting development that has recently been brought to light.[12] His original language-oriented conception of hermeneutics, with which we are acquainted through material published in 1959, was replaced in his later reflection by a much greater emphasis on subjectivity and psychological factors in understanding. It was the latter conception that seems to have influenced Dilthey. He concluded his 1900 essay on hermeneutics with the significant observation that interpretation theory is to be regarded as a 'major component of the foundation (*Grundlegung*) of the *Geisteswissenschaften*' (v, 331). His own major contribution to the development of hermeneutics was his broadening of its application to all cultural sciences that employ the higher forms of understanding, which, of course, includes various sciences that do not deal with linguistic expressions.* Richard Palmer therefore speaks of the cycle of experience, expression, and understanding as 'Dilthey's hermeneutical formula.'[13] All expressions and externalizations of life were to be dealt with by hermeneutical means.

In practice, then, Dilthey expanded hermeneutics far beyond the sphere of language. But in his formal definitions of hermeneutics, he did not take this step. In the 1900 essay, he speaks of hermeneutics as the 'theory of the art of interpreting written remains' (*Kunstlehre der Auslegung der Schriftdenkmalen*).[14] In later notes, hermeneutics is the science of the art of interpreting 'remains of human existence contained in *writing*' (*Fortsetzung*, 217). Dilthey's caution in this regard should be noted, but we should also note the fact that hermeneutics as such is virtually never discussed in the post-1900 writings; it received more attention in the writings of the pre-1900 years. For some reason never made clear by Dilthey himself, the implicit identification of hermeneutics with the higher forms of understanding as applied in a scientific context was never carried through to the point of a new definition and characterization of the general science of hermeneutics. This is another of the loose ends in his thought.

Central to Dilthey's conception of hermeneutics and higher understanding is the relation between part and whole. Understanding, for Dilthey, is not always oriented towards the genesis of expressions and does not necessarily involve a re-tracing of the process by which the expression in question was constituted. Thus it is a mistake to speak of the 'psychological hermeneutics' of Dilthey,[15] as though the meaning of an expression could be equated with a psychological process in the mind of its author. Unlike Schleiermacher, Dilthey did not regard the process of understanding as a 'reversal' (*Umkehrung*) of the process of creation or expression, although he never denied that an investigation of the conditions under which an expression was born can be relevant to our understanding of it. Because of his unflagging interest in the relation between part and whole in the social-historical world, higher understanding as he practised it focuses largely on the significance of the part for the whole and the whole for the part. It is for this reason that insight into contexts, structures, systems, and connections is so important to scientific understanding as conceived of by Dilthey.

---

* Dilthey was aware of the potential significance of hermeneutics for the cultural sciences long before he published his pivotal essay of 1900. In an article of 1892–93 he wrote: '... it can be said that hermeneutics even represents a starting point of the highest value for the modern effort to lay a foundation for the *Geisteswissenschaften*. That is why I have devoted special attention to its history. Hermeneutics prepares the way for my own effort to lay such a foundation' ('Das natürliche System,' II, 115).

The connection between higher understanding and the hermeneutical tradition becomes especially clear when we consider the centrality of the problem of the hermeneutical circle in the former. This is the problem of the '... relationship of parts to the whole, in which the parts receive meaning (*Bedeutung*) from the whole, and the whole receives sense (*Sinn*) from the parts ...' (*Fortsetzung*, 265). Dilthey spoke of this problem as the 'central difficulty of the entire art of interpretation (*Auslegungskunst*).' Unfortunately, it can only be overcome partially: 'Theoretically we encounter the limits of all interpretation (*Auslegung*) here; it fulfills its task only to a certain degree. Thus all understanding remains only relative and can never be completed.'[16] To the extent that this problem can be solved, Schleiermacher has solved it:

... all understanding begins with what Ast called a *hunch* (*Ahndung*), that is, with a working hypothesis about the coherence (*Zusammenhang*), just as all production begins with a germinal resolution. This gives us a procedure that can be regarded as *the technique of this method*, as Schleiermacher never tired of pointing out. The first reading of a text is only intended to establish provisionally the main idea in its essential relations; the understanding which it gives us is only provisional. It is the second *reading* that first reproduces the whole.[17]

Because the problem of the hermeneutical circle is central to Dilthey's reflection on historical understanding, the distinction between a critical approach to history focusing on historical knowledge and a speculative approach interested in the meaning of history (see p. 16 above) cannot be used to elucidate his thinking. First of all, historical knowledge and understanding, in Dilthey's view, cannot be separated from the apprehension of meaning and sense. Secondly, historical knowledge must move in the direction of a comprehension of the meaning or sense of the whole, of the totality of a historical development or tradition. Dilthey points out that it is in the interaction between part and whole that the ambiguities in our knowledge are gradually eliminated. Therefore, reflection on the sense of the whole is an inescapable part of the historian's task: 'Again and again, the present casts a new light on the past and creates new interest in it. The past appears different in every age and requires a different presentation.'[18] The past – or much of it – must be seen as part of a whole or totality still in the process of development. The further this development advances, the deeper and more complete – in principle – our knowledge and understanding of the past will be. But it will never be total, for it will always remain open to correction and revision.

One would have to await life's end and could not survey the whole on the basis of which the relations between the parts can be determined until the hour of death. One would have to await the end of history in order to possess the complete material for the determination of its meaning. On the other hand, the whole only exists for us insofar as it becomes understandable on the basis of the parts. Understanding always hovers between these two approaches (*Fortsetzung*, 233).

This amounts to an admission on Dilthey's part that the third of the objections to historical science raised in the first chapter (p. 10) cannot be countered. Historical knowledge is always provisional in essence and contains a degree of speculation, for historical investigation is impossible without certain general preconceptions about the whole. Therefore, the meaning of history (i.e., the sense of the whole) cannot be separated completely from our knowledge of historical particulars. If Dilthey is correct on this point, the division between critical and speculative approaches to history is untenable.

The train of thought of the preceding paragraph makes it apparent that the distinction between hermeneutical and non-hermeneutical thinking is hard to draw. In a recent book on hermeneutics we read: 'The problem of hermeneutics is the problem of understanding.'[19] Dilthey did not make the same explicit identification, but his conception of hermeneutics is open to it, for the problem of part and whole in understanding, which is central in his thinking, has traditionally been regarded as a hermeneutical problem. This problem was originally formulated and explored by hermeneutical theorists, and it is now widely recognized that it plays a role in much of our thinking about man, history, and society. In Dilthey and in many thinkers after him, then, the problems and methods of hermeneutics can no longer be strictly distinguished from the problems and methods of the historical and cultural sciences. Dilthey's achievement in relation to hermeneutics is basically that he brought the wisdom and insights of the hermeneutical tradition to bear on these sciences. His work, like that of Schleiermacher, represents a convergence of previously separate streams in the history of scholarship.

It is important to emphasize that Dilthey's conception of hermeneutics and understanding is flexible and unfinished, for this is one of its chief merits. It has proven to be open to further development by later thinkers, some of whom have moved in directions not entirely in harmony with Dilthey's own practice as a historian. His thought is open, for example, to the notion of a 'depth hermeneutics,' a method of interpretation that yields knowledge of individuals by studying dreams, memory lapses, slips of the tongue, and other such phenomena which have traditionally been regarded as meaningless. Because Dilthey did not possess the insight into the role of unconscious or subconscious factors in mental life that Freud achieved, he was not able to develop a depth hermeneutics. Yet, as we have seen (p. 78), he did acknowledge the importance of the unconscious; hence the interpretation of material stemming from the unconscious to augment or even direct our understanding of the mental life of others is certainly compatible with his outlook.[20] The addition of a depth hermeneutics to Dilthey's method of gaining knowledge of mental life would support his conviction that in principle it is possible to understand others better than they understand themselves.

Dilthey's outlook on hermeneutics is also open to the idea that we should use hermeneutical techniques in our quest for self-knowledge. Because the depths of mental life are best explored by examining the expressions that arise from them, self-knowledge as well as knowledge of others is dependent to some degree on the process of expression and understanding. Since these two types of knowledge employ similar procedures, both are facilitated by engaging in dialogue. Dialogue has become a popular theme in recent decades, but the term is hardly to be found in Dilthey's writings. Yet this does not mean that the idea is entirely absent. Cultural life as conceived of by Dilthey is an endless cycle of experience, expression, and understanding, a dialogue in which the many members of the human community can and should participate. As a cultural and intellectual process, understanding is part of a dialogical situation in which I grow in my knowledge of others and of myself, thereby opening myself to the prospect of being formed and changed both by the present and by the past. However, understanding as a scientific technique is not essentially a dialogue, for Dilthey does not fuse explication and application in the work of the historian and cultural scientist. The task of the cultural scientist is to grasp and restore the meaning and sense of expressions. Therefore Dilthey does not and cannot *identify* understanding and dialogue, despite the fact that the idea of dialogue is central to his conception of the role of the higher forms of understanding in non-scientific life. The life of the poet, who is the 'true man' for Dilthey (see p. 87 above) would be inconceivable without dialogue.

UNDERSTANDING IN THE HISTORICAL SCIENCES

The so-called method of understanding, which has been discussed by various thinkers in connection with the social sciences as well as the cultural sciences, has become the focus of a considerable amount of controversy in the twentieth century. The discussion of the status and nature of this mysterious process, which seemingly defies definition,[21] has also had an effect on Dilthey's image in the English-speaking world. Thus one writer complains that '... Dilthey's notorious "Verstehen" places the historian in a special position ...,'[22] and another declares: 'We cannot accept the position associated with the name of Dilthey which divides the sciences into *Naturwissenschaften* and *Geisteswissenschaften* and bases the latter on some direct, mysterious and uncontrollable power of understanding. Such understanding, since it could not be validated empirically, would be merely private and serve no common purpose.'[23] There is a certain amount of ground for such complaints, for Dilthey does maintain that understanding rests on personal abilities not shared by all to the same degree; he himself, as many of his contemporaries observed, possessed exceptional abilities in understanding others. Thus, insofar as his own success as a historian and biographer cannot be accounted for completely in terms of a method that could be taught to others who would then be able to achieve similar results, talk of a 'mysterious method' is partly justified. Dilthey also held that the special abilities required for the historical and cultural sciences are possessed to a unique degree by the German people in general. It was no accident, he maintained, that the *Geisteswissenschaften* blossomed in Germany: 'Only our nation (*Volk*) possesses historical consciousness in the highest sense.'[24]

We must be careful not to overemphasize this side of Dilthey's thinking, for personal genius and 'divination' are not as important in *his* conception of hermeneutics and understanding as in that of Schleiermacher. Dilthey did write that understanding rests on a 'particular personal genius' (*Genialität*), but in the very next sentence he continued: 'Because it is an important and abiding task as the foundation of historical science, this personal genius becomes a technique, and the technique develops with the development of historical consciousness' (*Fortsetzung*, 216–17). All understanding is 'irrational' (p. 218), but the process of understanding can be tamed and brought within the confines of a technique or method. It is the movement towards a method or a regular procedure that transforms higher understanding into something scientific. Dilthey's view of science (*Wissenschaft*) is fairly flexible, and he admits that the boundary between scientific and non-scientific knowledge is sometimes hard to draw: 'Who is to say at what point the striving for knowledge which is operative in all purposive social systems becomes science?' (*Weltanschauung*, 94). The higher understanding that Dilthey calls 'rule-directed (*kunstmässig*) understanding' is the explication and interpretation essential to the cultural sciences.[25]

At the heart of Dilthey's conception of historical understanding is a conviction he shares with many other German theorists of history, including Friedrich Meinecke, who declared: 'The immediate understanding of one person by another ... is also the source of all further understanding for the historian ...'[26] But such immediate understanding is to be achieved only by way of expressions, that is, documents, texts, and various other remains of man's past. In other words, the method of understanding can be used only when there are historical data to be studied; it must not be thought of as a mode of intuition or insight operating in a vacuum. Therefore, the criticism, purification, and restoration of sources is the 'fundamental historical science' (*Grundwissenschaft der Geschichte*) (*Fortsetzung*, 261). Both understanding or interpretation and the criticism of sources are indispensable for the historian: 'Reliable historiography first begins with a criticism of the sources, which establishes the true facts of the case from the remains of the act itself and the reports about it, and true historiography first begins with an interpretation of the sources, in which we understand the facts of the case as an expression of inner human life.'[27] This criticism of sources is one of the factors making objectivity in the historical sciences possible. Dilthey's emphasis on the importance of the sources must be balanced against his claim that understanding is the 'procedure that lays the foundation for all further operations of the *Geisteswissenschaften*.'[28] His view of historical science is somewhat more mundane and conventional than some of his critics seem to believe.

Through the use of hermeneutical techniques and the higher forms of understanding, the historian seeks to establish contact with figures in the past. Precisely because he studies the past, there is always some temporal distance between him and the object of his interest, and probably some cultural distance as well. It has long been the goal of hermeneutics to combat cultural distance, to remove barriers to understanding. Thus, to the extent that the historian is successful in his application of hermeneutical techniques, he overcomes the cultural distance and is then able to build up his knowledge of figures in the past in much the same way that he gains knowledge of his contemporaries, that is, by understanding their expressions. (Of course, there is also an important difference: the historian usually has no opportunity to question the object of his investigation directly.) The historian lives in the same world as his contemporaries; he shares a language, customs, and a general outlook with them, all of which facilitates his understanding of them. But if the historian is to understand the expressions of figures in the past, this knowledge of context and background must be built up artificially. This requires the use of historical imagination. In the *Einleitung*, Dilthey wrote:

We understand when we restore life and breath to the dust of the past out of the depths of our own life. If we are to understand the course of historical development from within and in its central coherence, a self-transposition from one position to another, as it were, is required. The general psychological condition for this is always present in the imagination; but a thorough understanding of historical development is first achieved when the course of history is re-lived (*nacherlebt*) in imagination at the deepest points at which the movement forward takes place (p. 254).

Because this re-animation of the past on the basis of our own experience is an inescapable part of the historian's work, Dilthey rejects the notion that objectivity can be achieved by eliminating subjective factors.[29]

Another reason why there is a good deal of confusion about Dilthey's conception of historical understanding is that understanding has a double object, as we saw earlier (p. 49). It is because the cultural sciences study expressions as bearers of meanings that they are possible as sciences and can attain a fair degree of objectivity. This might make it appear that historical understanding aims to construct a history of man in the form of a history of what man has said and done, that is, a history of human expression. However, although some cultural sciences may be content to study expressions without reference to the particular author or person behind them, history is not prepared to limit itself in this way. The historian seeks to penetrate to the very mind and experience of the past. The task of the historian, Dilthey declared, is 'to grasp inwardness.'[30] In the unfinished continuation of the *Aufbau* he wrote: 'We seek the mind (*Seele*); this is the final goal at which we have arrived after the long development of historiography' (*Fortsetzung*, 282). Historical understanding, then, is at bottom an understanding of persons. The understanding of expressions, on which the work of the historian rests, must be seen as preparatory and must not be identified with the task of history as such.*

Understanding, as we have seen, is possible only on the basis of a common or shared sphere. The necessary common element between the historian and the object of his investigation is established by way of methods and techniques developed in the hermeneutical tradition. But the ultimate ground for the possibility of establishing a common sphere is the fact that we in the present who seek to understand the past are human beings just as well as those whom we seek to understand. To this extent, the idea of a common

* This is not to say that for Dilthey the history of philosophy becomes a series of psychological biographies, as Suter maintains (see *Philosophie et histoire chez Dilthey*, 153). A philosophical system is more than an event in the life of its creator. If something is left unclear here, the problem is to be sought in the concept of the history of philosophy rather than in Dilthey's conception of expression and understanding. Is the philosophy whose history we write the *activity* of thinking or the finished *result* of thought?

human nature is retained by Dilthey as the ground for the possibility of understanding – although it is not enough in itself. Nonetheless, the *basis* for a solution is to be sought along these lines: '... the first condition for the possibility of historical science is that I myself am a historical being, that the one who investigates history is also the one who makes history' (*Fortsetzung*, 278). The mode of knowledge which Dilthey called understanding, then, represents his answer to the problem of historical knowledge. Historical knowledge is simply a species of our knowledge of others and is gained by the same methods.

HISTORICAL METHOD AND OBJECTIVITY

In Chapter 2 we noted Dilthey's preoccupation with individuality and the individual. We also saw that larger wholes or totalities are important in his thought. Much of his thinking revolves around the question of the relation between the individual and the whole or wholes of which he is a part. But despite his recognition of the importance of wholes, Dilthey's steadfastly empirical attitude – which is not to be equated with empiricism – led him to lay heavy emphasis on the individual in historical method. When I speak of 'the individual' in this context, I mean the human individual, whom Dilthey regarded as the basic unit of history (see p. 37 above). 'Individual persons,' he declared in 1907, form the primary subjects of all statements in the *Geisteswissenschaften* (*Philosophie*, 340). The question is: 'The individual is only the point of intersection of the cultural systems and organizations with which his existence is interwoven: how can these cultural systems and organizations be understood out of the individual?' (*Fortsetzung*, 251). Unfortunately, Dilthey never answered this question adequately. But as part of his legacy, he did bequeath to posterity a conception of historical method that we could characterize as 'methodological individualism.' The human individual, in this view, is the starting point for historical investigation. What does this mean for the historian?

First, biography is the basic historical science, for it focuses on the basic unit of history. It is the 'presentation of that which interests us most, i.e., human existence.'[31] Dilthey did not maintain that history is composed simply of the biographies of all significant figures in the past, but he did regard biography as the safest and most fundamental type of history. The human individual is given to us in a way that nations, epochs, and the various other groups and totalities in which the historian is interested are not. Thus biography is closer to the sources and data. But although its subject is individual, its significance is not so limited: 'The person, as the fundamental fact of all history, forms its object. Although it describes something singular, it still mirrors within it the universal law of development' (*Ideen*, 225).

Second, all expressions are the expressions of individuals. The doctrine that expression draws its material from lived experience strongly suggests such a conclusion – for experience is individual – but Dilthey was nevertheless attracted by the view that some expressions can be traced back to more than one person. No poet, he declared in the *Aufbau*, is the 'exclusive creator of his work.' What he has to say is influenced by and derived from others – in part, at least: '... he receives his conception of the meaning of life from the national consciousness (*Volksbewusstsein*) or from outstanding individuals ...' (p. 167). Dilthey speaks of a 'tracing back to the common mind' (*Zurückführung auf den Gemeingeist*) in connection with the historical school's treatment of religion, morals, and law and calls it a 'great discovery' (p. 96). In an essay of 1891–92, the term 'individual' is used to cover nations: everything in history, Dilthey writes there, is 'individual, that is, living, people and nations (*Menschen und Völker*).'[32] But he did not follow up the implications of these few scattered observations. Superindividual minds (*Volksgeister* or *Zeitgeister*) in the sense of the historical school are not permitted in his vision of history; he recognized only individuals as the authors of expressions.

Third, Dilthey's conception of historical method also emphasizes the individual in that he is accorded a trans-individual significance. Individuals are the sole authors of their expressions, but we are sometimes justified in regarding a particular individual together with his expressions as typical of his age and therefore as the key to understanding that age. The outlook (*Geistesverfassung*) of an entire epoch can be represented in a single individual, according to Dilthey; he speaks of such individuals as 'representative personalities' (*Ideen*, 236). In the *Aufbau* he observed that important historical individuals take on their meaning in relation to the spirit of their age:

Their creative action does not reach into the historical distance but draws its goals from the values and meaning-context of the age itself. It is precisely the limitation of the people of a particular period to its horizon that gives the productive energy of the nation in that period its highest power. Their work serves to realize that which constitutes the fundamental direction of the age. Thereby they become its representatives (p. 186).

Thus the historian can focus on certain historically significant individuals as representatives of their era. Moreover, their lives are interwoven with much of what is happening in their time, for the human individual as an isolated entity (*Einzelmensch*) is a mere abstraction, according to Dilthey (*Philosophie*, 375). A biography of an important person would then tend to become a history of his times as well. Dilthey's biography of Schleiermacher illustrates this, for it can be read as an intellectual history of the period dominated by the figure of Goethe.

Because of the restriction of expression to individual human beings, it was important that the idea of representative or typical persons be emphasized. Dilthey developed this idea further through his doctrine of types, which is also a by-product of his theory of art. A type, for Dilthey, is not reached through abstraction based on induction; rather, it is something common in the sense of representative. The type retains the full concreteness (*Bildlichkeit*) of the individual and must therefore be distinguished from the mere regularity and abstracted commonness in which the natural sciences are interested. 'Art, particularly poetry,' writes Dilthey, 'brings forth the typical, which plays an important role in our imagining (*Vorstellen*). The typical takes its place alongside the lawful. The lawful is that which expresses a universal state of affairs in nature. The typical is that which expresses a universal state of affairs in a single case.'[33]

Dilthey's types should not be called 'ideal types,' for the typical individual is simply an actual individual whom we recognize as representative. Developing an eye for types is important in art, for every genuine portrait is a type.[34] But the *historian* must also develop an eye for types, since the concepts used in the *Geisteswissenschaften* represent types: 'Thus the formation of concepts is not a simple process of generalization that wrests the common element from a series of individual instances. The concept expresses a type' (*Aufbau*, 188). Types are also important in historical narration, which employs modes of presentation akin to those of the artist. 'The writing of history is always art,' Dilthey declares.[35] In history as well as in art, then, the type mediates between the individual or particular and the whole or universal.

Dilthey's doctrine of types makes it apparent that his emphasis on the individual does not entail a neglect of the whole. We use the individual to get at the whole, and it is the whole, in turn, that makes the individual properly understandable. This means that the historian should select a typical or representative figure to gain a preliminary understanding of the age. Such figures are often to be found among artists, for '... as a rule, the substance of a new epoch develops first in the concrete vision (*bildliche Anschauung*) of the artist.'[36] Through the representative figure, the historian achieves a provisional understanding of the age. This provisional understanding serves as the necessary background of his investigation; it is the working hypothesis or pre-understanding (*Vorverständnis*) without which the understanding of particular expressions would be impossible. The historian's study of particular expressions and persons will eventually force him to make certain corrections and refinements in his provisional conception of the age, and thereby the working hypothesis will gradually be transformed into a research result. The improved understanding of the whole will in turn shed further light on the particulars contained within it, and so on. Thus there is no end to historical understanding. Furthermore, the age itself can and should be understood against the background of the larger course of history, and a similar relation of part and whole manifests itself on this level.

It is apparent from this sketch of historical understanding that Dilthey applied the term 'understanding' to a variety of rather different operations, namely, our comprehension of particulars, of wholes, and of the relations between them – to say nothing of the elementary forms of understanding and the other types of higher understanding outside the historical and cultural sciences. Therefore, there is a certain amount of justification for saying, as one commentator does, that Dilthey uses 'understanding' as a generic term covering a wide variety of processes.[37] Understanding as applied to the historical sciences can best be regarded as a series of operations which *together* yield significant results. It includes the apprehension of meanings within the context of an assumed background (immediate understanding), the exploration of a personality to see what light it might cast on a puzzling expression, the study of an age to see how it informs the expressions of a particular person, and other mental endeavours of this sort.

Dilthey's belief that the understanding of the part and the understanding of the whole can and do correct one another is based on an important assumption, namely, that of the spiritual homogeneity of the epoch, nation, individual life, or whatever whole the historian selects as the background for understanding particular expressions. This assumption is by no means arbitrary, and it must not be taken to mean that there are no discordant voices in such a background. It must be seen not as a factual assumption but as a transcendental and methodological assumption. Because understanding is only possible within a common, shared sphere or against a background assumed and understood in advance, we must interpret various expressions coming from the same source on the presupposition that they are in harmony with one another – unless we have explicit reason to do otherwise. More specifically, we understand expressions in the light of one another, and we can only understand them in this way. A person who deliberately utters expressions that contradict one another is not understandable to any great extent. Orthodox biblical hermeneutics is based on the assumption that the Scriptures together form a coherent whole and are to be interpreted and understood in the light of one another. Underlying this principle, of course, is the doctrine of the divine inspiration of the Scriptures, but this hermeneutical assumption is likewise based on the nature of understanding. In understanding we always proceed from the assumption of harmony between expressions from a common source, and we use the various expressions to elucidate one another. If and when we discover that there is a fundamental *disharmony*, we seek harmony within smaller wholes. To return to the Scriptures as our example, some modern theologians claim to have found irreconcilable disharmonies between the epistles of Paul and the teachings of Jesus as recorded in the Gospels. Hence they argue that the New Testament is not to be understood as a unified whole, and they proceed to break up this collection of writings into a number of smaller wholes. To take Kant's writings as another example, the *Critique of Pure Reason* cannot be used to determine the meaning of unclear passages in the pre-critical writings – although it may shed some light on them. No philosopher or writer would be understandable to a significant extent if there were no prospect of using our knowledge of his background and our knowledge of other texts as we seek to understand and interpret the text before us at a given moment. The entire enterprise of understanding as conceived of by Dilthey and others is dependent on this assumption of unity.

Up to this point, our discussion of historical method has remained within the bounds of hermeneutical thinking. The historical method described, in which the relation of part and whole is central, is suited to cultural and intellectual history, but it is not applicable to all other branches of history. Dilthey points out that history does not deal only with individual human beings: 'The logical subjects about which we speak in history include individual persons as well as communities and systems' (*Zusammenhänge*).[38] But the question must be raised: '... how does such a community become a subject that operates in a unified way like an individual?' (*Fortsetzung*, 264). The answer is that the historian must seek to grasp the social-historical world as a series of 'dynamic systems' (*Wirkungszusammenhänge*); the historian, Dilthey writes, '... cannot renounce the attempt to understand history out of itself on the basis of an analysis of various dynamic systems.'[39] Ultimately the entire historical world must be understood as a totality in the sense of a 'dynamic system' (*Aufbau*, 155). Therefore Dilthey devoted the last of his major works to the structure and construction of the historical world. Unfortunately, he did not live long enough to complete this work, although he did publish the first part. He pointed to the objective, but he failed to reach it himself.

The superindividual systems and structures of which the social-historical world is composed are produced by individual persons working together, but they cannot be identified as the product or expression of any single individual. It is the lack of a bond with a single living individual that seems to place these 'dynamic systems' outside the range of the method of understanding used in cultural and intellectual history. H.G. Gadamer puts his finger on the problem when he observes with reference to Dilthey: 'It is very significant that he turned to biography, and especially autobiography, when it came time to explain the possibility of interpreting history and understanding the logic of events clearly, for in this sphere the *Wirkungszusammenhang* (a Diltheyan term that cannot be translated), that is to say, the connection of events that form the resulting whole, is not without a lived connection in the memory of personal experience.'[40] The 'dynamic system' formed by the mind or an individual life can be understood by way of expression and understanding, but a system of law, which is built up over a number of years through the co-operation of numerous people, cannot. This is part of what is involved in Dilthey's individualism and his rejection of any 'common mind' (*Gemeingeist*). And we have little reason to suppose that he might have solved this problem if he had lived a few years longer.

Because Dilthey failed to develop a theory of the inter-subjective constitution of the social-historical world and was not able to give an account of our knowledge of this world, the historical method reflected in his writings is applicable only to cultural and intellectual history. This point is important when we consider what objectivity means for Dilthey and how it is to be attained. Some critics of Dilthey complain that historical understanding precludes the possibility of objective checking or verification,[41] but we shall see that this charge is unfair. Throughout this chapter, I have emphasized that Dilthey's conception of the historian's procedure was heavily influenced by hermeneutical thinking. Hence it is to hermeneutics that we should turn for an account of objectivity in historical understanding.

We should note first that the materials with which the historian works are accessible in principle to all; Dilthey does not claim any mysterious, direct, inner contact between the historian and the past. The objectivity of the results of the historian's labours must be sought in the objectivity of his understanding and interpretation of these sources. And there are two chief canons or criteria against which we can measure any interpretation. Both were recognized by Schleiermacher, and both have been incorporated into the hermeneutics of Emilio Betti. The first is the canon of immanence or autonomy, and the second is the canon of totality or coherence.[42]

The first major rule for historical interpretation is that the expression or the person behind it is to be understood in terms of itself or himself. Dilthey does not deny that historical understanding and interpretation should rise ultimately to the level of a universal historical perspective, as we shall see, but he does insist that interpretation is not to become a translation into a foreign idiom, e.g., the outlook of our own time. In other words, 'demythologizing' is not permitted in historical interpretation. In a discussion of Goethe as historian, Dilthey declared: '... the historical object can only be understood out of the whole in which it is contained; to grasp its causal relations and its meaning, the historian must always keep the universal historical context in mind. He must place the object at a distance from himself as a world in itself with which he deals in an impartial way.'[43] Dilthey's contention that we must try to understand an author better than he has understood himself is to be read in the light of the canon of immanence, for he writes:

The problem of the idea in a poem can be solved on the basis of the rule that we must understand an author better than he has understood himself. The idea is present (not as an abstract thought, but) in the sense of an unconscious coherence (*Zusammenhang*) that is operative in the organization of a work and through whose form the work is understood. A poet does not need the idea – indeed, he never becomes fully conscious of it; the interpreter points it out, and this is perhaps the greatest triumph of hermeneutics.[44]

The important point here is that the author is not conscious of all that shapes his expression, and this is the basis for the possibility of 'Besserverstehen.'

The possibility of 'Besserverstehen' should not lead us to overlook the main point, namely, that we must understand the author in his own terms. In other words, the act of historical understanding does not represent a 'fusion of horizons' but a 'transposition' (*sich versetzen*). Gadamer, who affirms the former notion and rejects the latter, is thereby also led to reject the idea of understanding an author better than he has understood himself: 'In truth, understanding is not a better-understanding ... Suffice it to say that we understand *otherwise* (*anders*) *when we understand at all.*'[45] Much of the disagreement between Gadamer and Betti revolves around the issues implied in the canon of immanence.

We are to understand historical figures in terms of themselves, then, and not in terms of ourselves. But this canon by itself is not sufficient to guide the historian's labours. The historical school was certainly faithful to the canon of immanence, but it overlooked the canon of totality: 'The limits of the historical school lay in this, that it achieved no relation to universal history.'[46] It is not enough to interpret a historical figure in terms of himself; he must also be understood in relation to the larger stream of events of which his life and work form a part. Only the two perspectives together make understanding an author better than he has understood himself a realistic possibility. The movement back and forth between part and whole should result ultimately in a universal historical perspective. 'The understanding of a part of the course of history,' Dilthey writes, 'is ultimately completed only by relating that part to the whole, and the universal historical view of the whole presupposes an understanding of the parts that are united in it' (*Aufbau*, 152). The idea of universal history is not quietly abandoned by Dilthey, as one commentator suggests,[47] but it is re-formulated somewhat. Dilthey stated his commitment to the importance of a universal historical perspective as early as the *Einleitung*: 'Universal history, insofar as it is not something suprahuman, would form the crown of this whole of the *Geisteswissenschaften*' (p. 95).

The affirmation of the canon of totality or coherence entails that historical understanding is an endless task, for world history, which is the ultimate background and context for understanding particular historical figures, is always advancing. Therefore new perspectives on the past are always possible in principle. In practice, however, dramatic new insights and interpretations occasioned by the unfolding of events are relatively rare; the passage of time instead tends to make our interpretations more complete and more internally coherent. In general, the historian's understanding of the object or objects of his interest grows and deepens until the understanding and insights which he has achieved begin to seem somewhat obvious and even trivial to him. The temporal distance between the historian and the figure whom he is studying helps to bring about an ever more balanced perspective. When our understanding of a historical figure begins to seem somewhat obvious and trivial, we have reason to believe that it is essentially correct – provided we have made painstaking efforts to understand him in terms of himself and against the background of his times and of the social-historical world in which he lived. The ideal is that historical understanding be straightforward and direct, just as elementary understanding is simple and obvious.

Historical understanding as conceived of by Dilthey is objective in roughly the same way that the interpretation of texts is or can be objective: anyone who disputes an interpretation can check it against the sources in the light of the canons of autonomy or immanence and totality or coherence. This is perhaps not as complete an objectivity as many historians might wish. It is certainly doubtful whether the term 'universal validity' (*Allgemeingültigkeit*) should be used in connection with it. Dilthey uses this imposing term sporadically in his writings – most often in the 1900 essay on hermeneutics – and nowhere rejects universal validity as a scientific ideal appropriate for the

Geisteswissenschaften. Yet there seems to be little place in his conception of historical understanding for the claim to universal validity. Therefore this claim can best be dropped from Dilthey's thought as a remnant of the positivistic conception of science, provided that the claim to objectivity is not abandoned in the process. This, at least, is the solution proposed by various students and interpreters of Dilthey.[48]

THE ISSUE OF 'BESSERVERSTEHEN'

When we consider Dilthey's controversial claim that it is – or must be – possible to understand an author *better* than he has understood himself, we should be careful neither to overemphasize it nor to underemphasize it. It is significant that he was by no means the first thinker to make such a claim.* He mentions this claim often enough to assure us that he was serious about it but not often enough for us to be justified in regarding it as the cornerstone of his doctrine of understanding. Although understanding has 'Besserverstehen' as its *ultimate* aim – which is no doubt why Dilthey did not speak of 'Besserverstehen' more often – the two should not be fully identified.

We have already seen that Dilthey means different things by the term 'Verstehen,' which is, among other things, an ordinary and much used German word. Three of the major uses must be distinguished if we are to gain clarity with regard to 'Besserverstehen.' One of these is understanding as the grasping of a meaning by way of a sign that stands for or represents what is meant. A second is understanding as 'nacherleben,' as a re-experiencing of feelings and experiences which we believe others to have had, on the basis of accounts of those experiences embodied in expressions accessible to us in the present. A third meaning of understanding is the grasping of the significance of a statement, action, or event in the light of a larger context, e.g., a person's entire life.

The first of these senses of understanding is of undisputed importance and is widely recognized. Yet it has nothing to do with 'Besserverstehen,' for to grasp a meaning by way of a sign is not to understand anything better than anyone else: it is simply to understand what was meant in the first place. The second sense of understanding mentioned above is also very important, for it is the basis for the possibility of the historian's craft as Dilthey conceived

* Kant, for example, argues that '... it is by no means unusual, upon comparing the thoughts which an author has expressed in regard to his subject, whether in ordinary conversation or in writing, to find that we understand him better than he has understood himself' (*Critique of Pure Reason*, Smith translation, A314/B370).

of it. But understanding in this sense does not leave room for 'Besserver-stehen' either, for it is not a matter of degrees. Like understanding in the first sense, it aims at identity: we must try to think or feel exactly what was originally thought or felt – nothing more and nothing less.

It is only when we turn to the third of these senses of 'understanding' that we see why Dilthey insisted on the possibility of 'Besserverstehen.' The meaning in context, the significance, the implications of a statement, an action or an event can never be fixed and finished. History is a complex web of patterns, connections and relationships that can never be properly comprehended by a single mind. In the lives of each of us there are many important factors of which we are not even aware. Grasping these factors and the connections between them is an endless task. It is the work of the historian as well as the aim of any individual who reflects seriously on the course of his own life. A man's understanding of his own life and of the forces operative in it is never complete. And this leaves open the possibility that a historian covering the same ground many years later will attain a fuller understanding of him (that is, of his major expressions and actions taken together) on the basis of a more complete knowledge of the relevant forces and circumstances, for more knowledge generally becomes available after a period of years has elapsed. This fuller understanding on the part of the historian is Dilthey's 'Besserverstehen,' and it is the implicit aim of every historian who seeks to understand figures in the past. If this were not the case, the statesman's memoirs would be definitive with regard to what they cover, and there would be no need to write a critical account of his life and work. The critical account that historians should write and do write may even take a psychoanalytical approach – although Dilthey did not foresee the rise of psychoanalysis – for the appeal to unconscious or subconscious factors is one example of how historians can seek to understand historical figures better than they have understood themselves.

It should also be noted that such 'Besserverstehen' is possible only to the extent that the expression or event to be understood is a product and reflection of external factors and circumstances. Hence the statesman is an apt example. It is less clear, however, how one might understand a *philosopher* better than he understood himself, for the roots of philosophic expression are to be sought chiefly in the less accessible realm of the mind.

The possiblility of 'Besserverstehen' enhances the importance of the historian's work, which is never done. The narrow terms in which the historical individual understands and explains himself are transcended as we begin to view him more and more as responding to many forces and movements, including some of which he was not even aware. His life and work then take their place within a larger pattern that emerges only gradually with the passage of time. Hence 'Besserverstehen' is not to be conceived of in an absolute sense. What it means is that a fuller and larger vision of things is always possible.

7

Historicism and Relativism

Dilthey's overall philosophical position has inspired a general uneasiness in various circles – even among his sympathizers. Many critics are quick to dismiss him as a victim of the pitfalls of historicism and relativism. To weigh this assessment, we must first find out what Dilthey meant when he spoke of man's historicality and of the relativity of human cultural expressions, for both of these emphases are basic components of his outlook on life. This outlook itself is also worthy of attention, for it clears up a number of puzzling features of his philosophy and intellectual career. Through his fundamental openness, Dilthey was a living demonstration of what the quest for a larger self involves.

HISTORICISM AND HISTORICALITY

The term 'historicism' is more often used negatively than positively. Even renowned students of history and the historical outlook condemn 'historicism' in blunt terms. Friedrich Meinecke points out that historicism is often identified with a declining culture: according to its critics, historicism understands all worldviews but has no worldview of its own.[1] We are also told that historicism can be seen as a suspension of normative considerations (*Absage des Normativismus, Entnormierung*) in connection with our knowledge and thought.[2] Heinrich Rickert goes further: 'All historicism, when it is consistent, results in relativism, indeed, in nihilism, or it hides its worthlessness and emptiness by arbitrarily singling out this or that particular form of historical life in order to draw from it the content for a worldview ...' Historicism, he complains, makes a principle of its very lack of principles.[3]

Whether any such accusations can be made to stick in Dilthey's case remains to be seen, but this much is clear: Dilthey is often characterized as a historicist. In a book on the history of the philosophy of history, we read that Dilthey's 'total conception' represents the 'most refined historicism.'[4] One writer goes so far as to describe Dilthey as 'the greatest of all historicists.'[5] Even Ernst Troeltsch, who speaks of Dilthey as his 'teacher,' assures us that he is 'the most ingenious, distinguished and animated representative of pure historicism.'[6] If we are to investigate this matter, the concept of historicism will first have to be defined. Only against such a background would it make sense to ask whether Dilthey fell prey to the alleged shortcomings of historicism.

The best study of the roots and development of the historicist outlook is still Meinecke's classic work *Die Entstehung des Historismus*. It is to be preferred not only because Meinecke was a fine historian but also because he was an open advocate of the outlook whose history he traced. Historicism, he declared, is 'one of the greatest spiritual revolutions that occidental thinking has undergone'; it is the 'highest level in the understanding of things human reached up to now.'[7] The two fundamental concepts of historicism, according to Meinecke, are individuality and development.[8] These two ideas must be understood in relation to one another: development is the development of an individual totality.

The outlook that is based on these two ideas has its roots in a great many thinkers, but one of them is of particular importance for understanding the development of historicism: Meinecke followed Dilthey's lead in maintaining that it was Leibniz who had prepared the way for the new historical way of thinking. Dilthey himself hailed Leibniz, 'who cannot be highly enough praised,' as the 'founder' of German philosophy and declared: 'Just as Descartes gave the French spirit its direction and Locke determined the English spirit, Leibniz became the leader of our spiritual culture.' Thus the roots of historical thought are to be found in Leibniz,[9] but not in his work as a historian. It was rather his theory of monads, which was not intended as a theory of history, that proved fruitful for historical thought. The monads are individual and unique. Each develops autonomously without acting on other monads or being affected by them. In the picturesque language of Leibniz, the monads are 'windowless,' although they 'mirror' one another.

The conception of the historical world as made up of 'monads' of some sort must be viewed as the background of historicist thought. In early historicist thinking, the idea of historical 'monads' as *individualities* was dominant, and therefore early historicism can indeed be defined as the outlook of the historical school or simply as the characteristically German approach to the historical world and the writing of history. At this stage, historicism was the awareness of and emphasis on the individual, and it paved the way for the new view of the *Geisteswissenschaften* as independent of the natural sciences in subject-matter and method. In this early phase of historicism, one could almost speak of 'l'histoire pour l'histoire.' In the excitement of the rediscovery of various earlier epochs and cultures, an antiquarian attitude towards history certainly manifested itself.[10] Every individual, according to this conception of history, is to be understood and judged in terms of itself. Thus Meinecke speaks of the 'right to life' (*Lebensrecht*) of individualities in history.[11]

Early historicism, it seems, does not manifest the same strong tendency towards relativism that is apparent in later historicism. The reason for this is also to be sought in Leibniz. Coupled with the theory of monads is the doctrine of the pre-established harmony. This belief reappears in early historicism in the form of a faith that God oversees and governs all development. It has been maintained that historicism – at least in the healthy sense of the term – is inconceivable without religious convictions of some sort,[12] yet the historical outlook was, in fact, largely secularized as the decades went by. At the same time, the idea of *development* tended to gain in prominence in relation to the idea of individuality. Autonomous development, of course, is also an intrinsic part of the theory of monads, which continued to play a role in later historicist thinking.[13] Although belief in the divine origin and guidance of the historical process slowly faded away, all development was still regarded as necessary and therefore as justified. To be 'progressive,' according to this outlook, is to move willingly with the flow of time and history, and to be 'conservative' is to try to slow down the tempo of this movement in order to assure the preservation of the accomplishments and gains of the past. Historicism leaves room for both of those social-political attitudes and sees no basic conflict between them. To be 'reactionary,' however, is simply to resist the inevitable. Because of the dominance of the historicist way of thinking, these definitions of the terms 'progressive,' 'conservative,' and 'reactionary' long governed debate on social and political issues; even in our own time, the conception of change and development which they embody has by no means lost all its influence.

Understanding, within the context of a historicism oriented towards development, really amounts to grasping phenomena in the light of their origin.[14] Understanding in this sense carries with it the implication of a relativistic outlook – 'Tout comprendre c'est tout pardonner.' Historicism so understood can be equated with the view that the historical world is the sphere of autonomous development, of 'evolution,' and it would then have to be approached by way of a mode of knowledge that focuses on development and grasps phenomena in terms of their place within a development. Furthermore, since norms and laws are identified with historical actuality, since 'the rational' is equated with 'the real,' historicism also represents a rejection of natural law. It rejects laws and norms of transcendent origin and eternal validity but affirms laws in the immanent sense. The 'unique value (*Eigenwert*) of every historical epoch and individuality,' which Meinecke spoke of as the 'central idea of historicism,'[15] must be understood to include the 'Eigen-gesetzlichkeit' or 'auto-nomy' of historical individualities.

This doctrine of the full autonomy of historical individualities in their development is a dangerous idea, for the forces that make up history are not in fact 'windowless monads' that carefully refrain from acting on one another or interfering with one another's development. The major events of the twentieth century, beginning with World War I, have once again reminded us that history is the arena of conflict and collision. This awareness has led to a strong reaction against the historicist tendency to assume that existing historical trends, developments, and forces are healthy and progressive. But the significance of the principle at issue was realized long before the grim reminders of the twentieth century. As early as 1883, Wilhelm Windelband warned against the 'genetic approach' in blunt terms:

Change is not progress. That sounds very trivial and obvious. Yet to express this triviality is perhaps to insert a finger into an open wound of our time. For the more the purely genetic approach becomes accepted, the more easily the illusion is created that what is new in the cultural development of mankind is likewise better and more worthy of recognition. From the standpoint of explanatory theory, there is only earlier and later, there is only change: whether a particular change represents progress cannot be determined via a genetic investigation; for this we need a criterion, the idea of a goal by reference to which the value of the changes can be measured.

Windelband pointed to the danger of historical relativism and called for a 'critical' approach: 'In order to trace reason in history, we must be acquainted not only with history but also with reason.'[16]

Such arguments were not without effect on the leading historicists, but a complete abandonment of historicism was out of the question. The answer to the inner crisis of historicism was to be sought in the historical outlook itself; historicism, Meinecke wrote, '... must itself seek to heal the wounds which it has caused.'[17] Meinecke could even contemplate the possibility that historicism might soon reach the end of the road. But if so, this would not mean death in the sense of complete dissolution: 'Historicism contains seeds for new formations – even if the ripe, perhaps overripe, fruit of its present form falls by the wayside.'[18] Yet Meinecke himself was not willing to draw the ultimate relativistic conclusions that historicism seemed to imply. In his own thinking he gave priority to the idea of individuality,[19] and his loving account of the history of the historical outlook dealt only with early historicism. Nevertheless, the danger of relativism and nihilism loomed large in his mind. His official answer was a reaffirmation of the historicist faith: 'Full historicism also includes the capacity for resignation and demands respect for destiny.'[20] Yet in the sphere of ethics, where the problem of historicism perhaps assumes its most painful form, he counselled a moral faith. He appealed to conscience as 'that in which we are most like God' (*das Gottverwandteste in uns*) and argued that conscience gives an eternal significance and substance to the historical moment: 'All eternal values in history stem ultimately from the decisions of conscience made by man in action.'[21]

Although Meinecke was born in the heart of the nineteenth century (1862), he lived long enough to witness the German catastrophe and humiliation of Hitler's Third Reich. In his reflection on this tragedy, the historicist outlook recedes visibly, and his moral faith comes to the foreground. He writes that the 'high mission of German historical writing for the future' is '... to give evidence of both love and severity for our past and to proceed to the task of maintaining what was truly good in it, recognizing what was valueless and taking warning from it when one has to take action.' Meinecke points to conscience as the 'sun of our moral day' and as '... the original source of everything that we regard as divine in and around us ... Therefore so long as conscience is active in mankind and in the individual nations, it will guard itself against this march to the abyss.' Meinecke's reason for refusing to sanction the Nazi movement is not simply that it failed to triumph in the end: 'For what is a man profited,' he asks, 'if he shall gain the whole world, and lose his own soul?'[22]

We see a similar development in Troeltsch, for whom the ethical question was central to the problem of historicism.[23] After the disillusionment of World War I, Troeltsch finally abandoned the hope of a grand cultural-historical synthesis and began instead to emphasize the direct relation of each separate human individual to God. Thus the inner crisis of historicism leads ultimately to a new affirmation of morality and personal faith. The inner life of the individual is thereby granted priority over the larger course of events, and the way is prepared for a religious or ethical existentialism.

This survey of the historicist way of thinking and its consequences shows us that the emphasis falls more and more on the concept of development. By itself this should not surprise us, for it could be argued that development is the single most important concept employed by the historian. This concept has even been used as a 'common denominator' to define historicism. Yet, not every thinker who emphasizes development is to be branded a historicist.

Historicism operates with a specific conception of historical change. For historicism in the narrower sense (i.e., the historicism that leads to historical relativism), historical change is immanent, necessary, and directional. The subject of change, on this view, is the historical individual, a category that includes nations, institutions, societies, persons, systems of law, and other such phenomena studied by historians. It is the retention of the category of individuality (in the sense of individual totality) that separates classic historicism à la Meinecke from historicism in the broad sense, the sense the covers virtually every major historical thinker.

If we raise the question whether Dilthey can be called a historicist in the narrower sense outlined above, the answer must be no. He shares with historicism the emphasis on and interest in individual totalities, and to that extent he could almost be viewed as a late representative of early historicism. But insofar as the concept of development conceived as progress and unfolding is taken as determinative, Dilthey is not a historicist. The historicist belief in progress, as we have seen, was made possible by a faith in a divine pre-established harmony or in a divine dominion over the course of human history. But Dilthey was neither a Christian nor any other kind of theist, and nowhere in his writings did he express the kind of faith in the transcendent guidance of history that animated Ranke, for example. The progress of history towards a goal ordained by God was out of the question for Dilthey. There is indeed purpose (*Zweckmässigkeit*) in history, but it '... does not realize a goal (*Zweck*) set for it by nature or God ...' Talk of goals is rather to be understood in the sense of striving towards a goal (*Zielstrebigkeit*).[24] Hegel's 'dream' that the periods of history represent stages in the development of reason is to be rejected (*Fortsetzung*, 288). Dilthey goes even further: 'We must leave behind us any doctrine of a development advancing in stages' (p. 244). What, then, are we to take the concept of development to mean? It means that the present is filled by the past and bears the future within it, but it does not mean '... that we can apply to the individual or the nation or mankind the concept of a goal that is realized here; this would be an approach that goes beyond the object and could thus be rejected' (p. 232). Dilthey's term 'development' is to be understood in a weak sense and does not include the idea of progress: 'What the individual human being experiences and comprehends gives us no indication of a development as progress' (p. 253).

Dilthey's rejection of the belief in progress must be seen as an application and manifestation of his resolutely empirical approach to the sciences, which banishes metaphysical thinking and allows no appeal to transcendent beings and influences. Yet he was personally optimistic about the course of human events, and he did recognize a progress of sorts in history, although he did not argue that it is inevitable or necessary. In one sphere of human life, at least, there has been steady progress: 'The progress of the sciences continues all through history. This progress is steady, uninterrupted, irresistible, for what it depends on is that concepts can be handed on without loss from person to person and from age to age. In the entire sphere of the understanding of expressions of life, such a transferability (*Uebertragbarkeit*) is to be found only here.' Thus a similar progress in the sphere of culture is not to be expected. But the progress of the sciences includes that of the *Geisteswissenschaften*, and this in turn makes another kind of progress possible: 'The objectification of the spirit in expressions of life increases as time goes by. Thereby the material for historical understanding grows continuously. Ever more encompassing coherences (*Zusammenhänge*) become visible. Thus, within certain bounds, a progress in historical knowledge is present ...'[25] The triumph of science in all its branches penetrates to many aspects of life and elevates them by improving the conditions under which we live and by vastly enlarging the range of our knowledge and experience. The elevation and enlargement of our existence made possible by understanding leads Dilthey to affirm the '... superiority in the sense of life (*Lebensgefühl*) of any one of us compared with the greatest thinkers and heroes, the most elevated religious spirits of the ancient world.'[26] Development, then, can sometimes include progress in a general, cumulative sense because much of the past is retained within the present.

Although development is a key historical concept, Dilthey did not define history in terms of it. In fact, he avoided defining the historical process in specific terms at all, but a definite view of it does emerge from his writings. The 'essence of history,' he wrote in his diary in 1865, is 'historical movement itself.'[27] Four years earlier he had written:

What goes on in *the historical process*, seen in general terms, is that inner features of our ethical-cultural existence (*sittlich-geistige Dasein*), as common to many, create forms of this commonness, but that these forms, like all forms, do not satisfy the productive spirit, which is a progressing infinity, and rise up against the spirit because of various impulses such as the opposition between parties and schools. Thus it comes about that all cultural (*geistig*) matter threatens to become form, and the formed matter again becomes mere matter for the spirit (*Der junge Dilthey*, 147).

This bold, somewhat metaphysical formulation reveals to us the motor driving the historical process onward. In terms of Dilthey's philosophy of life, we could say that life itself is the underlying ground of history and that the human spirit, as an individual manifestation of life, drives history forward through its restless quest to achieve an adequate expression of its inward content or substance. But because the spirit is transformed in the very process of expression, it quickly becomes dissatisfied with its expressions. Consequently, the matter that has taken on form once more becomes matter to be used in the shaping of new expressions. The historical *process* should therefore be viewed as a restless stream, and it is through historical *thought* that we create a certain amount of order in this flow: 'The river of life which carries everything into the past is overcome by memory, and the contingency of events is overcome by the coherence (*Zusammenhang*) of what is thought.'[28]

Dilthey's concept of history, like every other important idea in his writings, must be understood in terms of his 'philosophy of life.' As we have seen (p. 73), Dilthey restricts the term 'life' to the human world; indeed, history and life are to be understood in terms of one another. History is a determinate manifestation of life: 'At every point in history we find life. And it is of life of every kind in the most varied relationships that history consists. History is simply life conceived of from the standpoint of mankind as a total coherence' (*Fortsetzung*, 256). In an early article, Dilthey identified history as understood in the German tradition with 'everything in the realm of the spirit (*alles Geistige*), language, law, and customs.'[29] He liked to associate himself with the German tradition, and he adopted this view as his own. The realm of history is simply the realm of the spirit, and the terms 'geistige Welt' and 'geschichtliche Welt' are therefore used interchangeably in many passages in the later writings. Furthermore, Dilthey never specified the relation between the historical sciences and the larger body of sciences called the 'Geisteswissenschaften.' In practice he tended to equate the two – by speaking of the 'Geisteswissenschaften' when he really meant the historical sciences – thereby neglecting or overlooking the systematic social sciences. History gives us a general knowledge of the realm of the spirit, according to Dilthey, and 'genuine universal history' seeks '... to arrive at a knowledge of what man is via the forms of the historical life of mankind.'[30] The 'universal historical aspect' of Dilthey's thought, as one of his students points out, must be conceived of in the light of his 'desire to understand everything' (*Allesverstehenwollen*).[31] It does not represent world history in the grand style of the believer in inevitable progress.

Dilthey's conception of history must be sharply distinguished from the historicist conception, for the latter lays great emphasis on development. Corresponding to this difference are two distinct conceptions of historical understanding, which are not to be confused with one another. For the historicist, to understand is to trace the genesis and development of the particular phenomenon under consideration. Because this development is viewed as necessary and progressive, understanding tends to lead to implicit or explicit approval. In virtue of his conception of science, of course, the historicist is at least a *methodological* relativist, but insofar as he identifies laws and norms with historical actuality, and insofar as he regards the end towards which a development is moving as decisive for assessing its meaning, we must go further and conclude that for the historicist, to understand all is indeed to forgive all. However, understanding so conceived is far from what Dilthey has in mind when he speaks of understanding as the basic cognitive operation of the *Geisteswissenschaften*. For Dilthey, understanding does not always focus on genesis and development; it focuses rather on structures, systems, connections, and coherences – in short, on *Zusammenhänge*. 'We understand only *Zusammenhang*,' Dilthey writes. '*Zusammenhang* and understanding correspond to each other' (*Fortsetzung*, 257). Strictly speaking, this statement must be qualified, for it does not apply to elementary understanding: 'If we take the specified forms of higher understanding together, we see that what they have in common is that they enable us to understand the coherence (*Zusammenhang*) of a totality via an inductive inference from given expressions' (p. 212). Basic for Dilthey is not the development of an individual totality but the relation of part and whole.

Dilthey's doctrine of understanding and its relation to his notion of 'Zusammenhang' is the real evidence that he is not to be regarded as a historicist in his view of historical knowledge and the historical process. (I leave open the question whether he might be called a historicist in some other, more narrowly philosophical sense.) Development as such is only a secondary idea in his thinking; it represents one form of 'Zusammenhang.' There are static 'Zusammenhänge' as well as dynamic ones. A development within a historical process can be regarded as a 'Zusammenhang' or whole in terms of which a particular is to be understood, but a written text – and even a single sentence – also constitutes such a 'Zusammenhang.' The understanding of development is part of historical science, but it does not entail the approbation of every historical trend, for Dilthey did not regard development as automatically justified or necessary. (Of course, Dilthey, too, can be spoken of as a methodological relativist, but only if we take this to mean that the scientific attitude adopted by the historian requires impartiality.)

Understanding is bound to 'Zusammenhänge' because life, as something intelligible, is given to us in this way: '... life exists everywhere only as *Zusammenhang*' (*Ideen*, 144). Dilthey's own practice as a historian also reflects the emphasis on 'Zusammenhänge,' which take on many different concrete forms in history. Particulars are to be grasped in context and in relation to other historical phenomena, but ultimately they must be understood in terms of themselves and not as mere steps or links in a development. As historian, Dilthey refused to subordinate the particular completely to a larger process or development from which it would then derive its meaning. As one of his own students noted as early as 1912, this is simply not the kind of approach that one would call historicism.[32]

But to say that Dilthey is not a historicist is by no means to deny that he is a historical thinker interested in the historical side of man's existence and in the historical process as a revelation of what man has become. In other words, there is a doctrine of 'historicality' to be found in Dilthey. But what did Dilthey mean by this elusive term?

To begin with, we should note that the term itself is a noun built on an adjective that is in turn built on another noun, i.e., 'history.' Dilthey's use of this term is varied. He writes that through the work of the historical school, the nineteenth century recognized the 'historicality' of man and of all social orders.[33] He also writes that nineteenth-century thinkers conceived of the state as an organic formation undergoing continuous development and grounded in the spirit of a people. The task was then to develop a science of the state '... which would take into account the historicality of the state and the right of the social arrangements that have emerged in history.'[34] In this context, 'historicality' means that the institutions and structures making up the social-historical world are products of 'historical growth,' and therefore the term can also be applied to Christianity as one religion among others.[35] In a narrower sense, 'historicality' can mean that which is 'historically conditioned' as opposed to the eternally or universally valid (*allgemeingültig*). Thus Dilthey speaks of the 'historicality' of aesthetic ideals,[36] of educational ideals,[37] and even of literary and poetic techniques.[38] Everything that man makes and does is conditioned in part by non-natural circumstances. Dilthey speaks of this as the 'complete (*allseitig*) conditionedness of man, his dependence on the social order around him, his historicality.'[39]

Dilthey comes closer to the most interesting and significant conception of historicality operative in his thought when he applies the term to consciousness, experience, and thinking. The rise of the *Geisteswissenschaften* and the historical sciences in Germany is one of the factors making such a conception of historicality possible. Thus Dilthey speaks of the 'historicality of German thought' in the sense of its historical orientation and even of 'inner historicality' as a superior feature of German thinking.[40] He also speaks of the 'historicality of consciousness' in the sense of historical consciousness pervaded by an awareness of the past but not permitting itself in an uncritical spirit to be completely dominated by it (*Philosophie*, 380). Historicality in the sense of historical awareness is a 'fundamental characteristic' (*Grundeigenschaft*) of consciousness.[41] Even more significant is his claim that historicality is a characteristic (*Merkmal*) of life (*Ideen*, 196) and that life itself is 'historically conditioned' (*Individualität*, 275).

Dilthey, then, regards man as a thinking, living, responding being, that is, as a *historical* being. The intention of spelling out what this means goes back to the very beginning of his philosophical career. In a diary entry of 1860 he wrote that the 'contemporary German spirit' is characterized by its effort '... to grasp man as an essentially historical being, whose existence is only realized in community' (*Der junge Dilthey*, 124). The struggle for the autonomy of the *Geisteswissenschaften* must be seen in this light. It represents a rejection of naturalism and of any conception of man that fails to acknowledge the centrality of the life of the spirit. And the life of the spirit, as we have seen (p. 129 above), is in turn identified with the realm of history. This emphasis on history and the spirit must not be read as a denial that man is part of the system that we call nature but only as an affirmation that man transcends nature. In Dilthey's own terms, man's historical nature is his higher nature.[42] And this historical nature is essentially undetermined: man is only given to us in terms of realized possibilities, as Dilthey puts it (*Fortsetzung*, 279). To say that man is a historical being is to say that he has a history rather than a fixed nature. This doctrine must be seen not as a finished anthropology but as a manifestation and expression of an empirical approach to the question of man. Dilthey does not mean that man can become whatever he chooses but only that we must wait and see what he becomes: man represents an 'undetermined type' (*Aufbau*, 159). History is our chief source of knowledge about man's higher nature, and thus we are justified in making statements about what man is only on the basis of our knowledge of what he has become: 'What man is only his history tells him,' Dilthey declares.[43] This emphasis is one of the central components of his doctrine of the historicality of man. The 'historicality of free human nature' must be accepted as a 'fundamental fact of the *Geisteswissenschaften*' (*Poetik*, 108).

A second meaning of Dilthey's claim that man is a historical being is that he contains something of the past within him: '... the spirit is a historical creature; that is, it is filled with the memory of the history of the entire human race ...' (*Fortsetzung*, 277). This statement is a piece of Diltheyan hyperbole and is not to be taken literally, but its thrust is clear: man transcends the natural order. Because he grows up in the awareness of a past, he always finds himself in a specific situation and set of circumstances. He never begins his active life only with what nature has given him and placed before him. It is in this sense that human life is historically conditioned. But in order that the term 'historically conditioned' not be misunderstood, we must immediately go on to specify a third sense in which we can speak of man as a historical being. Man is also historically *aware*; that is to say, he possesses a *historical* consciousness, and this is precisely what enables him to *transcend* (in the sense of see beyond) the conditions of his own history. The developed historical consciousness as described by Dilthey includes an awareness of the *relativity* of all historical phenomena. A knowledge of the variety present within the social-historical world and a proper conception of the development and changes which the components of this world continuously undergo prevents us from becoming bound irrevocably to anything in the past or present. Thus the truth about man as a historical being is not only that he is historically conditioned but also that he is free. The very growth of historical awareness represents an increase in human freedom: 'The *historical consciousness* of the *finitude* of every historical phenomenon, of every human or social condition, of the relativity of every kind of faith, is the final step in the liberation of man' (*Fortsetzung*, 290). The growth of historical knowledge achieved through historical understanding – which always retains a certain detachment, however helpful sympathy may be – must lead ultimately to an ever more comprehensive grasp of what man has been and become, which will in turn reveal to man his own possibilities. Through historical consciousness, man frees himself in principle from the past in order to appropriate and develop some of the possibilities revealed to him by historical understanding. When Dilthey says that man is a historical being, then, we must think of the historical attitude as facing the future and not as gazing into the past.

This picture of the historicality of human life is strikingly similar to the views of various twentieth-century existential thinkers. It is among these thinkers that we must seek Dilthey's successors – and not among phenomenologists and historicists. Herman Nohl, one of Dilthey's own students, realized this when he declared in 1935 that philosophy of life had assumed a new form in existential philosophy (see p. 71 above). Dilthey's philosophy can be read, then, as a philosophy of existence, simply by regarding his characterization of 'the life lived by man' as an elucidation of human 'existence.' The terms 'life' and 'existence' are often used as synonyms in everyday German as well as English, and in Dilthey's writings we often find 'Dasein' or 'Existenz' where we would expect to read 'life.' But this is not to say that

Dilthey intended his philosophy to be understood as a philosophy of existence. As I have emphasized, he intended it as a philosophy of life, but as we shall see later, he really did not succeed in constructing a philosophy of life. The connection between Dilthey and the existential thinkers of the twentieth century is not that the latter shared his basic philosophical intentions but that many of his insights into the nature of human life or existence were eventually incorporated into their work.* This, too, is a reflection of Dilthey's individualism. What he struggled to say about the larger structures that make up the social-historical world had no lasting impact, but his doctrine of the historicality of the existence of the human individual has become the common property of many thinkers of the twentieth century.

RELATIVISM AND RELATIVITY

If Dilthey cannot be classed as a historicist in the strict sense, is he perhaps a relativist? Many of his critics have concluded that he is. In one book we read that Dilthey was an 'avowed relativist'[44] and in another that he eventually recognized his 'capitulation to historical relativism.'[45] Such claims are simply mistaken, for Dilthey did not intend to preach relativism, nor did he ever declare that relativism is the logical outcome of his thought. That he believed the contrary is clear from his correspondence with Husserl. In a famous article of 1910 entitled 'Philosophie als strenge Wissenschaft,' Husserl commented on the rise of a new kind of 'worldview philosophy' (*Weltanschauungsphilosophie*) which represents a 'transformation of Hegel's metaphysical philosophy of history into a skeptical historicism,' and he brought up Dilthey's name in connection with this philosophy. 'One can easily see,' he wrote, 'that when historicism is thought through consistently, it turns into an extreme skeptical subjectivism. The ideas of truth, theory and science, like all ideas, would then lose their absolute validity.' Husserl admitted that Dilthey had expressly rejected historical skepticism, but he claimed to see no grounds in Dilthey's thought for such a rejection.[46] Some three months before his death, Dilthey responded to this criticism by way of a letter to Husserl dated 29 June 1911.[47] He complained that Husserl's article was really a 'polemic' and claimed that his own published works, in particular *Das Wesen der Philosophie* (1907), showed Husserl's criticisms to be unjustified. Dilthey wrote that he denied the possibility of metaphysics but not the

---

* This is not to say that those thinkers all came by these insights by reading Dilthey. Important ideas often arise simultaneously in more than one quarter, and this was no doubt the case with regard to some of the ideas common to various existential thinkers.

possibility of knowledge. He agreed that the inquiry into historical conditions and origins must be distinguished from the inquiry into validity and went on to affirm '... that any statement from the sphere of worldviews (e.g., a religious statement) can be investigated with regard to its validity just as well as a scientific statement.' Dilthey therefore protested: 'I am neither a philosopher of intuition nor a historicist nor a skeptic ...' and added that Husserl's argument failed to show that his (Dilthey's) thought leads to skepticism.

Much of the talk of Dilthey's 'relativism' results from his regular use of the term 'relativity.' The terms 'relativity' and 'relativism' are then confused, in the apparent belief that any recognition of the relativity of historical phenomena amounts to an affirmation of relativism. Even Meinecke is guilty of this careless use of terms. He writes, for example: 'Herder's genuine historical greatness lay in this, that although he, too, fell into a false idealization of earliest history, from the beginning he emphasized the impossibility of reviving it, thereby also emphasizing its *relativity*, and that he then applied *the same relativism* to all historical formations.'[48] The identification of relativism with the recognition of relativity is a dangerous procedure. During the last 200 years in particular, European civilization has been overwhelmed by a flood of evidence demonstrating the relativity – in the sense of variety, at least – of human customs, beliefs, and institutions. One conceivable answer to the implicit threat posed by this situation is to declare that one way of life in this multiplicity (i.e., our own) is correct and in harmony with the eternal laws of God and nature, while all the rest are false and immoral. A more realistic and popular approach is to grant a certain amount of validity to most – if not all – forms of life and to try to define values and norms in a more flexible way that takes this diversity as well as the unfolding of history into account. This approach in turn requires making a strict distinction between relativity and relativism, in order that the former may be affirmed and the latter rejected. Hence much of the historical and social thought of the nineteenth and twentieth centuries has focused attention on various aspects of the question how such a distinction is to be drawn and upheld. This question is of the greatest importance, for the health of our civilization – and even its very survival – may depend on it.

One way to deal with the problem of relativity is to develop a 'sociology of knowledge,' i.e., a theory of the 'situational' and 'positional' determinants of our knowledge and experience. All knowledge would then be related to factors on the side of the subject apart from which it could not be understood, although it would not by any means be explained or accounted for solely in terms of such factors. Karl Mannheim, a leading proponent of sociology of knowledge, characterizes such a view of knowledge and experience as 'relationism,' which is to be distinguished from relativism. 'Relationism,' he writes, 'does not signify that there are no criteria of rightness and wrongness in a discussion. It does insist, however, that it lies in the nature of certain assertions that they cannot be formulated absolutely, but only in terms of the perspective of a given situation.' Relationism '... becomes relativism when it is linked with the older static ideal of eternal, unperspectivistic truths independent of the subjective experience of the observer, and when it is judged by this ideal idea of absolute truth.'[49]

Although Dilthey himself was not a sociologist of knowledge, we can consider Mannheim and other thinkers of similar persuasion as carrying on part of his tradition. Dilthey was concerned with the factors conditioning our experience of the social-historical world, and he laid particular emphasis on the previous experience, background, and pre-understanding that we bring to our encounters with the world of nature and culture. What we are able to see in the physical world and understand in the cultural world depends on our background knowledge. In a discussion of the importance to the historian of notes, letters, written plans, and early drafts of manuscripts, Dilthey observed that one never knows '... what a particular page might be able to tell us if only the right person sees it.'[50] In this sense, all our knowledge of the social-historical world is relative, that is, relative to our background knowledge and experience. Thus Dilthey speaks of the relativity of human thought and of theories,[51] but he also speaks of the relativity of historical forms of life, of all worldviews, of every kind of faith, of historical phenomena, of all existence (Dasein), of historical convictions, of answers to the riddle of the world, of metaphysical systems, of religious doctrines, and of human conceptions of the coherence of things.[52] Thus his doctrine of relativity applies to every kind of expression, cultural creation, and form of life.

The relativity of historical forms of life was also a favourite theme among historicists. In fact, the discovery of the diversity and variety of historical forms of life from place to place and from age to age was one of the factors that contributed heavily to the rise of historical thinking. But for historicism, relativity means something different than for Dilthey. On the historicist outlook, every form of life is relative to the development of which it forms a part. Its validity and significance is limited in that it will inevitably be superseded by later, higher forms of life within the same development. But Dilthey, as we saw above, was no believer in necessary and inevitable development in a certain direction. On his conception of the world of history and the spirit, every expression and form of life is relative instead to the totality of life which it reflects in part and to which it responds as well as to the fullness of man's nature. For Dilthey, to be relative means to be incomplete and partial. Therefore, the validity of an expression or form of life is not unconditional or absolute, but must rather be regarded as relative. Particular expressions are grounded in particular aspects of man's being and experience. They are superseded not because the development goes on but because other aspects of man's being and experience call for recognition. Although Dilthey sometimes speaks Hegelian language in this context, we must be careful not to interpret his conception of relativity as allowing for a Hegelian 'Aufhebung.'[53] It is the restlessness of the finite human spirit, which never achieves full and adequate expression of what it is and what it has lived, that drives history forward. 'The totality of human nature exists only in history,' Dilthey writes; 'the human individual enjoys it and becomes conscious of it only when he gathers the spirits of the past within himself.'[54] The human spirit in search of itself therefore moves from one expression to another. In other words, through its expressions the spirit seeks its own substance or content, which can never be presented totally in a direct consciousness. No single expression can be fully adequate or final, and what the spirit gains at one point in history can be lost from its view at another.

Although Dilthey believed that adding together or summing up the relativities present in history would yield something of more than passing significance and value, he also recognized definite dangers inherent in the historical way of thinking. He worried about the 'chaos of relativities' and the 'anarchy' of systems, of thought, of convictions, and of views of life that he saw in the world around him.[55] He even worried about the dangers of skepticism in relation to his own thought.[56] His final and definitive response to such doubts was his belief in the sovereignty of the human spirit: 'Not the relativity of every worldview is the final word of the spirit that has gone through them all but the sovereignty of the spirit over against any one of them and furthermore the positive awareness that the one reality of the world exists for us in the various attitudes (*Verhaltungsweisen*) of the spirit' (*Philosophie*, 406). If relativism were philosophy's last word, Dilthey wrote, '... then d'Alembert's superior amusement about the revelations would also be the definitive mental attitude of every truly honest man.'[57] But relativism is *not* the last word, and Dilthey wished to remain open to revelations of some sort, even if they are not always to be taken at face value.

Because of the dangers of relativism, the word 'relativity' has taken on some unpleasant connotations in our time. But this was not yet so in Dilthey's time – at least, not to the same extent – and Dilthey personally conceived of the awareness of the relativity of historical phenomena more as liberating than as threatening. It did mean that the European forms of life sanctioned by the Christian tradition were not absolutely and eternally valid and binding, but it also meant that the many diverse forms of life outside this tradition have a value and significance of their own. The latter idea represented an intriguing prospect to Dilthey, for he was an optimistic soul who had written enthusiastically in his youth that the 'finitude of life' and the 'relativity' of time mean that each day represents 'a completely unlimited (*ungemessen*) good' (*Der junge Dilthey*, 191). Because of his basically optimistic outlook, he would no doubt have insisted that the glass of water about which optimists and pessimists debate is half full rather than half empty. His conception of the relativity of everything historical must be viewed in the light of this optimism. Dilthey was much more inclined to be impressed by the values which have already been realized in history than to be dismayed at what had not yet been achieved. In this sense he is indeed a 'conservative thinker,' as one of his students characterized him.[58]

It is sometimes argued that Dilthey did not deal adequately with the question of truth.[59] This is certainly so insofar as his works do not contain any explicit, systematic discussion of the concept of truth. Yet this should not be taken to mean that Dilthey is a relativist after all. Because of his underlying ontology, the question of truth became secondary. Dilthey did not discuss his own ontology explicitly, but he did make it clear as early as the *Einleitung* of 1883 that the new favourable attitude towards the *Geisteswissenschaften* (which he himself represented) and the underlying conviction that knowledge of the individual is possible rest on a rejection of Spinoza's metaphysical principle that all determination is negation.[60] For Dilthey and other thinkers of similar persuasion, determination does not constitute negation or some sort of insufficiency in being; it represents rather an enrichment of being. In other words, in Dilthey's thought there seems to be an implicit neo-Platonism at work, according to which all that actually exists is good and true insofar as it exists. It is this conception of being that makes the question of truth secondary. And it also requires that all spiritual, cultural, and historical existence be regarded as relative, that is, as relatively good. The ultimate criterion for the goodness and truth of an expression would then be sought not in its formal qualities or in its correspondence with reality and ideals but in its fullness; that is to say, the highest and best cultural expressions would be those that reflect the totality of life in some substantial way and draw extensively on man's nature and experience. Of course, expressions are not to be measured against one another in strictly quantitative terms, for the ideal of fullness also compels the recognition of novelty as a norm. This means that the author of an expression must not be content simply to bring together as much as possible of what man has lived in the past; he must also probe new dimensions of experience and aspects of life that are then to be made accessible to others by way of the cultural and intellectual expressions which he creates. This in turn implies that our judgments about the worth of expressions are relative to the historical situation. But the expressions themselves are relative in principle to the totality of life, which transcends our experience and imagination and can never be adequately reflected in an expression. Thus all expressions are limited in value. Everything historical is relative, Dilthey declares.[61]

This doctrine of relativity comes to expression in Dilthey's 'philosophy of philosophy' and in his outlook on religion as well. According to Dilthey, religions as well as philosophical systems are rooted in 'worldviews' (*Weltanschauungen*). The recognition that worldviews are relative and limited takes the sharp edges off the conflict between the various religions and philosophies.

Dilthey's doctrine of worldviews includes a division into three basic types, namely, naturalism, idealism of freedom, and objective idealism, which correspond respectively to the dominance of thought, feeling, and will (*Philosophie*, 403). Through this division into types, Dilthey was able to bring a certain amount of order into the diversity and sheer multiplicity of worldviews.

All worldviews contain something valuable and true, but all are one-sided. How are we to get at what is valuable in each? We can only approach worldviews through the forms in which they are expressed, the most important of which are art, religion, and philosophy, as Hegel noted. Each work of art reflects a worldview, but works of art do not normally claim to give a complete expression of the worldview which they embody. Therefore, the conflict of worldviews does not assume as acute a form in art as in religion and philosophy. Nonetheless, there is a problem here, and Dilthey worried about the 'anarchy of taste,'[62] which is bound up with the diversity of worldviews. A parallel problem is the struggle between competing religions based on different worldviews. Dilthey believed that the one-sided affirmation of a particular religion with its worldview, e.g., Christianity and the idealism of freedom,[63] would have to be replaced by a recognition of the relativity of all worldviews and the openness towards other religions that must accompany such a recognition. But perhaps because organized religion has steadily declined in influence in the modern world, Dilthey gave no further attention to this problem. Instead he focused on the relativity of worldviews as reflected in the diversity of philosophical systems. In his youth he had already raised the prospect of carrying Kant's unfinished work further by means of a 'philosophy of philosophy.' Great philosophical systems, he wrote, are 'one-sided, yet true (*aufrichtig*) revelations of human nature.'[64] This philosophy of philosophy, on which he resumed work during the last fifteen years of his life, really represents a 'philosophy of philosophies,' as one of Dilthey's students put it.[65] More specifically, it is an attempt to account for the diversity of philosophical (i.e., metaphysical) systems and also for the possibility of learning from each of the systems.

Dilthey's theory concerning the diversity of philosophical systems contains three major points. First, we must remember that all philosophers

... have before them one and the same world, the reality that appears in consciousness. The sun of Homer shines forever. Plato beheld the same reality as Thales. From this it follows that the unity of all philosophies is grounded ultimately in the identity (*Selbigkeit*) of the outer and inner world. Because of this identity, the same basic relationships are seen again and again.

All philosophies are bound together, then, by the fact that they focus on the same world. 'We must proceed from what they have in common ...,' declared Dilthey hopefully.[66] But this brave beginning for a philosophy of philosophy cannot be carried through in exactly the way which this passage suggests. Dilthey also wrote that all philosophers and philosophies deal with the riddle of life and the world. Because we encounter this riddle in connection with specific experiences (e.g., the mysteries of birth and death), it does not confront every thinker as the same. Furthermore, the claim that Hegel lived in the same world as Aristotle is a partial truth at best. Homer's sun may have shone on both of them, but the social-historical world had undergone many fundamental changes during the centuries that separate these two thinkers. Therefore, we must understand the claim that all philosophers face the same reality in a more limited sense. Each philosopher grasps and brings to expression a few of the many sides of the totality of reality, and no philosopher can claim a total experience of reality. Thus the various philosophers do not have as much in common as they might at first appear to have.

A second element in Dilthey's philosophy of philosophy is his theory of the types of philosophical or metaphysical systems. If the many systems cannot be traced to a single, identifiable common ground, they can at least be divided into fundamental types that appear again and again in the history of philosophy. The three types of philosophical systems, corresponding to the three types of worldviews, are naturalism, idealism of freedom,[67] and objective idealism. The third of these, of course, represents the classic metaphysical outlook: the 'bulk of all metaphysics,' Dilthey declares, falls into this category (*Weltanschauung*, 112). It would be useful to know the law by which these metaphysical systems develop, but we have no way of discovering any such law. Since a priori insight into the essence of the history of philosophy is not granted us, we must content ourselves with a knowledge based on mere comparison. Therefore the typology of metaphysical systems must be regarded as provisional, Dilthey cautions us: 'The central thing here can only be the intuition that has resulted from working with the metaphysical systems for a long time ... This distinguishing of types is only intended to enable us to look more deeply into history – and that from the standpoint of life.'[68]

This theory of the three types of philosophical systems[69] must be taken for what it is – a classification. It must not be regarded as a relativism applied to the history of philosophy.* Neither is it a philosophy of the history of philosophy à la Hegel,[70] for it really has nothing to do with the *history* of philosophy as such. The three types of systems have existed side by side since the time of the Greeks, and we have no reason to believe that they are moving towards a synthesis. Objective idealism might look like a synthesis reconciling the tensions between determinism and freedom as embodied by naturalism and the idealism of freedom respectively, but Dilthey himself gave no indication that we are to read the history of philosophy along such lines. Although each of the three types of philosophies undergoes a certain amount of internal development, and although the three exercise some influence on one another, they march on through history without merging and without destroying one another. Dilthey apparently believed that there would always be different types of persons who would be attracted to different kinds of philosophies. Rather than a philosophy of the history of philosophy, one might even argue that this typology represents an essentially *unhistorical* approach to the diversity of worldviews and metaphysical systems.[71]

Third, Dilthey's philosophy of philosophy includes the conviction that we can learn from every metaphysical system. In this regard it picks up themes about metaphysics that had already been developed in Book II of the *Einleitung* (see Chapter 4 above). Dilthey did not, however, maintain that the truths expressed in the various metaphysical systems could somehow be taken together or added up to form the whole truth or the closest possible

---

* With reference to Dilthey, Rickert complains: 'The various types of worldviews are lined up next to each other peacefully as though independent philosophizing was a thing of the past, as though philosophy had lived out its life or come to the end of the road by turning into a series of forms that are now regarded as immobile ...' He then adds: 'Indeed, the belief that the world is nothing but a great picture book and that paging through this picture book is the only activity worthy of man could also be called a "worldview"' (*Die Philosophie des Lebens*, 48, 49).

human approximation to it. Such a philosophy of the history of philosophy would be incompatible with his conception of the puzzling 'countenance of life' which the philosopher tries to read (see p. 60 above). First of all, the totality appears to different persons in such a way that irreconcilable contradictions between the various worldviews and philosophies come about. Furthermore, antinomies sometimes arise when worldviews are expressed in philosophical form. But the contradictions and antinomies disappear when we reduce the worldviews to their roots in the human subject and in the totality of life. In this context Dilthey even speaks of the various worldviews as surviving in an 'aufgehoben' form.[72] But a truly Hegelian 'Aufhebung' in which the truth of each worldview and philosophy is preserved on a higher level was not what Dilthey had in mind. Such an 'Aufhebung' would require a conception of knowledge which he would be forced to rule out, for he maintained that it is not granted us to grasp the various sides or aspects of the totality in one all-embracing view.[73] 'Aufhebung' is possible only on a limited scale, for two reasons.

First, the totality of life and reality simply does not appear to us in a unified way which we can penetrate rationally. Life, Dilthey writes, '... is not only given in our experience in an incomplete (lückenhaft) way, but it is many-sided as well; oppositions produced by our thinking about life appear, and in the attempt to overcome these oppositions via thinking in concepts, they turn into contradictions ...'[74] In a fragment on the problem of the conflict between worldviews, we read: 'When someone with an impartial mind seeks to combine everything that he is able to re-live (nacherleben) within himself, when he seeks to look the world in the face, as it were, in order to understand it inwardly, then features appear to him that cannot be reconciled in a unified understanding.'[75] Here we encounter Dilthey's irrationalism, which includes not only a belief in the importance of the irrational factors in the life of the mind but also a conception of reality as beyond straightforward logical comprehension and explanation.[76] The world appears to us again and again in a 'new light' (Weltanschauung, 81), writes Dilthey, but we must not interpret such talk in a perspectivistic sense, as though we could get at the whole truth by adding up all partial truths. The 'truth-content' (Wahrheitsgehalt) of each metaphysical system is to be understood not as a perspective on reality but rather as an experiential possibility.

The second reason why only a limited 'Aufhebung' of earlier philosophical systems is possible is rooted in the very nature of our understanding of the social-historical world and all that is produced within it. Understanding, as we have seen, is not a merely intellectual operation: it involves the 'totality of our mental powers.' It is rooted in lived experience, and without a broad range of experience, there is little that we will be able to understand. This means that the 'truth-content' of past metaphysical systems cannot simply be read out of a book. The true metaphysicians have lived what they write (*Einleitung*, 358), and if we are to understand what they have to say, we must live it after them. Metaphysical systems can neither be appropriated nor disposed of on a purely intellectual plane: we must 'think through' them – and even 'live through' them (p. 126). Because metaphysical thought has its roots in 'metaphysical' or 'philosophical experience,'[77] we must approach it by the method of the understanding of expressions, hoping thereby to extract its truth and value. But such understanding is an arduous process. It simply does not allow us to work quickly through the entire history of Western philosophy in order to master all that is valuable in it and make it our own. We are inevitably forced to choose and to immerse ourselves fully in only a few thinkers, just as Dilthey chose to concentrate on Schleiermacher and Hegel. Because we have so much history behind us, we can and should be superior in general philosophical insight and awareness to the Greeks, but an adequate comprehension and appropriation of man's entire intellectual past is beyond the grasp of the individual human mind as presently constituted. The philosophy of philosophy must limit itself to pointing out the wealth that is there for our enjoyment and enrichment. Each of us must personally undertake the labour of understanding and absorbing that which appeals to him in the history of philosophy.*

DILTHEY'S OWN OUTLOOK ON LIFE

Earlier in this chapter we saw that Dilthey did not surrender to relativism and that his recognition of the relativity of everything historical is not his last

---

* This philosophy of philosophy, like so many other branches of Dilthey's thought, leaves various questions unanswered. Among them is that of the relation between worldviews and philosophies. Dilthey is generally unclear on what philosophy is and is not, and he does not always distinguish it clearly from metaphysics (see p. 84 above). Worldviews come to expression in metaphysical systems, but Dilthey does not tell us whether philosophy in general (e.g., his own philosophy of life and the philosophy of philosophy based upon it) is also to be regarded as the expression of a worldview. This question of the 'welt-anschaulich' element in philosophy is dealt with in a Diltheyan vein by G.A. van der Wal in *Wereldbeschouwelijk denken als filosofisch probleem* (The Hague: Kruseman, 1968). Because Dilthey was reluctant to embrace the view that philosophy as such contains a 'welt-anschaulich' element – he tried to confine this element to metaphysical thinking – his endless efforts to define philosophy are unconvincing. What he implies about philosophy throughout his writings (i.e., a view like that of Van der Wal) is not fully in harmony with what he declares philosophy to be.

word on this matter. The decisive point is rather the *sovereignty* of the human spirit over against all that it has produced: there is nothing alien to the spirit to which it must subordinate itself. This belief in man's sovereignty is central to Dilthey's reading of the cultural and intellectual history of the West. The human spirit's realization of its autonomy, he wrote, represents the most difficult and perhaps the greatest of its advances.[78] By affirming man's sovereignty and autonomy, Dilthey places himself in the mainstream of modern Western thought. In this outlook, the Humanist belief that man is his own legislator (Kant) is combined with the belief that man is essentially an undetermined being whose limits have not been reached and are not known to him. The latter belief then becomes the basis for the hope that man can make of himself whatever he chooses. This specifically modern understanding of man was formulated in classic fashion as early as the time of the Renaissance. In Pico della Mirandola's 'Oration on the Dignity of Man,' we read that man is a 'creature of indeterminate nature.' After God created man, he told him:

Neither a fixed abode nor a form that is thine alone nor any function peculiar to thyself have We given thee, Adam, to the end that according to thy longing and according to thy judgment thou mayest have and possess what abode, what form, and what functions thou thyself shalt desire. The nature of all other beings is limited and constrained within the bounds of laws prescribed by Us. Thou, constrained by no limits, in accordance with thine own free will, in whose hand We have placed thee, shalt ordain for thyself the limits of thy nature ... Thou shalt have the power to degenerate into the lower forms of life, which are brutish. Thou shalt have the power, out of thy soul's judgment, to be reborn into the higher forms, which are divine.[79]

The divine Creator soon vanished from this picture, leaving a creature who has to survey his own history to find out what he is. This vision of man created the faith in the sovereignty of the human spirit which has dominated the Western thinkers who have turned their backs on orthodox Christianity and traditional theism. It is in this tradition that we must view Dilthey, with his emphasis on man's autonomy and on the historical character of existence, and it was this outlook that he affirmed in the face of relativism. Indeed, insofar as sovereignty and autonomy represent attributes of divinity, we could say that the divine is brought down to earth and is now to be sought in man.

Dilthey's personal outlook on life, of course, took on a somewhat more specific form. It was not his task as a philosopher to advocate a particular worldview, but in his non-philosophical writings especially, his preference became clear. 'I have no solution to the riddle of life,' he told his friends, 'but I want to share with you the *feeling about life* (*Lebensstimmung*) which has arisen within me through my *reflection on the consequences* of historical consciousness.' He then proceeded to do so by relating a dream which he claimed to have had at the home of his friend Count Yorck some years before. In this dream the three types of philosophical systems again appear, and Dilthey feels strongly attracted to each of them, to the point, he declared, that '... the unity of my being seemed to be torn ...'[80] But the comments which he appended to his account of this dream make it clear that he had personally chosen for the worldview of the thinkers who attracted him most (i.e., Schleiermacher, Goethe, and Hegel). In other words, his own outlook represents what he called objective idealism. This has been recognized by various commentators on his thought, some of whom have spoken of an implicit or hidden pantheism in his work.[81]

The pantheistic background of Dilthey's thinking illuminates some key statements in his writings and clears up certain features of his somewhat puzzling character as well. One might expect that Dilthey, as an intellectual deeply immersed in culture, art, and ideas, would be a source of easily recognizable values and an advocate of definite convictions; that is to say, one would picture him as a man who 'knows what he stands for.' But this is not the picture of Dilthey painted by those who knew him well. One of his students wrote that his inner life was a riddle not only to his students but even to his own children.[82] Another of Dilthey's students declared not long after his death: 'I do not know whether anyone is able to say that he has known Dilthey.'[83] This is a strange statement to make about a man who stated that outside of philosophy, friendship as the ancients conceived of it is the highest good in life, and who spoke of his 'insatiable need of friendship.'[84] Yet this same man also felt a deep need to be alone: 'Much as I love sociability and happy as I am to find friends with similar goals,' he confessed, 'I can nevertheless say that by nature I am solitary, that solitude always seems to me to be my best friend.'[85] Dilthey claimed that the emotional side of his own life was deeper than that of most other people, but he admitted that he remained reserved in spite of this: '... in general it is the consequence of a life turned inward that the intensity of what one feels increases, while the need and ease of expression diminishes' (*Der junge Dilthey*, 170). It was in part because of his underlying pantheistic outlook that Dilthey did not need human companionship to the same extent that many other people do – despite the fact that he loved and enjoyed his fellow men. He felt a unity with them on a deeper level, and he encountered them in ways that are not real and available to all of us, for he possessed remarkable powers of understanding. The long hours in the study were not spent alone in the strict sense: Dilthey was in the company of his beloved Schleiermacher, or perhaps Hegel, or some other writer or thinker whom he revered. As one of Dilthey's students observed, he lived the life of others as much as his own.[86] His pantheist belief in the deeper unity of mankind enabled him to lose himself so completely in the thought and writings of others that he finally seemed to have no specific inner life or convictions of his own. Thus in Dilthey's historical works, the contributions and insights of valued thinkers like Schleiermacher are presented in such a way that Dilthey's own standpoint with regard to them is hard to discern. This is no doubt what prompted Max Scheler's comment that Dilthey had the childlike nature of a person who has seen much more than he is able to express.[87] Fritz Heinemann attributes a 'feminine nature' to Dilthey and speaks of his boundless need to give himself (*hingeben*) to the other, to lose his being in the other, and eventually to recover it in elevated form.[88]

Heinemann's use of the word 'hingeben' is deliberate, for Dilthey often used it in this sense. He counselled a surrender, an unconditional giving oneself up to the historical process, which is like the surrender to the object which we see in the work of the historian and the artist. 'Self-surrender (*Hingebung*),' he wrote, 'makes the inner life of the true, born historian into a universe which mirrors the entire historical world.'[89] The great historian combines the power and breadth of life with '... an unbounded need to give himself (*hingeben*) to that which is outside of him and to lose his own selfhood in it ...' (*Fortsetzung*, 201). The same concentration and disregard of self is necessary in art: 'Poetic genius gives itself (*hingeben*) to the experience, to the image, with a peaceful satisfaction in contemplation ...' (*Poetik*, 132–3). We also read that genius '... gives itself (*hingeben*) to the objects without considerations of utility, thus without interest' (pp. 198–9). The same total self-surrender is the key to human happiness in general. Historical consciousness, Dilthey writes, enables man '... to wrest from each experience its content, to give himself (*hingeben*) to it fully and impartially, as if there were no system of philosophy or faith that could bind man' (*Fortsetzung*, 290–1). In 1907 Dilthey affirmed: 'Everything works together in order that man may become more free and open to resignation and to the happiness of surrender (*Hingebung*) to the great objectivities of life' (*Philosophie*, 409). In the meditation on the meaning of life appended to his account of his dream, we find Dilthey's clearest expression of his personal outlook on life:

Yes, my friends, let us strive for the light, for freedom and for the beauty of existence. But not in a new beginning, shaking off the past. We must take the old gods with us into every new home. Only those who sacrifice themselves live life to the full ... Man frees himself from the agony of the moment and the fleetingness of every joy only by surrender (*Hingabe*) to the great objective forces that history has produced. Surrender to them, and not the subjectivity of willfulness and enjoyment, is the reconciliation of the sovereign personality with the way of the world.[90]

Another word which is important for understanding Dilthey's outlook on life is 'resignation.' However, we must be careful not to interpret the attitude of resignation which he recommends as despair or as the product of despair.[91] Because of his pantheist outlook, Dilthey did not believe that the course of a man's life is entirely in his own hands; that is to say, he was not a Fichtean idealist of freedom and personality who believed that the heroic individual can bend the world to his will. Thus he wrote in his diary in 1861: 'It is necessary that one become resigned on the whole, once and for all, in order to become free of resignation in specific cases' (*Der junge Dilthey*, 141). But such resignation must be understood against the background of a generally optimistic and hopeful attitude towards life: '... I am happy when I am striving,' Dilthey wrote, 'and I hardly doubt that, if God permits me the strength, I will achieve as many of the goals of my life as one could reasonably expect' (pp. 51–2). Resignation does not by any means involve abandoning one's major goals. In an early essay Dilthey wrote that every great life is like an '... unceasing resignation. So many branches of the spirit that sprout in youth die off – whether because the time is not right or because of the shortness and the limitations of man's existence – in order that those that remain may grow freely!'[92] Consequently, when Dilthey himself reached old age, he could face the prospect of dying on the road to the goal which he had set for himself,[93] for he believed that the course of history does not depend primarily on what the individual achieves, however illuminating the study of the historical individual may be. We must believe instead that there is something greater and more encompassing than ourselves.

Dilthey's essentially pantheistic outlook is important for understanding the role which death played in his philosophical thinking. As the antithesis of life, death is beyond our understanding. It is both the most fearful and the most fruitful of the riddles which we confront; it represents 'something horribly foreign' (*ein schauerlich Fremdartiges*) which '... has such an effect that every person of a more thoughtful nature can recall how thoughts about death and immortality first occupied his philosophical or religious reflection.'[94] The phenomenon of death confronts us in its most painful form in the death of one's father: childhood comes to an abrupt end, and the world suddenly takes on alien features.[95] But although Dilthey did not believe in personal immortality,[96] death did not pose a great threat to him – apart from the fact that it would probably prevent him from finishing his work.[97] His

pantheistic outlook did not permit him to regard death as the ultimate anni-
hilation of personality.

This pantheistic outlook and the attitude towards death which it made
possible must be kept in mind when the question of Dilthey's relation to
existential philosophy is considered. A number of existential themes are
mentioned in his writings without being developed to any great extent, and
death is one of them. Dilthey even speaks of the relationship '... which determines the sense (*Gefühl*) of our existence in the deepest and most general
way, that of life to death (*das des Lebens zum Tode*), for the limitation of our
existence by death is always decisive for our understanding and estimation of
life.'[98] Because of his underlying pantheism, however, this insight was not
developed into a philosophy of the consequences of human finitude. In
other words, Dilthey's pantheism prevented him from developing his thinking in the direction of an atheistic existentialism, despite the fact that there
are various elements in his thought that could be incorporated into such a
philosophy of existence. His pantheism also prevented him from moving
towards a Christian or theistic existentialism in which the responsibility and
potential creativity of the individual in his direct relation to God are emphasized. The pantheistic outlook simply does not permit us to make moral or
religious choice the ultimate imperative. If Dilthey's pantheist conception of
human life resembles anything in the current religious world, it is the religiosity of Buddhism, with its emphasis on the union of the individual with the
whole and the passivity of the individual in the face of the course of events
in his life. Perhaps because Dilthey emphasized the cultural world rather
than the natural order as the setting in which life is lived, this affinity has
generally been overlooked.*

---

* That Dilthey himself thought of Buddhism in these terms is apparent from *Philosophie*,
   410. But the Buddhist religious world has a long history which includes a great deal of
   diversity. Dilthey's outlook on Buddhism may have been too closely tied to an occidental
   perspective. Helmuth von Glasenapp claims that '... the attempt to apply the three types of
   worldviews established by Wilhelm Dilthey to India runs into difficulties: earlier
   Buddhism can be characterized neither as sensualistic naturalism nor as idealism of freedom nor as objective idealism but represents a separate type' (*Die Philosophie der Inder*,
   Stuttgart: Alfred Kröner Verlag, 1949, p. 8).

8

Provisional Individualism

Throughout this study I have pointed to Dilthey's emphasis on the individual. At certain junctures I have even spoken of his thought as a species of 'individualism,' usually qualifying it as 'methodological.' But such a characterization can be misleading, for we are to regard Dilthey's 'individualism' not as a goal or result but as a provisional stage in his thought, a stage he hoped to move beyond. He never did in fact get beyond it, but we should nevertheless speak of '*provisional* individualism' whenever we use the term 'individualism' to characterize his thought. The two words 'provisional' and 'individualism' are the key to the shortcomings of this thought, to which I now turn in conclusion.

DILTHEY AS PHILOSOPHER

A survey of the various criticisms of Dilthey would lend considerable support to a curious claim made by one student of his thought, namely, that Dilthey is the most misunderstood of the major philosophers of the nineteenth century.[1] It is certainly true that some of the criticisms are misleading (to say the least), that many are superficial, and that few get to the heart of his thought. One common line of criticism is that Dilthey was torn between two philosophical tendencies – one rooted in German thought or in Romanticism and the other in the positivist tradition with its conception of science.[2] On this view, Dilthey's thought is not clear because he was unable or unwilling to choose between these two irreconcilable ways of thinking. Unfortunately, it must be admitted that this complaint is by no means groundless when it is made with reference to Dilthey's earlier writings, but it does not apply in principle to the post-1900 writings in which he left his early positivist sympathies farther and farther behind him. The same can be said of the complaint that Dilthey remained mired in psychological – or perhaps 'psychologistic' – considerations and problems. These criticisms can be set aside simply by recognizing the development of his thought, especially the significant shift that occurred after the publication of the two psychological treatises of the 1890s.

A more promising line of argument against Dilthey is that he overlooked some significant aspect of human reality. Such criticisms, of course, usually proceed from a philosophical standpoint other than Dilthey's own. Thus Marxists complain (with some justification) that he was blind to the role of social and economic factors in the life of the human spirit and reproach him for not dealing with the work of Marx and Engels.[3] Other criticisms of Dilthey from an external standpoint were made during the National Socialist period by adherents of the view that there is a 'connection' (*Zusammenhang*) between 'blood' and history: 'He did not yet clearly realize the meaning of the blood-connection (*Blutzusammenhang*) and the original spiritual determination of the individual bound up with it.'[4] But such indications of disagreement are only of limited value to those who seek to understand the thinker being criticized; the truly telling criticisms come from within and must adopt – provisionally, at least – the thinker's own point of departure. In other words, just as Dilthey must be understood in terms of himself, he must be criticized first of all on the basis of his own philosophical intentions and of the philosophical principles which he affirmed.

Another important charge against Dilthey is that he was more of a historian than a systematic philosopher. Heinrich Rickert praises Dilthey for his abilities and achievements as a historian and then adds that he '... did not possess the capacity for rigorously conceptual thinking to the same degree.'[5] In evaluating this charge, we should note first of all that Dilthey had already manifested a suspicion of philosophical systems at the outset of his career: 'We spurn construction, love investigation, and take a skeptical attitude towards the machinery of a system,' he wrote in his diary in 1859.[6] This aversion to systems manifested itself throughout his philosophical career in the conviction that the philosopher must begin with concrete phenomena: 'We no longer get at life through the system but proceed instead from the analysis of life' (*Fortsetzung*, 276). Thus Dilthey's failure to proceed as systematically as Rickert might wish should be seen in part as a deliberate philosophical decision. But the complaint about lack of system takes on a more drastic and blunt form. In one article we read that there are no conclusions in Dilthey's works,[7] and even Georg Misch, Dilthey's son-in-law and defender, writes: 'One longs for a final word and searches in vain.'[8] A case can be made in support of this strong charge, but only if the charge is limited to Dilthey's failure to carry out his basic philosophical intentions, for on one level, of course, there are many conclusions in his works. On the deepest level, however, his philosophy is about 'life,' and thus we must ask what conclusions about life he reached.

Here I must emphasize again that the effort to grasp 'life' is Dilthey's fundamental philosophical concern and the most important unifying factor in his work (see pp. 40 and 63 above): at the very end of his life he still insisted that the governing impulse in his philosophical thinking was the attempt to understand life out of itself.[9] We must be careful not to translate this talk of 'life' into the language of philosophical anthropology; Misch rightly warns against such an identification and argues that Dilthey's 'life' was to take the place of the 'being' of the Greeks and the transcendental subject of Kant.[10] Philosophy must deal with what Dilthey called the 'totality of life' and the 'unity of life'[11] – and not just with particular, limited manifestations of life. To use Ortega's term, philosophy requires 'totality of theme.'[12] Dilthey himself wrote that philosophy seeks to unite everything knowable in *one* coherent system, that the philosophical mind seeks '... the elevation of isolated knowledge or rules into a system (*Zusammenhang*) that strives to combine all that can be combined and does not rest until this unity is achieved.'[13] The function of philosophy, he maintained, is to sum up, universalize, and ground our scientific reflection on life.[14] Thus philosophy must be philosophy of life.

The methodological problem of Dilthey's philosophy is how we are to get at 'life.' The general answer is that we approach it through its particular manifestations, for life, as Dilthey put it, is present in countless forms in our knowing (*Weltanschauung*, 78). Therefore we attempt to grasp life first as it appears in concrete form in the realm of history and culture; this is what Dilthey means when he declares that history is to teach us what life is (*Fortsetzung*, 262). The specific question that Dilthey leaves unanswered is how we get beyond the level of the particular to a philosophical position that would enable us to draw total or universal conclusions about 'life.' The failure to work out a satisfactory answer to this question represents the central failure of Dilthey's work as a philosopher. In this sense his talk of a 'philosophy of life' must be seen as an unfulfilled promise; it is the destination he never reached. And it is in this light that some of the most serious charges against Dilthey should be understood. Karl Jaspers complains about Dilthey's 'neglect of genuine philosophy' and claims that in Dilthey the seriousness of the philosophical enterprise was given up in favour of a mere comprehension (*verstehendes Wissen*) of past philosophies.[15] If this charge is taken not as a comment about Dilthey's original philosophical intentions but as a judgment about what he did and did not achieve, it must be admitted that there is substance to it. The long awaited conclusion or 'final word' was never produced by Dilthey. Thus even Ernst Troeltsch – in a book dedicated to the memory of Dilthey and Windelband – speaks of Dilthey's capitulation to the individuality of the historical.[16] He did not succeed in transcending individuality, which he spoke of as the 'mystery of the world.'[17]

The central unresolved philosophical problem for Dilthey is that of the relation between the individual and the whole. As early as 1870 he wrote that the 'focal point of biography as well as of life itself' is to be sought in 'the relationship between the individual and the totality within which he develops and which he in turn affects.'[18] Near the end of his life he was still forced to ask: 'The individual is only the point of intersection of the cultural systems and organizations with which his existence is interwoven: how can these cultural systems and organizations be understood out of the individual?' (*Fortsetzung*, 251). If this question had been properly answered, there would also have been some hope of moving from individual life to the totality of life. But because it was not answered, Dilthey was unable to write a 'philosophy of life' or even to clarify the concept of philosophy. Although he regarded philosophy in general as life reflecting on itself (see pp. 75–6 above), he was unable to specify how it goes about its task – beyond pointing out that it must begin with the individual as the concrete particular that is given to us. I have spoken earlier of Dilthey's tendency to focus on and proceed from the human individual as 'individualism.'[19] It now becomes apparent that this individualism is *provisional* in character and not a matter of principle. Dilthey's emphasis on the individual appears one-sided only because he was unable to go on from there to deal with the whole, with life itself, which has no ground or meaning other than itself (*Fortsetzung*, 234). Finally he began to give serious consideration to the possibility that life as a totality, as something infinite, is unfathomable and beyond human expression (a conclusion which he had already stated in an unpublished writing of the 1890s).[20]

Dilthey's individualism should be regarded as provisional because it is coupled with a belief in the insufficiency of the individual or the single manifestation of life. The individual as such must be transcended; we must seek to move in the direction of the universal and the whole. Dilthey sought to do this first of all by emphasizing that the whole is somehow present in the individual. There is a 'totality of mental powers' at work in expression as well as in understanding. Furthermore, expressions – in certain instances, at least – must be seen as man's total response to the totality (see p. 83 above). To this extent, then, the whole is indeed present in the individual.

Dilthey was even tempted to use the Leibnizian doctrine of monads to express the idea of the presence of the whole in the individual,[21] and some students of his thought have spoken of the individual as a microcosm reflecting a more encompassing macrocosm.[22] The individual also moves in the direction of the whole by absorbing as much as possible of what is outside him: through understanding and art, we achieve an elevation and enlargement of our existence. This, too, is an indication of the insufficiency of the individual. But the individual never reaches the whole or becomes the whole by means of this slow process of growth. A philosophy of life in which life is understood not just as the source of meaning but also as the whole encompassing us all is simply not to be found in Dilthey's writings. As he foresaw on his seventieth birthday, he died on the road to the goal he had set for himself.[23]

HISTORICAL KNOWLEDGE

The first point to be made in a critical examination of Dilthey's account of historical knowledge is that it does not cover the entire range of the historical sciences. We have seen that understanding as applied within the sphere of science and scholarship is central to the work of the historical-cultural sciences, and it is in this area that Dilthey's major contribution to the epistemology of the sciences must be sought. Understanding also plays an important role in the work of the other historical sciences, but by itself it is not a sufficient basis for what these sciences seek to achieve. H.P. Rickman, a translator of Dilthey whose own thinking owes a great deal to Dilthey's inspiration, argues: 'An epistemology which stands on the single leg of perception has endless difficulties in explaining our knowledge of other people. Understanding opens up the human world for us ...'[24] But it must likewise be recognized that an epistemology of the historical sciences will do no more than limp if it is restricted to the single leg of understanding. Thus Raymond Aron, who is also a student of Dilthey's work, calls for 'collaboration' between understanding and causality, which he speaks of as 'the two possible modalities of all explanation.'[25] Insofar as Dilthey has not dealt with the interplay of understanding and causal explanation in the work of the historian, his account of historical knowledge is incomplete and therefore limited in its application.

Having noted this limitation of Dilthey's doctrine of understanding, we now proceed to a more central difficulty related to his 'individualism.' Jürgen Habermas points the way when he observes: 'It was not by chance that Dilthey chose biography as the point of departure for his analysis of understanding; the reconstruction of a lived historical *Zusammenhang* that can be remembered is the model for the interpretation of symbolic *Zusammenhänge* in general.'[26] Thus the meaning that we seek to grasp in understanding as conceived of by Dilthey is first and foremost the meaning which the expression assumes in relation to the life of its author. In other words, understanding must be guided by the canon of immanence or autonomy (see pp. 116–17 above); it must seek to comprehend the other (and his expressions) in terms of himself, which is what the best biographers have always tried to do. This claim, which may appear innocent at first glance, merits careful attention, for it issues from the very heart of Dilthey's (unfinished) philosophy of life. In more abstract terms, the claim is that the meaning, rationality, or intelligibility which understanding seeks to grasp is not a universal (i.e., trans-individual) rationality rooted in a divine creation order or in being as such but a particular rationality as concretized in an individual life and its awareness of itself. The other whom we seek to understand, then, is the centre and embodiment of the rationality in terms of which we attempt to explain him. He represents 'life,' and there is no ground outside of life from which (his) life derives its meaning and intelligibility.

Thus the Diltheyan biographer understands and explains the subject of his biographical research in terms drawn originally from his subject's self-understanding. (Of course, the biographer should ultimately go somewhat beyond this in order to try to understand his subject better than he understood himself.) But a Diltheyan biography, as we saw earlier (pp. 112–13), quickly expands beyond the limits of an individual life, for the life of the historically significant individual is intricately interwoven with the events of his time. Therefore, the biography tends to turn into a treatment of the age and the historical world in which the subject of the biography lived. To take an example, a Diltheyan biography which seeks to understand Hitler in terms of himself would inevitably become something of a history of World War II. The rationality in terms of which the war is explained would then be the peculiar rationality that governed Hitler's life and was reflected in his understanding of himself and his mission. Such a treatment of World War II would, of course, differ markedly from one arising out of the biography of Churchill or Stalin or Roosevelt. The debate about A.J.P. Taylor's controversial book *The Origins of the Second World War* gives us an indication of what consternation such an approach to historical understanding would cause among historians;[27] most historians seem to think that it must be possible to produce an account of a series of events like World War II which transcends the self-understanding of Hitler, Churchill, Stalin, Roosevelt, or any other participant in that war. The issue is not so much determining 'what really happened' as ascertaining its relation to some larger, trans-historical scheme or framework of reference and intelligibility.

This problem also manifests itself in intellectual history, but in a less acute form, for there is much less interaction and joint action in the life of the mind. That a Diltheyan intellectual biography dealing with Kant and his age might conflict in some respects with such a treatment of Hegel and his age would not appear to be a cause for alarm: both Kant and Hegel, obviously, must be understood in terms of themselves. But how could one proceed to write a history of 'the German mind' or of 'the German philosophical tradition'? Can such entities or traditions be understood in terms of themselves? As we have seen (pp. 38–9 above), Dilthey rejected the notion of a superindividual 'Volksgeist' which could conceivably provide the self-understanding and centre of rationality and meaning for a history of the German mind or of German philosophy. Nor did he develop a *problemgeschichtlich* method *à la* Nicolai Hartmann, a method in which philosophical problems or perhaps concepts could be regarded as the abiding source of trans-individual intelligibility in the history of philosophy or the history of ideas. Dilthey, in short, had no answer to the question of how to write a history of the German mind.

There is no easy way out of this dilemma for Dilthey, for it arises directly out of his conception of understanding. Meinecke speaks of the principle that we understand only what we love,[28] and Dilthey, as we saw earlier (p. 95), used similar language at one point. However, I argued that love ultimately is *not* a prerequisite for understanding in Dilthey's view. What understanding requires instead is an *acceptance* of the other as the centre and source of rationality, intelligibility, and meaning in relation to his expressions of life. (This is the grain of truth behind the claim that understanding is inseparable from love.) Of course, I can also accept *myself* as the source of rationality – which is what I do when I reflect on the meaning of my own life – and then seek to understand the expressions which have arisen out of my own past life, some of which now seem foreign to me. Thus Dilthey writes: 'We conduct ourselves in an understanding way (*verstehend*) over against life – our own as well as that of another' (*Fortsetzung*, 196). Such an understanding of myself – unless it involves expressions from the distant past that has largely faded from memory – is immediate. Yet when we emphasize the necessity of *seeking* a centre of rationality in order to make understanding possible and then also emphasize the intellectual effort required to grasp this centre of rationality, we could well reach a different conclusion, namely, that we do not *understand* ourselves: 'Experience of ourselves, but we do not understand ourselves,' Dilthey writes as well (p. 225). The apparent contradiction, of course, is simply the result of differences in perspective and emphasis in the two cases: in one sense we can be said to understand ourselves, and in another sense we cannot. The important point illustrated by this surface contradiction is that understanding is not fragmentary: it seeks the unity that only a centre of rationality – whether it is given to us immediately in our own self-understanding, or arrived at by way of a process of ratiocination – can provide. What the higher forms of understanding have in common, Dilthey writes, is that '... they enable us to understand the coherence (*Zusammenhang*) of a totality via an inductive inference from given expressions' (p. 212). The difficulty, as we have seen, is that there are potentially as many centres and embodiments of rationality as there are persons; this, I take it, is what lies behind Dilthey's assertion that understanding always 'opens up a world.'[29] Thus, anyone who seeks to understand others encounters a plurality of perspectives, of worlds, of systems of meaning. How, in the face of this plurality, are we ever to arrive at the meaning of 'life' itself? Dilthey was not very hopeful about this prospect. 'We understand life only in a continuous approximation,' he wrote, 'and because of the nature of understanding and of life, the latter, in its passage through time, shows us highly varied sides at the various points at which it is grasped' (p. 236).

This drives us back to the basic Diltheyan question: how is the whole to be understood out of the individual? Is there a trans-historical source and pattern of meaning and rationality that represents the real truth about life and history, and, if so, is it somehow accessible to us? Dilthey's confidence that there is somewhere a meaning and rationality of this sort supported him in his life-long struggle to lay bare the structure of the social-historical world. It is also the faith behind his declaration that understanding represents a '... rediscovery of the I in the Thou; the spirit rediscovers itself at ever higher levels of coherence ...' (p. 191). The search for this kind of meaning is the quest for a 'philosophy of life,' for Dilthey did not seek only to understand lives (plural) in terms of themselves: the governing impulse in his philosophy, he insisted, was the effort to understand *life* in terms of itself.[30] Had he managed to succeed in this, he would have found a centre and source of rationality that would enable us to write a history of the German mind as well as a definitive account of World War II (which, of course, includes much more than the events in which any one individual participated). This in turn would have paved the way – in principle, at least – for universal history understood not just as the perspective of the whole (see p. 118 above) or as a general knowledge of man as he is revealed to us in history (see p. 129 above) but as a cohering account of the entire history of mankind. And it would have silenced the critics who complained about Dilthey's neglect of the question of truth.[31]

We see, then, that Dilthey's failure to produce a fully articulated philosophy of life has serious consequences for his doctrine of understanding and his account of historical knowledge. (This is the reason why it was necessary to devote so much attention to Dilthey's statements about 'life.') Yet, in O.F. Bollnow's study of Dilthey we read that Dilthey's philosophy of life necessarily becomes a philosophy of history.[32] It was certainly Dilthey's intention to produce a philosophy of history – although he rejected the term itself – but Bollnow overlooks the failure of Dilthey's philosophy of life, which in turn was the cause of his failure to produce a philosophy of history. Although Dilthey was preoccupied to the very end of his life with the structure of the social-historical world and with our knowledge of it, he has given us no general theory of history – beyond the view that life as manifested in the restlessness of the human spirit is somehow the driving force pushing the historical process onward (see pp. 128–9 above). What Dilthey offers us in place of a philosophy of history is a philosophy of biography, or perhaps a philosophy of the historical individual. However valuable and interesting his reflections on historical knowledge, the historical process and the historicality of human existence may be, they remain fragmentary and do not add up to a philosophy of history.

By this point the connections between the major shortcomings in Dilthey's thinking should be sufficiently clear. His hesitance on the ontological side compounded his difficulties on the epistemological side, and this in turn left questions unanswered in the further branches of his thought. By repeatedly postponing the systematic exposition of his 'philosophy of life,' he condemned his early epistemological investigations to incompleteness and inadequacy. He had hoped to distinguish clearly between our knowledge of nature and our knowledge of the world of the spirit, assigning the former to the realm of 'explanation' and the latter to the realm of 'understanding.' But he did not fully confine this distinction to the epistemological level, for it seemed to point implicitly to an ontological separation of nature and culture. This separation, however, was in conflict with the 'imperialistic' tendency of his philosophy of life: although Dilthey stopped short of an explicit identification of life and being, his readers could hardly be blamed for assuming that his endless talk about 'life' represented an ontology – or at least an interpretation of being that had not yet been given its final formulation. And if being is life, then understanding must be the sole mode of knowledge – think of Heidegger – for understanding, as Dilthey emphasized, is the only cognitive operation adequate to the inherent dynamism, complexity, and interrelatedness of life. And this would again undermine the distinction between the natural sciences and the *Geisteswissenschaften* and would force us to face the prospect that nature, in the final analysis, is to be understood rather than explained – a conclusion which Dilthey expressed at least once in his published writings (see p. 183, note 76).

This train of thought leads to the conclusion that Dilthey's doctrine of historical understanding has not been given an adequate ontological foundation. If understanding is always the grasping of a 'Zusammenhang,' and if the category of 'Zusammenhänge' is sufficiently broad to include the semantic structure of a sentence, a national economic system, and world history, it would seem that an account of the knowledge which history and the *Geisteswissenschaften* give us requires an analysis of the types of 'Zusammenhänge' and of the rationality and intelligibility inherent in each. One would like to know, for example, whether formal mathematical relationships also count as 'Zusammenhänge,' and whether we can be said to 'understand' them. (Is the 'totality of our mental powers' operative in mathematical thought?) Until this doctrine of 'Zusammenhänge' is provided, the question of the uniqueness of historical knowledge will remain open, and 'methodological naturalism' will remain unrefuted.

UNRESOLVED METAPHYSICAL ISSUES

I have already argued that Dilthey's projected 'philosophy of life' was a destination which he never reached. His philosophical writings seem to point in the direction of certain metaphysical affirmations which he refrained from embracing explicitly, and this is what leaves the student of his philosophy feeling unsatisfied. One winds up wondering just what it is that Dilthey has left undone. Hence I now propose to raise the question what sort of metaphysical underpinnings his doctrine of understanding seems to require.

Such an inquiry must begin with the individual mind or spirit, which is the agent of understanding. The question to be asked is whether this mind is more than individual, whether several minds or perhaps even all human minds might be regarded as forming some sort of whole larger than the sum of its parts. Dilthey's use of certain terms and phrases suggests such a view, but his rejection of all metaphysics as lacking validity seems to rule it out. The problem is that instead of deciding on this issue in an unequivocal manner, Dilthey uses language in a way reminiscent of certain wily theologians who dodge the question of God's transcendence. Such theologians like to speak of God in the language used by those who affirm transcendence without actually committing themselves to any such view of the divine. When pressed they are forced to admit that in speaking of God they are really only speaking of man or of his potential for development. Dilthey, similarly, likes to speak of 'the spirit' (*der Geist*) in general, by which he presumably means something that transcends the limitations of the human individual, yet he stops short of affirming this sort of transcendence outright. The position assumed in his philosophical writings is rather that we have no grounds for positing the existence of any type of mind or spirit more ultimate than that of the human individual.

We have seen in Chapter 7 that Dilthey's non-philosophical or prephilosophical outlook on reality is pantheistic. This by itself signifies little, but when it is coupled with an analysis of what his doctrine of understanding seems to presuppose or imply, we are led to the conclusion that there is an unresolved metaphysical issue here. In various different ways, Dilthey gives expression to the view that what the human mind or spirit 'understands' is not completely other and alien: the spirit, as he puts it, '... understands only what it has itself created' (*Aufbau*, 148). Understanding represents a special kind of knowledge which is possible only because of a certain common sphere or an overcoming of otherness that is present – to some degree, at least – from the outset. If such knowledge is to be possible throughout the entire human world, then we must have an ontology which explains how it is possible that this entire world be familiar and not alien. Do I as an individual human being somehow participate – perhaps not consciously – in a larger human mind or spirit that has created and is creating the entire world of history, society and culture? Something like this, it seems to me, is what Dilthey must embrace philosophically if understanding as he spoke of it in his more elevated moments is to be possible. Of course, it might also be possible to build a theory of understanding on the basis of a theistic philosophy,* but a theistic separation between the divine and the human was foreign to Dilthey's way of thinking. The peculiar knowledge called understanding is possible not because a divine Creator has established a harmony between the knower and the known, intending them for each other, but because the otherness which we seem to experience is only apparent. Thus Dilthey's thinking seems to require the presupposition that nothing in the human world can be truly alien. Only if we accept this assumption does the doctrine of understanding assume the proportions he hints at.

If we were to follow this route, the problem of the status of nature (which Dilthey left unresolved) could also be settled. A clear choice would have to

---

* My own commitment is to the Christian faith and a theistic philosophical outlook, and therefore I cannot follow Dilthey in his quest for a 'philosophy of life,' despite my deep sympathy for the ethical motives behind his doctrine of understanding.

be made between two possibilities. Nature could be regarded as something ultimately alien and other, and hence as knowable only to a lesser extent – or perhaps not knowable at all. This would leave us with a dualistic view of reality in which there are two separate realities – nature and spirit. The problem with such an outlook, of course, is where the points of contact between the two are to be sought, and how the interaction between them is to be interpreted. What connection is there between body and mind, and how is it possible for spirit to have knowledge of nature? A second possible view, which might have more success in answering such questions, would be a monistic outlook in which nature and spirit are one, spirit then counting as a higher, more developed level of reality. Because nature excludes consciousness, it is not amenable to the same sort of knowledge from within that we have of the realm of history and culture. Thus, while 'understanding' of nature might remain an ideal, we would have to be satisfied with a more external, explanatory knowledge, until such time as reality develops further and nature is transformed.

The second view, it seems to me, represents a metaphysical outlook and background of the sort that Dilthey would have to provide if his doctrine of understanding were to be placed on a foundation adequate to what the doctrine promises. Understanding would then be given the ultimate status of self-awareness; it would then be a true 'rediscovery of the I in the Thou' (*Fortsetzung*, 191). But for reasons to which I have already referred, Dilthey refused to take the steps sketched in this section. He would have felt compelled to reject the metaphysical background or framework outlined here as speculation that could never be substantiated. Together with many thinkers of his time, he accepted the apparent collapse of the metaphysical enterprise as an accomplished historical fact. His appreciation of metaphysics was limited to its experiential foundation: one tries to re-live what the metaphysician has seen and experienced, but one does not seriously consider the metaphysician's claims at face value. So strongly did Dilthey believe this that he chose to leave his major philosophical doctrine (i.e., that of understanding) without a proper foundation rather than risk the dangers of unwarranted speculation. The student of his philosophy might wish that Dilthey had been more courageous and venturesome, but who is to say where prudence ends and foolhardiness begins? Dilthey, in any event, bowed to his own caution. He was aware of the difficulties raised in this section, but he never managed to resolve them once and for all. Hence we must be content to accept Dilthey – for better or worse – on the basis of what he said rather than on the basis of what he might have said or ought to have said, and we must judge him accordingly. Speculation about the metaphysical background of his theory of understanding remains just that – speculation.

Notes

INTRODUCTION

1 See *Gesammelte Schriften*, Vol. VIII, pp. 220–6. The dream itself, without Dilthey's introductory comments, is available in English translation in *The Philosophy of History in Our Time*, ed. Hans Meyerhoff (Garden City, New York: Anchor Books, 1959).
2 *Being and Time*, 429.
3 See 'A Chapter from the History of Ideas,' 131, and 'History as a System,' 216.
4 *No Souvenirs: Journal, 1957–1969*, trans. Fred H. Johnson, Jr. (New York: Harper and Row, 1977), p. 120.

CHAPTER 1

1 'The Presuppositions of Critical History,' in *Collected Essays* (Oxford: Clarendon Press, 1969), p. 33.
2 *What is History?*, 62.
3 See 'Uebersicht meines Systems,' VIII, 176; see also the 1887 Antritts-rede, where Dilthey declares that he has come 'from history' (V, 10).
4 'Einleitungen zu Untersuchungen über die Geschichte des Naturrechts,' XVIII, 45–6.
5 See his remarks in 'Rede zum 70. Geburtstag,' V, 7–8.
6 V, 27. See also Dilthey's comments in a letter to his parents in 1858 (*Der junge Dilthey*, 50) and 'Frühe Aphorismen aus der Berliner Zeit,' XVIII, 206.
7 See 'Zur Philosophie der Philosophie,' VIII, 206, 219.
8 V, 42–3. Various passages from this essay reappear, usually in somewhat revised form, in the *Einleitung*. A somewhat pragmatic outlook on the *Geisteswissenschaften*, together with the example of the knife, appears in *Einleitung*, 85. See also the unfinished drafts in XVIII, 1, 47.
9 Quoted from the Nachlass by Misch in 'Dilthey versus Nietzsche,' 392.
10 See his remarks in the preface to the *Einleitung*, p. xvii.

11 On this rejection, see the 1875 essay, v, 47, 35–6; *Einleitung*, 86–112, 120; 'Schlosser,' XI, 154; the Zusätze to 'Uebersicht meines Systems,' VIII, 266; see also '28. Literaturbrief,' XVII, 195. Dilthey upheld this stand in the later years of his life (see *Fortsetzung*, 284). He criticized what he called 'sociology' on similar grounds (see *Einleitung*, 86–112), although he was not opposed to the idea of a science of society as such (see *Einleitung*, Zusätze, 420–3; 'Geschichte und Naturwissenschaft,' XVI, 106; and the book review essays, XVII, 41–2, 76, 185).

12 See *Briefwechsel*, 223, 224, 251. Dilthey did, however, speak of traditional philosophy of history as the 'old philosophy of history,' thereby suggesting that there was room for a new approach to this branch of inquiry ('Einleitungen zu Untersuchungen über die Geschichte des Naturrechts,' XVIII, 39).

13 *What is History?*, 13.

14 The other figures dealt with in this book are Rickert, Simmel, and Weber. See also Michael Ermarth's recent book on Dilthey.

15 *The Philosophy of Wilhelm Dilthey*, p. 1; see also p. xiii.

16 See *La philosophie critique de l'histoire*, 27.

17 In the dedication to Count Yorck, he writes: 'In our earliest discussions I explained to you the plan for this book, which at that time I still ventured to characterize as a "critique of historical reason."'

18 'Zur Philosophie der Philosophie,' VIII, 207.

19 'Rede zum 70. Geburtstag,' v, 9.

20 See *Fortsetzung*, 278.

21 J.F. Suter, for example, sees the influence of Kant as the key to Dilthey's work: 'It was in effect by transposing the critical inspiration to history that Dilthey tried to overcome the opposition between the two influences – idealist and positivist – that were present in his thinking' (*Philosophie et histoire chez Wilhelm Dilthey*, p. ix).

22 See the 1887 Antrittsvorlesung, v, 12, 13, 27, and the Vorrede to Vol. v, p. 5.

23 Hellmut Diwald touches on the most important differences in *Wilhelm Dilthey*, 23–4, 26–8, 37, 44, 77. In the preface to the *Einleitung* Dilthey writes: 'In the veins of the cognitive subject construed by Locke, Hume and Kant flows no real blood but only the diluted fluid of reason as pure thinking' (p. xviii).

24 Thus Aron sees Dilthey's 'Kantianism' in the affirmation '... to attain the truth, philosophical thought must appeal to the only immediate certainty – inner experience' (*La philosophie critique de l'histoire*, 23). As we shall see, Dilthey was later to give up his belief in inner experience as fundamental.

25 See Carlo Antoni, *From History to Sociology*, 18–19.

26 *Einleitung*, 92, 97.

27 *Philosophy of History*, 11.

28 *Aufbau*, Zusätze, VII, 341.
29 *Von deutscher Dichtung und Musik*, 6.
30 See 'Friedrich der Grosse und die deutsche Aufklärung,' III, 131.
31 'Leibniz und sein Zeitalter,' III, 62.

CHAPTER 2

1 'Erkenntnistheoretische Fragmente,' XVIII, 197.
2 Rickert, *Die Probleme der Geschichtsphilosophie*, 33.
3 See *Kulturwissenschaft und Naturwissenschaft*, 77.
4 *Probleme*, 33.
5 *Die Grenzen der naturwissenschaftlichen Begriffsbildung*, 227 – spaced in original; see also *Kulturwissenschaft*, 55–6.
6 *Kulturwissenschaft*, 15; see also *Grenzen*, 220.
7 *Kulturwissenschaft*, 97.
8 *Kulturwissenschaft*, 21.
9 *Grenzen*, 708.
10 *Grenzen*, 322.
11 *Kulturwissenschaft*, 87; see also *Probleme*, 61.
12 Rickert simply mentions this point but does not pursue it very far (see *Grenzen*, 28–9).
13 See *Kulturwissenschaft*, 31. As a neo-Kantian, Rickert rejected the notion of knowledge as an 'Abbilden' of reality.
14 Rickert died in 1936, and Aron wrote in 1938: '... his thought is dead – deader than the thought of Dilthey, or even of Simmel. After having been the object of a long

quarrel, his position is no longer being discussed. People are now starting to ignore it' (*La philosophie critique de l'histoire*, reprinted in 1968, p. 139).
15 See his comments in 'Das 18. Jahrhundert und die geschichtliche Welt,' III, 223–4. Also revealing of Dilthey's attitude is Yorck's praise of Dilthey's method: 'Here is an instance of rigorous analytical method, which may even set an example for natural scientists' (*Briefwechsel*, 2). Finally, we must not forget Dilthey's admiration for the physiologist Hermann von Helmholtz (see *Briefwechsel*, pp. vi, 36, 37).
16 As late as 1868, Dilthey admitted that physiology and mathematics were 'entirely new disciplines' to him (*Der junge Dilthey*, 261; see also 280).
17 See Misch, Vorbericht to Vol. V, p. xxvi, and Ulrich Herrmann, Vorbericht to Vol. XV, p. xiii.
18 See *Einleitung*, p. xvii. Yet Dilthey was careful not to identify himself as a latter-day representative of the historical school (see pp. 27, 49, 80–1; see also *Poetik*, 189). Instead of simply defending this school, he hoped to reconcile it – or its achievements, at least – with other streams of thought in the history of science and scholarship.
19 See V, 53
20 See the 1875 essay, V, 54–5.
21 *Die Jugendgeschichte Hegels*, Zusätze, IV, 250n.

22 See *Einleitung*, 81–2, 145.

23 See *Ideen*, 236, and *Individualität*, 271.

24 Because all three combated 'methodological naturalism,' they are often lumped together and sometimes even confused. (See Calvin Rand, 'Two Meanings of Historicism,' 510, and Suter, *Philosophie et histoire*, 142.)

25 Dilthey did, however, make regular use of the term 'apperception,' as contrasted with mere sensory awareness below the level of organized experience. In the *Poetik* he characterized apperception as the '... simplest case in which the system of mental life affects an individual mental event and is affected by it in turn' (p. 144). See also his comments on the experience of the artist in *Individualität*, 282, and his use of the term 'apperception' in *Fortsetzung*, 230–1.

26 The most important discussion of the two kinds of perception and experience occurs in *Individualität*, 243ff. The relation between inner perception and inner experience is not defined precisely by Dilthey: 'By *inner experience* we generally mean an aggregate of mental events such that one or more inner perceptions are brought together by discursive thought in a coherence of a certain sort, a coherence in which these mental facts are then elevated, opening the way to a better understanding whereby our knowledge of the inner world is expanded' (p. 245).

27 See, for example, *Leben Schleiermachers*, XIII–1, 33; *Einleitung*, 186, 369; and the '10. Literaturbrief,' XVII, 74.

28 'Der Strukturzusammenhang des Wissens,' VII, 27.

29 'Archive für Literatur,' XV, 5.

30 1887 Antrittsrede, V, 11; see also '1. Literaturbrief,' XVII, 2.

31 In a later polemical note to *Ideen*, V, 237.

32 *Schleiermachers System als Philosophie*, XIV–1, 152.

33 Compare *Aufbau*, 119 with *Individualität*, 264. The omission of the word 'erfahren' in the later version supports my contention about the role of the terms 'Erlebnis' and 'Erfahrung' in Dilthey's thought.

34 See 'Die Abgrenzung der Geisteswissenschaften,' VII, 70–1; *Aufbau*, 118, 131, 136, 148; *Weltanschauung*, 101.

35 See *Die Entstehung des Historismus*, 8, 20, 36, 181, 235n, 469, 471.

36 See *Individualität*, 271, 273, 310, 315.

37 See *Ideen*, 229–30.

38 1887 Antrittsrede, V, 11; see also Dilthey's foreword to his life of Schleiermacher, XIII–1, p. xxxiii.

39 See *Ideen*, 225; 1887 Antrittsrede, V, 10–11; 'Archive der Literatur,' IV, 564; *Fortsetzung*, 246. Dilthey also speaks of the 'Erlebnis' as the 'Urzelle' of the historical world (see *Aufbau*, 161).

40 See, for example, *Von deutscher Dichtung und Musik*, 86, 45–6; 'John Stuart Mill,' XV, 246; *Schlei-*

ermachers System als Philosophie,
XIV–1, 52, 85, 394, 424; *Weltan-*
schauung, Zusätze, VIII, 136–7.
41 *La philosophie critique de l'historie,*
106; see also 46–7.

CHAPTER 3

1 Vorrede to Vol. V, 4.
2 See *Einleitung,* 380.
3 See 1867 Antrittsvorlesung, V, 13;
Leben Schleiermachers, XIII–1, 192,
207, 250, 251, 380, 473; *Versuch*
einer Analyse des moralischen Be-
wusstseins, VI, 7; 'Novalis,' in
Erlebnis, 212, 213; 'Adolf Bastian,'
XI, 205, 206; 'Arthur Schopenhauer,' XV, 53; 'Materialismus und
Naturwissenschaft,' XVI, 440, 444;
'Die Grundzüge der Weltord-
nung,' XVI, 448; see also *Der junge*
Dilthey, 241, 256.
4 *Einleitung,* 5; see also 'Einleitungen
zu Untersuchungen über die Geschichte des Naturrechts,' XVIII, 41
and 50, where Dilthey states that
he uses the term 'Geisteswissenschaften' for the sake of brevity.
5 The misconception that Mill had introduced some such term as 'Geisteswissenschaften' lingered on well
into the twentieth century. Heinrich
Rickert still included it in the final
edition of *Grenzen* (see pp. 25,
514), published in 1929.
6 See, for example, *Ideen,* 142–3.
7 For Rickert's discussion of these matters, see *Probleme,* 15–16, 23, 25–6;
Kulturwissenschaft, pp. x, 24n; *Gren-*
zen, 121, 122n, 179–80, 182, 525–6.

8 *Aufbau,* 81. See also 'Die Abgrenzung der Geisteswissenschaften' –
erste Fassung, VII, 304.
9 Dilthey avoided the term 'cultural
sciences' because of his somewhat
limited view of the meaning of the
term 'culture.' He certainly did not
use the latter term in Rickert's
sense (see his comments in his lectures on ethics, X, 105).
10 This 'Vorrede' was appended to the
Gesammelte Schriften edition of the
Einleitung (I, 410–11).
11 The *Poetik* has been reprinted in
Vol. VI, and the notes towards the
revision, which Dilthey did not live
to complete, are appended to this
volume. The quotation is from
p. 311.
12 One is Raymond Aron's book *La*
philosophie critique de l'histoire,
which devotes some 90 pages to
Dilthey. Aron touches on the question of development only briefly,
distinguishing three periods (see pp.
13, 28, 64n, 102, 273). Hünermann devotes 160 pages to Dilthey
in *Der Durchbruch geschichtlichen*
Denkens im 19. Jahrhundert and
divides Dilthey's thinking into four
periods, adding a division within
what I have called the first period.
On pp. 13 and 28 above, I have
mentioned some of the changes
within this first period, but I have
chosen not to discuss Dilthey's earliest writings in any detail.
13 Hans Sommerfeld declares of the
Einleitung, the major publication of
Dilthey's first period: 'In this work

Dilthey's philosophical outlook comes to its purest expression.' But his summary of what Dilthey says in the *Einleitung* draws on themes that were only developed in the post-1900 years (see *Wilhelm Dilthey und der Positivismus*, 5, 11–12). His reading of the *Einleitung* amounts to a 'Hineininterpretation.'

14 Notes towards a revision of the *Poetik*, VI, 317.

15 *Fortsetzung*, 279; see also pp. 194–5, 231, 250; *Aufbau*, 86–7; 'Das 18. Jahrhundert und die geschichtliche Welt,' III, 210; 'Die 3 Grundformen der Systeme,' IV, 528–9; 'Ueber die Möglichkeit einer allgemeingültigen pädagogischen Wissenschaft,' VI, 57; 'Grundlinien eines Systems der Pädagogik,' IX, 173; Notes towards a revision of the *Poetik*, VI, 317–18. Dilthey was already moving toward such a position in *Ideen* (see p. 180).

16 'Der Traum,' VIII, 226.

17 At least one student of Dilthey attributes a greater role to Nietzsche. Kamerbeek, in an intriguing article entitled 'Dilthey versus Nietzsche,' suggests that Dilthey was engaged in some sort of rivalry with Nietzsche, and that some of the images which he used to criticize Nietzsche were inspired by the latter's own writings. He even suggests that it was Nietzsche's work that showed Dilthey the inadequacy of introspection. For Dilthey's comments on Nietzsche, see 'Die 3 Grundformen der Systeme,' IV, 528–9; 'Das 18. Jahrhundert und die geschichtliche Welt,' III, 210; *Philosophie*, 379, 412; 'Die Kultur der Gegenwart,' VIII, 200–1; *Briefwechsel*, 238–9; and his note on Nietzsche's *Menschliche, allzu Menschliche* in XVII, 390. For contrasting views of the relation between Dilthey and Nietzsche, see Misch's reply to Kamerbeek, also entitled 'Dilthey versus Nietzsche,' and Suter, *Philosophie et histoire*, 145n, 148.

18 See 'Die 3 Grundformen der Systeme,' IV, 531.

19 In letters to his parents (see *Der junge Dilthey*, 229, 243).

20 See *Einleitung*, 34, 45, 59, 67; *Leben Schleiermachers*, XIII–1, 380; 'Novalis,' in *Erlebnis*, 213–14; 'Charles Dickens,' in *Die grosse Phantasiedichtung*, 299.

21 See *Einleitung*, 29; see also Misch, Vorbericht to Vol. V, pp. lxx, lxxvi-lxxvii.

22 See *Einleitung*, pp. xviii, xix, and the 1887 Antrittsrede, V, 11.

23 *Ideen*, 172. Also: 'In this living through (*Erleben*) and understanding, the totality of our mental powers is operative, which is why this fullness of inner life is echoed even in the most abstract statements made in the *Geisteswissenschaften*' (*Individualität*, 263–4). This 'totality' is also fundamental to poetic expression: '... the poet (*Dichter*) draws on the totality of his powers as he writes' (*Philosophie*, 396). See also *Einleitung*, 137, 148, 152, 186, 266, 359, 371, 395, 401.

24 In a diary entry of 1861 (*Der junge Dilthey*, 150).

25 See *Individualität*, 274–5; *Philosophie*, 394; *Poetik*, 116; 'Briefe von und an Hegel,' xv, 311. See also *Ideen*, 152; Vorrede to Vol. v, 4; 1867 Antrittsvorlesung, v, 17; 'Die 3 Epochen der modernen Aesthetik,' vi, 276; 'Lessing,' in *Erlebnis*, 50; 'Goethe,' in *Erlebnis*, 139; 'Leibniz und sein Zeitalter,' iii, 8; 'Die grosse Phantasiedichtung,' in *Die grosse Phantasiedichtung*, 37.

26 Vorrede to Vol. v, 4.

27 'Shakespeare und seine Zeitgenossen,' in *Die grosse Phantasiedichtung*, 53.

28 *Schleiermachers System als Philosophie*, xiv–1, 469.

29 They have been reprinted in Vols. ii and iii of the *Gesammelte Schriften*.

30 'A Chapter from the History of Ideas,' 139.

31 *Introduction aux sciences humaines*, 7, 8. Erich Rothacker, one of Dilthey's own students, admits that the *Einleitung* remained a 'torso' (see his *Einleitung in die Geisteswissenschaften*, 269). Other students of Dilthey have emphasized the sympathy for the positivist outlook manifested in the *Einleitung* (see H.L. Friess, 'Wilhelm Dilthey,' 22, and Husserl, *Phänomenologische Psychologie*, 34). Dilthey himself pointed out that his sympathy for positivism came to expression especially in the 1875 essay (see Vorrede to Vol. v, 4). One author even

maintains that the *Einleitung* is Dilthey's most important work (Ludwig Stein, 'Historical Optimism: Wilhelm Dilthey,' 330).

32 See Kuypers, *Theorie der geschiedenis*, 20. Eduard Spranger also uses this contrast in *Lebensformen*, 9.

33 See *Ideen*, 168.

34 Ebbinghaus, 'Ueber erklärende und beschreibende Psychologie,' 173.

35 The notes towards this reply are appended to *Ideen* (v, 237–40).

36 See Hodges, *The Philosophy of Wilhelm Dilthey*, 284n.

37 *Philosophie et histoire*, pp. x, 73, 105; see also pp. 1, 106. Carlo Antoni writes: 'Dilthey never came to realize that history and psychology were basically irreconcilable in the same system.' 'Thus, tired but undefeated, the old philosopher continued to seek the key to the science of history in psychology to the very end' (*From History to Sociology*, 7, 24, 25).

38 See Bollnow, *Dilthey*, 215–16. Liliane Frey-Rohn speaks of Dilthey's pre-1900 thought as 'psychologistic' (see *Die Grundbegriffe der Dilthey'schen Philosophie*, 94, 58). Hans Sommerfeld also calls Dilthey a proponent of 'psychologism' and charges that Dilthey reduces all questions of values and culture to questions about the psyche (*Wilhelm Dilthey und der Positivismus*, 62, 66). Because of the lack of general agreement about the meaning of the term 'psychologism,' I see little

point in using it to characterize Dilthey's earlier thought.

39 See Coreth, *Grundfragen der Hermeneutik*, 28, 129; Bollnow, *Dilthey*, 5; Brock, *An Introduction to Contemporary German Philosophy*, 22; Herman Nohl, *Einführung in die Philosophie* (Frankfurt am Main: Verlag G. Schulte-Bulmke, 1960), p. 84; Klapwijk, *Tussen historisme en relativisme*, 172, 311n; Kamerbeek, 'Dilthey versus Nietzsche,' 76; Gadamer, *Le problème de la conscience historique*, 22; Landgrebe, *Wilhelm Diltheys Theorie der Geisteswissenschaften*, 302; Sommerfeld, *Wilhelm Dilthey und der Positivismus*, 11, 52, 53; Liebert, *Wilhelm Dilthey*, 67, 75; Störring, 'Die Frage der geisteswissenschaftlichen und verstehenden Psychologie,' LVIII, 393, 403–4, 406–7; Schmied-Kowarzik, 'Diltheys und Sprangers verstehende Psychologie.'

40 See Jaspers, 'Philosophical Autobiography,' in *The Philosophy of Karl Jaspers*, ed. P.A. Schilpp (New York: Tudor Publishing Company, 1957), p. 18, and *General Psychopathology*, trans. J. Hoenig and Marian W. Hamilton (Chicago: University of Chicago Press, 1963), p. 301n.

41 See Hünermann, *Der Durchbruch geschichtlichen Denkens*, 225, and R. Bakker, *De geschiedenis van het fenomenologisch denken*, third edition (Utrecht and Antwerp: Aula-Boeken, 1969), p. 27.

42 Dilthey himself became suspicious of Husserl's 'Platonism' (see Misch's Vorbericht to Vol. V, p. cxii). And Husserl, ever conscious of methodological considerations, criticized Dilthey for lack of attention to method: '*Dilthey*, who was thoroughly grounded in the *Geisteswissenschaften* in his studies and was doubtless one of the great practitioners of those sciences in the nineteenth century, was much more a man of brilliant global intuitions than of analysis and abstract theorizing. The ability to carry out fundamental analyses of experience was not his special strength, any more than he excelled in logical precision and thinking in precise concepts of the sort that one learns in the mathematical natural sciences' (*Phänomenologische Psychologie*, 6). Dilthey '... did indeed see the problems that determined the goal and also the direction in which one would have to work, but he did not penetrate to any decisive formulation of the problem or any methodologically sound solution, however great the progress he managed to make in the last years of his life' (*Ideen*, Vol. II, The Hague: Martinus Nijhoff, 1952, p. 173).

43 Georg Misch, Dilthey's son-in-law, suggests this as a reason for Dilthey's use of this name (see Vorbericht to Vol. V, p. lxxiii).

44 See *Grundformen und Erkenntnis menschlichen Daseins*, 662n.

45 See *Die Jugendgeschichte Hegels*, IV,
3, 151, 153; 'Schleiermacher,' IV,
397; *Leben Schleiermachers*,
Zusätze, XIII–2, 34; *Schleiermachers
System als Philosophie*, XIV–1, 130,
131, 145; *Einleitung*, 395, 400, 406;
'Das Problem der Religion,' VI,
301. F.J. Schmidt speaks of Dilthey's method as an 'applied phenomenology' (see 'Das Erlebnis
und die Dichtung,' 204–5).
46 The psychologist F.J.J. Buytendijk,
writing in this vein, speaks of the
'frequently repeated complaint' to
the effect that '... introspection is
always retrospection, a later view, a
post-mortem (*grafrede*), and an interpretive one at that. But this need
not be the case! That which we live
through, which, as something living, belongs to itself, need not become the psychologist's prey, that
he tears to pieces and digests or
conserves and preserves in fixed
concepts. Like everything living that
we encounter, the inward can become something cherished, that we
respect and care for tenderly. This
is what phenomenology tries to
do ...' Buytendijk accepts introspection as a method for gaining knowledge of man, but it is not the only
method: 'Introspection is not sufficient by itself to give us knowledge
of human inwardness' ('Het kennen van de innerlijkheid,' in *Academische redevoeringen*, Utrecht and
Nijmegen: Dekker en Van de Vegt,
1961, pp. 88, 92).

47 'Rousseaus Entwicklungsge-
schichte,' XVI, 429; see also 'Ferdinand Christian Baur,' IV, 419.
48 Dilthey did not claim that his was
the first or only philosophy of life.
Philosophies of life appear from
time to time in the history of philosophy. 'And with each new
appearance they shake off more
metaphysical elements and unfold
more freely and independently. In
the last generation philosophy of
life has again become the dominant
force on the scene' ('Die Kultur
der Gegenwart,' VIII, 197). Dilthey
also used the term 'philosophy of
life' in a non-technical sense to
mean simply an outlook on life.
49 *Fortsetzung*, 268. This 'hunger' and
'thirst' must be understood not in
the sense of a zest for life but as a
passionate desire to encounter concrete reality: 'The most universal
feature of our age is its sense of
reality and the this-worldliness of its
interests' ('Die Kultur der Gegenwart,' VIII, 190). In the *Einleitung*
Dilthey spoke of an 'insatiable
hunger for reality' as the 'powerful
soul of contemporary scholarship'
(p. 123; see also *Poetik*, 105).
50 See the Vorrede to Vol. V, 4, and
'Goethe,' in *Erlebnis*, 142. 'The
history of literature (*Dichtung*)
manifests a growing effort and determination to understand life out
of itself' (*Philosophie*, 398; see also
Individualität, 280, and *Weltanschauung*, 93).

51 Quoted by Misch in his Vorbericht to Vol. v, p. liv.

52 See 'Die 3 Epochen der modernen Aesthetik,' VI, 287, and 'Der Traum,' VIII, 226. Dilthey also speaks of the 'countenance of life' in 'Goethe,' in *Erlebnis*, 142; 'Hölderlin,' in *Erlebnis*, 273; *Weltanschauung*, 80; and the Zusätze to the latter, VIII, 140.

53 Rudolf Bultmann complains: 'It seems to me indeed that Dilthey looks at history principally from an aesthetic standpoint as at a spectacle which the historian enjoys in perceiving all the different possibilities of the human being as his own' (*History and Eschatology*, New York: Harper and Row, 1957, p. 125; see also 128, 148). In a study of the later Dilthey we read: 'Dilthey's attitude toward history is antiquarian-aesthetic. Along with his entire epoch, which is under the impression of historical consciousness, he finds himself in the situation of a "collector." He collects historical phenomena as precious gems, as it were. He restores them as he interprets them and then finally offers them to a certain esoteric group in society, a group that has the intellectual tools and also the leisure time to be able to understand these exquisite gems. Such people can then enjoy those gems and use them to ornament their existence and elevate it' (Barbara Trill, *Kunstphilosophie als Metaphysik beim späten Dilthey*, 127–8; see also 3ff).

54 'Die Entstehung der Hermeneutik,' Zusätze, V, 336.

55 See 'Die 3 Epochen der modernen Aesthetik,' VI, 272; *Individualität*, 276; *Weltanschauung*, 92; 'Archive der Literatur,' XV, 4.

56 See Dilthey's 'Preisschrift' on Schleiermacher's hermeneutics in relation to earlier Protestant hermeneutics (XIV–2, 597–787). See also 'Das natürliche System der Geisteswissenschaften im 17. Jahrhundert,' II, 110–29.

57 *Aufbau*, Zusätze, VII, 334.

58 John Raphael Staude claims: 'Dilthey and his followers had abandoned philosophy and become sociologists and historians, devoting themselves to describing the plurality of intellectual systems in the world, but denying that philosophy could provide the norms by which to judge their worth and validity' (see *Max Scheler: An Intellectual Portrait*, New York: The Free Press, 1967, pp. 153–6).

59 Dilthey's unfinished essay on the problem of religion (see VI, 288–305) represents his most important post-1900 statement on religious expression. In this essay he made no secret of the fact that his view of religion was dependent on the thinking of Schleiermacher. For his comments on James, see pp. 293, 302. (James was also mentioned in *Ideen*, 167, 177.) Dilthey and James had met in 1867 (see p. 183, note 88), and they later corresponded.

60 'By *anthropology* we understand in
Germany the study of the whole man
in his relations both to nature and to
history,' wrote Dilthey in a book review essay of 1877 (XVII, 362).

61 Husserl, in a lecture in Berlin in
1931, declared: 'Wilhelm Dilthey's
Lebensphilosophie, a new kind of
anthropology, which is very influential at present and has even affected
the so-called phenomenological
movement, maintains that true philosophy should seek its foundations exclusively in man and, more
specifically, in the essence of his
concrete wordly existence' ('Philosophy and Anthropology,' trans.
Richard G. Schmitt, in *Realism and
the Background of Phenomenology*,
ed. R.M. Chisholm, New York: The
Free Press, 1960, p. 129). Husserl
again misrepresents Dilthey somewhat, but his statement does
convey to us the impression which
Dilthey's philosophical labours had
created.

62 See, for example, Suter, *Philosophie
et histoire*, 47, and Aron, *La
philosophie critique de l'histoire*, 42–3.

63 'Die Abgrenzung der Geisteswissenschaften' – zweite Fassung, VII,
311.

64 Dilthey's comments in *Ideen*, 236
might be used to support such an
interpretation of his conception of
history, but there history is contrasted not with the systematic *Geisteswissenschaften* but with the
natural sciences.

65 On the term 'culture,' see note 9
above. Dilthey maintained his opposition to the term 'cultural sciences'
to the very end of his life. It is to
be avoided, he claimed, because it
'... contains an unprovable and one-
sided suggestion that history has a
meaning and goal. This is an all too
friendly and benevolent conception
of man's being. The dark instincts
of oppression and destruction play a
very substantial role in human history' (*Aufbau*, Zusätze, VII, 323).
In the twentieth century, the term
'culture' no longer implies value or
implicit approval.

66 In a diary entry of 1860, Dilthey did
speak of 'Geschichte des Geistes'
(*Der junge Dilthey*, 141). In the 1875
essay and in the biography of Schleiermacher, he spoke of 'die Geschichte der geistigen Bewegungen'
(see V, 41, and XIII–1, pp. xliii, xlv).
This term is prominent in his essay
'Archive der Literatur' (IV, 555ff)
and is also used in a similar essay entitled 'Archive für Literatur' (XV,
6n) as well as in book review essays
(XVII, 32, 194; see also 225, 384).
Suter, misreading the passage referred to in note 65, mistakenly
claims that Dilthey preferred the
term 'Geistesgechichte' to 'Kulturgeschichte' (*Philosophie et histoire*,
132n). Dilthey did write what the
Germans call 'Geistesgeschichte' –
hence the title chosen for Vols. XV
through XVII of his *Gesammelte
Schriften*, in which various early

essays are reprinted, is 'Zur Geistes-geschichte des 19. Jahrhunderts' – but he did not use this term himself.

67 Despite the fact that Dilthey avoided the term 'Kulturwissenschaft,' terms like 'Kulturgeschichte' and 'kulturhistorisch' appear frequently in his early book review essays (see XVII, 29ff, 62, 83, 132, 159–60, 167, 184, 205, 219, 235, 260, 268, 293, 324, 399, 411, 413, 415, 444, 459–61).

68 XIII–1, p. xliii. The same idea comes to expression in a passage from the 1875 essay quoted above (p. 14).

69 *Fortsetzung*, 208; see also *Aufbau*, 151.

70 'Archive für Literatur,' XV, 4; see also 5.

CHAPTER 4

1 Liebert speaks of Dilthey's philosophy of life as a mixture in which positivism and metaphysics are interwoven (*Wilhelm Dilthey*, 5). In the intellectual climate of Dilthey's time, positivism and metaphysics were, in fact, the two elements from which he was trying to free himself!

2 *Being and Time*, 72.

3 *Aufbau*, Zusätze, VII, 331.

4 Schleiermacher's philosophy was a philosophy of life (see *Schleiermachers System als Philosophie*, XIV–1, 10–11). Dilthey also speaks of an eighteenth-century French philosophy of life ('Die Kultur der

Gegenwart,' VIII, 201), a philosophy of life in the Renaissance era ('Die Funktion der Anthropologie,' II, 417, and 'Auffassung und Analyse des Menschen,' II, 21–3), and even of a philosophy of life in Roman times (*Geschichte der Philosophie*, 143). See also p. 169, note 48 above.

5 *Einführung in die Philosophie* (Frankfurt am Main: Verlag G. Schulte-Bulmke, 1960 – first published in 1935), p. 70. See also Bollnow, *Die Lebensphilosophie*, 8.

6 'Erfahren und Denken,' V, 83 – second sentence spaced in original.

7 Aussenwelt essay, Zusätze, V, 136 – spaced in original.

8 *Ideen*, 194. In 'Erfahren und Denken,' Dilthey had written that we cannot get behind thought (V, 83).

9 'Grundgedanke meiner Philosophie,' VIII, 172.

10 *Fortsetzung*, 278. 'The individual enjoys and understands history as a bearer and representative of the common elements that are interwoven within himself. He understands history because he is a historical being himself' (*Aufbau*, 151).

11 'History as a System,' 213. This statement may well have been inspired by Count Yorck's definition of historicality: 'That the psychophysical entity lives rather than simply *exists* is the nucleus of historicality' (*Briefwechsel*, 71).

12 'History as a System,' 217 – italics omitted.

13 *Fortsetzung*, 228; see also Notes towards a revision of the *Poetik*, VI, 314.

14 See *Weltanschauung*, 78, and the Zusatze, VIII, 121.

15 'Das Problem der Religion,' VI, 304; see also 'Dichterische Einbildungskraft und Wahnsinn,' VI, 95.

16 *Weltanschauung*, Zusätze, VIII, 163; see also *Philosophie*, 378–9.

17 *Erlebnis*, 164. Of Wolfram von Eschenbach, Dilthey writes: '... he interprets life out of life itself and not out of books, and with the things he gladly communicates in addition the strong impressions that they evoke in him' (*Von deutscher Dichtung und Musik*, 109).

18 *Briefwechsel*, 221; see also 'Uebersicht meines Systems,' VIII, 179.

19 See 'Das geschichtliche Bewusstsein,' VIII, 69; *Weltanschauung*, Zusätze, VIII, 143, 144, 147, 163.

20 See *Briefwechsel*, 47.

21 'Goethe,' in *Erlebnis*, 128. Dilthey insisted on this point and repeated it in *Poetik*, 172; 'Dichterische Einbildungskraft und Wahnsinn,' VI, 99; and *Einleitung*, 377–8.

22 'Goethe,' in *Erlebnis*, 129.

23 See *Einleitung*, 377–8, and 'Goethe,' in *Erlebnis*, 128–9.

24 See, for example, the comments made by William James in his Gifford Lectures of 1901–2 (*The Varieties of Religious Experience*, New York: Modern Library, no date, pp. 228, 501). Dilthey was acquainted with these lectures. We should also bear in mind that the first edition of

Freud's book on the interpretation of dreams was published in 1900.

25 See his comments in *Ideen*, 178–9 and in the Anmerkung following it (p. 239).

26 Carlo Antoni, for example, speaks of Dilthey's 'total rejection of all metaphysics' (*From History to Sociology*, 3).

27 'Der Fortgang über Kant,' VIII, 174.

28 V, 11. That Dilthey accepted the collapse of metaphysics as a *fait accompli* is also apparent from *Philosophie*, 404, and his letter of 29 June 1911 to Husserl (Dilthey-Husserl correspondence, 434ff).

29 Antón Donoso, 'Wilhelm Dilthey's Contribution to the Philosophy of History,' 154.

30 *The Philosophy of Wilhelm Dilthey*, pp. 346, xviii.

31 See *Einleitung*, pp. xviii, 123–4, and 'Grundgedanke meiner Philosophie,' VIII, 171.

32 See *Leben Schleiermachers*, XIII–1, 96n, 102n.

33 See 'Erkenntnistheoretische Fragmente,' XVIII, 193–201.

34 'Wilhelm Dilthey,' in *Zur Theorie*, 358.

35 See Liebert, *Wilhelm Dilthey*, 52, and Robert P. Mohan, *Philosophy of History* (New York: Bruce Publishing Company, 1970), p. 126.

36 See Degener, *Dilthey und das Problem der Metaphysik*, 7, 32, 41. Degener's view of metaphysics is dependent on the thought of Nicolai Hartmann (see pp. 16, 18–19).

37 See Vorbericht to Vol. v, p. liv. See also Trill, *Kunstphilosophie als Metaphysik beim späten Dilthey*, 3ff, 130, note 8.

38 *Aufbau*, Zusätze, VII, 334.

39 *Einleitung*, 358. See also Dilthey's criticism of metaphysics in 'Die Kultur der Gegenwart,' VIII, 196–201, where we read that the various metaphysical systems are refuted by history, and that the metaphysicians ultimately wind up producing 'Begriffsdichtungen' that can lay no claim to universal or abiding validity.

40 'The entire foundation of the metaphysical method is a presupposition that cannot be proved or justified on purely scientific grounds ...' (*System der Ethik*, X, 20).

41 See *Einleitung*, 384, 398, 402, 403; 'Das geschichtliche Bewusstsein,' VIII, 3.

42 *Einleitung*, 405; see also *Aufbau*, Zusätze, VII, 334.

43 *Philosophie*, 401; see also *Weltanschauung*, 94.

44 *Die Jugendgeschichte Hegels*, IV, 55.

45 See *Ideen*, 228.

46 'It is true that a religious occurrence is first of all interwoven also with outward deeds of will: through his religious acts, man seeks to guarantee the success of his deeds ... But in the more developed cultures, those inner deeds of will became the actual kernel of the religious occurrence' (*Poetik*, 146). In the modern world, religion is virtually inseparable from morality: '... we have all become accustomed, with Lessing and Kant, to assess a religion in terms of the moral effects it brings about' ('Das Problem der Religion,' VI, 292).

47 'Zur Philosophie der Philosophie,' VIII, 208–9.

48 'Der Traum,' VIII, 224.

49 *Schleiermachers System als Theologie*, XIV–2, 486.

50 'Der Traum,' VIII, 224; see also Zusätze, VIII, 273; *Philosophie*, 405–6; 'Der moderne Mensch,' VIII, 235.

51 Poetry and metaphysics sometimes bring the same worldview to expression: 'The systems of Schelling, Hegel and Schleiermacher are only logically and metaphysically grounded elaborations of this view of life and the world developed by Lessing, Schiller and Goethe' (1867 Antrittsvorlesung, V, 13; see also *Weltanschauung*, 93).

52 This formulation is inspired by A.J. de Sopper, who defines philosophy as 'the intellectual deposit (*neerslag*) left by man's most personal total-reaction to the totality with which he is in communion' (see *Wat is philosophie?*, Haarlem: De Erven F. Bohn, 1950, pp. 168ff). De Sopper was originally a neo-Kantian, but his later existential outlook on philosophy and human expression is strikingly similar to that of Dilthey, whom he does not mention in this context. Dilthey himself speaks of an 'objectivized deposit of life' in the social-historical world (*Individualität*, 265).

53 See the editor's comments in VIII, 264.
54 'Zur Philosophie der Philosophie,' VIII, 208.
55 'A Chapter in the History of Ideas,' 163.
56 Weltanschauung, Zusätze, VIII, 140.
57 'Uebersicht meines Systems,' VIII, 176.
58 Philosophie, 407. 'Philosophy is the reflection of the spirit on all its modes of comportment, right down to their ultimate presuppositions' (p. 358). We also read: 'The philosophical mind is always characterized on the one hand by universal self-reflection, and also the formative and reforming power grounded in that self-reflection, and on the other by the strong tendency towards a grounding and coherence, which tendency seems to be inherent in the philosophical mind' (p. 407).
59 Weltanschauung, Zusätze, VIII, 140; see also Die Jugendgeschichte Hegels, Zusätze, IV, 218.
60 Compare Philosophie, 404 with Die Jugendgeschichte Hegels, Zusätze, IV, 218.

CHAPTER 5

1 'Goethe,' in Erlebnis, 126.
2 In the Aufbau Dilthey sometimes speaks of a 'Zusammenhang of experience, expression and understanding' and sometimes of a 'Zusammenhang of life, expression and understanding' (see p. 87). He

also speaks of 'going back ... to experience,' which means 'going back to life' (p. 83).
3 Poetik, 108. Dilthey may well have been influenced here by Count Yorck, who spoke of the 'inner historicality of self-consciousness' in connection with his criticism of the historical school (see Briefwechsel, 68–9).
4 See Der junge Dilthey, 24. He also writes: 'Luther and Schleiermacher, our two greatest theologians, realized that music is the nearest sister of religion, and that listening to music, when it is true music, is a religious act' (p. 9; see also 151). Of Beethoven's ninth symphony, he wrote: 'It does not have a single side of life as its special object; rather, life itself is its object' (Von deutscher Dichtung und Musik, 297; see also 262, 280–1, 286; Aufbau, Zusätze, VII, 341–2; 'Frühe Aphorismen aus der Berliner Zeit,' XVIII, 205).
5 Dilthey explicitly rejected the principle of 'l'art pour l'art' (see Notes towards a revision of the Poetik, VI, 320). Given Dilthey's standpoint, we could better say: 'l'art pour la vie.'
6 See Philosophie, 397; Weltanschauung, 99; Poetik, 131; 'Dichterische Einbildungskraft und Wahnsinn,' VI, 94, 98.
7 See Die Jugendgeschichte Hegels, IV, 178.
8 See 'Goethe,' in Erlebnis, 165–6; Aufbau, Zusätze, VII, 326, 329.

9 *History and Eschatology* (New York: Harper and Row, 1957), p. 128.
10 *Aufbau*, Zusätze, VII, 331; see also *Fortsetzung*, 224.
11 See Misch, Vorbericht to Vol. V, p. lx.
12 *Von deutscher Dichtung und Musik*, 89.
13 *Aufbau*, Zusätze, VII, 326.
14 'Goethe,' in *Erlebnis*, 165.
15 See 'Das natürliche System,' II, 243.
16 See *Fortsetzung*, 205.
17 See 'Die Abgrenzung der Geisteswissenschaften' – zweite Fassung, VII, 319–20; 'Das geschichtliche Bewusstsein,' VIII, 15; *Leben Schleiermachers*, XIII–1, p. xliii.
18 See 'Lessing,' in *Erlebnis*, 50; *Poetik*, 128, 161, 204, 206.
19 Quoted in the Vorbericht des Herausgebers, *Die grosse Phantasiedichtung*, 3.
20 *Aufbau*, 166; see also 'Goethe,' in *Erlebnis*, 139, 140; *Weltanschauung*, 92–3; *Philosophie*, 378, 394–5.
21 'Goethe,' in *Erlebnis*, 186.
22 'Shakespeare und seine Zeitgenossen,' in *Die grosse Phantasiedichtung*, 53–4; see also 'Goethe,' in *Erlebnis*, 142.
23 *Leben Schleiermachers*, XIII–1, p. xxxiii.
24 Dilthey writes that '... all understanding is a reliving, and all reliving has its initial material in the lived experiences themselves' (*Die Jugendgeschichte Hegels*, IV, 178; see also 'Lessing,' in *Erlebnis*, 45).
25 'Die Entstehung der Hermeneutik,' V, 331.

26 See *Fortsetzung*, 278.
27 See *Weltanschauung*, 82.
28 'Die Sprache,' XVI, 425.
29 See 'Die Entstehung der Hermeneutik,' V, 319; *Philosophie*, 392; *Fortsetzung*, 217.
30 See *Ideen*, 229, 236; 'Uebersicht meines Systems,' VIII, 176; see also *Weltanschauung*, 85, and *Fortsetzung*, 278.
31 See the Aussenwelt essay, V, 98, 102, 103; 'Archive der Literatur,' IV, 559; *System der Ethik*, X, 50, 104; *Briefwechsel*, 90.
32 *Weltanschauung*, 79; see also 85.
33 'Mens en geschiedenis bij Dilthey,' in *Verspreide geschriften*, I, p. 71; *Theorie der geschiedenis*, 150–1.
34 See Apel, 'Das Verstehen,' 158.
35 See F.J.J. Buytendijk, 'Over het verstaan der levensverschijnselen,' in *Academische redevoeringen* (Utrecht and Nijmegen: Dekker en Van de Vegt, 1961), especially pp. 14–15.
36 *Le problème de la conscience historique*, 41.
37 See Coreth, *Grundfragen der Hermeneutik*, 196.
38 See *Wahrheit und Methode*, 162ff.
39 *Grundfragen der Hermeneutik*, 166, 64ff; see also 55, 164–5, 184.
40 'Vom Zirkel des Verstehens,' 25, 29.
41 See *Einleitung*, 394, and 'Der Traum,' VIII, 224–5. There is also a hint of a pragmatist conception of truth in Dilthey (see *Fortsetzung*, 262). On the affinities between philosophy of life and the pragmatist

conception of truth, see Bollnow, *Die Lebensphilosophie*, 66.

42 'Le problème herméneutique,' 25.

43 See H.M. Kuitert, *De realiteit van het geloof* (Kampen: J.H. Kok, 1966), pp. 51, 55–8.

44 'Die Entstehung der Hermeneutik,' Zusätze, v, 332; see also *Einleitung*, 109, 119–20.

45 *Die Begegnungsphilosophie* (Freiburg and Munich: Verlag Karl Alber, 1970), p. 60.

46 Katsube, *Wilhelm Diltheys Methode der Lebensphilosophie*, 97; see also 45.

47 'Grundlinien eines Systems der Pädagogik,' IX, 201; see also 'Ueber die Möglichkeit einer allgemeingültigen pädagogischen Wissenschaft,' VI, 74.

48 *Individualität*, 266, and 'Die grosse Phantasiedichtung,' in *Die grosse Phantasiedichtung*, 10.

49 v, 318; see also Zusätze, v, 332; 'Die Abgrenzung der Geisteswissenschaften' – erste Fassung, VII, 309; and Rickert's criticism of this formulation of the doctrine of understanding in *Grenzen*, 560n.

50 See 'Die Entstehung der Hermeneutik,' Zusätze, v, 336.

51 See 'Die Entstehung der Hermeneutik,' v, 318; see also *Ideen*, 144.

52 See *Fortsetzung*, 226–7, and 'Die Entstehung der Hermeneutik,' v, 319.

53 Miller-Rostowska writes: 'In the last editions of *Grenzen*, Rickert tried to build in Dilthey's theory of understanding by way of his theory of in-

dividualizing concept-formation' (*Das Individuelle als Gegenstand der Erkenntnis*, 32).

54 Calvin Schrag, *Experience and Being* (Evanston: Northwestern University Press, 1969), p. 194n.

CHAPTER 6

1 *Historik*, 26.

2 See 'Geschichte und Wissenschaft,' XVI, 105.

3 *The Problem of Knowledge: Philosophy, Science and History since Hegel*, trans. W.H. Woglom and C.W. Hendel (New Haven: Yale University Press, 1950), p. 257. It should be remembered that the idea of understanding had already undergone considerable development even before Droysen, as Wach's three-volume work *Das Verstehen* makes clear.

4 See *Historik*, 26–7.

5 *Theorie des objektiven Geistes*, 36–7.

6 Kuypers therefore notes that there is a 'surprising' amount of agreement between Husserl, Dilthey, and Rickert on the question of meaning (see *Theorie der geschiedenis*, 79n).

7 See p. 90 above. The principle of 'Besserverstehen' can also be formulated with reference to the text: 'The text is to be understood by the interpreter better than the author was able to understand it ...' (see Thomas S. Seebohm, *Zur Kritik der hermeneutischen Vernunft*, Bonn: Bouvier Verlag Herbert Grund-

mann, 1972, p. 13). Bollnow claims that there is no essential difference between the two formulations: 'When we say that we understand an author, we mean the text he has written or the work he has composed ... For me the possibility of *Besserverstehen* applies only to the work ...' (*Das Verstehen*, 15).

8 This distinction between 'meaning' (*Bedeutung*) and 'sense' (*Sinn*) is clearly reflected in some important passages: see *Weltanschauung*, 83, and *Fortsetzung*, 240.

9 See *Hermeneutik*, 129–30.

10 Dilthey was well aware of the problem of generations (see the 1875 essay, v, 36–40; *Aufbau*, 177n; *Fortsetzung*, 284).

11 See *Allgemeine Auslegungslehre*, 52.

12 See Heinz Kimmerle's introduction to Schleiermacher's *Hermeneutik*, 14ff.

13 See *Hermeneutics*, 106ff.

14 v, 320. In the Zusätze he writes: 'This theory of the art of understanding fixed written expressions of life is called hermeneutics' (v, 332–3 – spaced in original).

15 See Carl E. Braaten, *History and Hermeneutics* (Philadelphia: Westminster Press, 1966), p. 154.

16 'Die Entstehung der Hermeneutik,' v, 330.

17 *Das hermeneutische System Schleiermachers*, XIV–2, 708. See also 'Die Entstehung der Hermeneutik,' v, 330, and 'Archive für Literatur,' XV, 5.

18 'Die Fürstin Galitzin,' XV, 178.

19 Coreth, *Grundfragen der Hermeneutik*, 55; see also 119, 184.

20 The question of Dilthey and Freud comes up in Habermas, *Erkenntnis und Interesse* (see especially 262ff).

21 See the comments made by Hughes in *Consciousness and Society*, 17, 30, 116–18, 120–2, 124, 187–8, 226–7, 263, 305–6, 310–12.

22 See Calvin Rand, 'Two Meanings of Historicism,' 510.

23 Philip Bagby, *Culture and History* (Berkeley and Los Angeles: University of California Press, 1963), pp. 67–8.

24 'Archive der Literatur,' IV, 557; see also *Einleitung*, 125; 'Das natürliche System,' II, 170; 'Das 18. Jahrhundert,' III, 267; Vorwort, XI, pp. xv–xvii; 'Eduard Gibbon,' XV, 85. See also Meinecke's 'Vorbemerkung' to *Die Entstehung des Historismus* and pp. 285, 581.

25 See 'Uebersicht meines Systems,' VIII, 183, and *Fortsetzung*, 217.

26 *Die Entstehung des Historismus*, 223.

27 'Das 18. Jahrhundert,' III, 219.

28 'Die Entstehung der Hermeneutik,' Zusätze, v, 333.

29 See *Individualität*, 281; *Einleitung*, 94; and 'Shakespeare und seine Zeitgenossen,' in *Die grosse Phantasiedichtung*, 88.

30 *Die Jugendgeschichte Hegels*, IV, 168.

31 '3. Literaturbrief,' XVII, 18.

32 'Auffassung und Analyse des Menschen,' II, 6–7.

33 'Grundgedanke meiner Philosophie,' VIII, 173.

34 See *Individualität*, 282, and 'Shakespeare und seine Zeitgenossen,' in
   Die grosse Phantasiedichtung, 89.
35 *Schleiermachers System als Philosophie*, XIV–1, 26.
36 'Leibniz und sein Zeitalter,' III, 8;
   see also *Individualität*, 275, and 'Die
   Funktion der Anthropologie,' II,
   437.
37 Morgan, 'Wilhelm Dilthey,' 364–5.
38 *Aufbau*, 135; see also 81.
39 *Aufbau*, 173; see also 138, 152ff;
   Fortsetzung, 246.
40 'Le problème herméneutique,'
   22; see also *Wahrheit und Methode*,
   210–11.
41 See Kon, *Die Geschichtsphilosophie
   des 20. Jahrhunderts*, I, 104–5;
   Hughes, *History as Art and as
   Science*, 13; see also pp. 107–8 above.
42 For Betti's discussion of these two
   canons, see 'Zur Grundlegung einer
   allgemeinen Auslegungslehre,'
   100ff, and *Allgemeine Auslegungslehre*, 218ff.
43 'Goethe,' in *Erlebnis*, 163.
44 'Die Entstehung der Hermeneutik,'
   Zusätze, V, 335.
45 Gadamer, *Wahrheit und Methode*,
   280. On the 'fusion of horizons,'
   see pp. 289–90.
46 *Aufbau*, 99; see also Dilthey's criticism of the 'abstract school' and the
   historical school in *Einleitung*, 49,
   and Ortega's comments in 'A Chapter from the History of Ideas,' 153.
   Also relevant here is Dilthey's criticism of Herder, whom he speaks of
   as the 'founder' of the historical

school (*Poetik*, 120), in *Die Jugendgeschichte Hegels*, IV, 165–6.
47 See Suter, *Philosophie et histoire*,
   166–8, 170, 190.
48 See Misch, *Lebensphilosophie und
   Phänomenologie*, 297–8; Bollnow,
   Das Verstehen, 78; Mekkes, 'Wilhelm Dilthey's "Kritik der historischen Vernunft" in de wending der
   eeuw,' 27; Baring, *Wilhelm Diltheys
   Philosophie der Geschichte*, 73. Josef
   Höfer deals with this problem by
   arguing that Dilthey uses the term
   'allgemeingültig' in a weaker than
   normal sense (see *Vom Leben zur
   Wahrheit*, 100–1).

CHAPTER 7

1 See 'Aphorismen,' in *Zur Theorie*,
   231.
2 See Brands, *Historisme als ideologie*,
   6–7, 9.
3 *Grenzen*, 8; *Probleme*, 130; see also
   12, 129, 132.
4 Johannes Thyssen, *Geschichte der
   Geschichtsphilosophie*, second edition
   (Bonn: H. Bouvier und Co., 1954),
   p. 125.
5 Werner Stark, *The Sociology of
   Knowledge* (London: Routledge and
   Kegan Paul, 1958), p. 206.
6 'Das religiöse Apriori,' in *Gesammelte Schriften*, Vol. II (Tübingen:
   J.C.B. Mohr, 1913), p. 754; *Der
   Historismus und seine Probleme*, 528.
7 *Die Entstehung des Historismus*, 1, 4.
8 See *Historismus*, 155, 159, 211. The
   better definitions of historicism re-

flect both these elements. Berkhof, for example, characterizes historicism as follows: 'The attitude that would do justice to the peculiarity of history in all its individuality, finality and variegation, and which appreciates all cultural phenomena as phenomena in a historical process, we call *historicism*' (*Christ the Meaning of History*, 28).

9 On Leibniz, see *Das hermeneutische System Schleiermachers*, XIV–2, 698; *Geschichte der Philosophie*, 165; 'Leibniz und sein Zeitalter,' III, 62; 'Das geschichtliche Bewusstsein,' VIII, 10; *Weltanschauung*, Zusätze, VIII, 124–5; 'Die Funktion der Anthropologie,' II, 469. For Meinecke's treatment of Leibniz, see *Historismus*, 27ff.

10 See Count Yorck's criticism of the historical school in *Briefwechsel*, 68–9. Ortega y Gasset picks up this criticism and accuses the historical school of 'positivism,' i.e., of 'mere seeing' without 'effective historical thinking' (see 'A Chapter from the History of Ideas,' 148–50, 153).

11 See *Historismus*, 155–6.

12 See, for example, Eberhard Kessel's introduction to Meinecke's *Zur Theorie*, p. xviii.

13 For the role of monadological thinking in Troeltsch, see Klapwijk, *Tussen historisme en relativisme*, 60–1, 79n, 398ff, 447ff.

14 Ricoeur writes: 'For historicism, understanding is finding the genesis, the prior form, the sources, the meaning of the evolution' ('Struc-

ture et herméneutique,' in *Le conflit des interprétations*, 35).

15 See 'Aphorismen,' in *Zur Theorie*, 244.

16 'Kritische oder genetische Methode?,' in *Präludien*, II, 119, 120.

17 *Historismus*, 496; see also 4, and 'Geschichte und Gegenwart,' in *Zur Theorie*, 94. Similar statements about the historical approach are to be found in Dilthey (see 'Der moderne Mensch,' VIII, 234, and 'Das Problem der Religion,' VI, 303).

18 'Aphorismen,' in *Zur Theorie*, 215.

19 See Kessel's introduction to *Zur Theorie*, p. xii.

20 *Historismus*, 337.

21 'Geschichte und Gegenwart,' in *Zur Theorie*, 101.

22 See *The German Catastrophe*, trans. Sidney B. Fay (Boston: Beacon Press, 1963), pp. 82–6, 93, 103, 108, 113.

23 See Klapwijk, *Tussen historisme en relativisme*, 184.

24 *Aufbau*, Zusätze, VII, 329–30.

25 *Aufbau*, Zusätze, VII, 346.

26 'Das 18. Jahrhundert,' III, 223–4.

27 *Der junge Dilthey*, 190. Many years later Dilthey wrote: 'History is movement' (*Fortsetzung*, 288).

28 *Aufbau*, Zusätze, VII, 329.

29 See 'Die Sprache,' XVI, 424–5.

30 'Das natürliche System,' II, 170.

31 See Groethuysen, 'Wilhelm Dilthey,' 90.

32 See Groethuysen, 'Dilthey et son école,' 21; *Introduction à la pensée philosophique allemande depuis Nietzsche*, 45.

33 1887 Antrittsrede, V, 11.

34 *Schleiermachers System als Philosophie*, XIV–1, 375.

35 See 'Auffassung und Analyse des Menschen,' II, 77.

36 See 'Jahresbericht über die im Jahre 1886 erchienene Literatur über die Philosophie seit Kant,' XV, 304.

37 See Dilthey's preface to his lectures on the history of pedagogy, IX, 10.

38 See *Poetik*, 190, 196, 228, 229, 231.

39 *Individualität*, 302; see also 'Das geschichtliche Bewusstsein,' VIII, 13.

40 See 'Auffassung und Analyse des Menschen,' II, 73, and 'Archive für Literatur,' XV, 2.

41 See 'Das geschichtliche Bewusstsein,' VIII, 38.

42 See 'Archive der Literatur,' IV, 560.

43 'Der Traum,' VIII, 226.

44 Masur, *Prophets of Yesterday*, 167; see also 'Wilhelm Dilthey and the History of Ideas,' 106.

45 J.P.A. Mekkes, *Radix, tijd en kennen* (Amsterdam: Buijten en Schipperheijn, 1970), p. 23.

46 See 'Philosophie als strenge Wissenschaft,' 293, 323ff.

47 See the Dilthey-Husserl correspondence, 434ff.

48 *Die Entstehung des Historismus*, 406 – italics mine; see also 414, 439–40; 526; 577ff.

49 *Ideology and Utopia*, trans. Louis Wirth and Edward Shils (New York: Harcourt, Brace and World, 1936), pp. 283, 300; see also 78–9, 85–7, 98n–9, 264–5, 282, 305–6.

50 'Archive der Literatur,' IV, 562.

51 See 'Der moderne Mensch,' VIII, 234, and 'Zu Schmollers Grundriss der Volkswirtschaftslehre,' XI, 256.

52 See *Die Jugendgeschichte Hegels*, IV, 31; *Einleitung*, 358; 'Rede zum 70. Geburtstag,' V, 9; *Philosophie*, 406; *Fortsetzung*, 290–1; *Weltanschauung*, 77; 'Die Kultur der Gegenwart,' VIII, 194; 'Lessing,' in *Erlebnis*, 123.

53 See 'Das geschichtliche Bewusstsein,' VIII, 12.

54 'Die Kultur der Gegenwart,' VIII, 204.

55 See *Einleitung*, Zusätze, I, 413; *Weltanschauung*, 78, and the Zusätze, VIII, 121; 'Rede zum 70. Geburtstag,' V, 9; 'Die Kultur der Gegenwart,' VIII, 194; *Philosophie*, 397.

56 See Misch, Vorbericht to Vol. V, p. cxii.

57 Quoted by Misch, Vorbericht to Vol. V, p. cx.

58 See Herman Nohl, *Einführung in die Philosophie* (Frankfurt am Main: Verlag G. Schulte-Bulmke, 1960), p. 66. Dilthey is also regarded as a 'conservative thinker' in Marxist circles: see, for example, Herzberg, 'Wilhelm Dilthey in der heutigen westdeutschen Philosophie,' especially pp. 92n, 94.

59 Rudolf Bultmann writes that '... for Dilthey the worrying question of truth remains without an answer.' But he also notes that Dilthey managed to avoid relativism and nihilism (see *History and Eschatology*, New York: Harper and Row, 1957, pp. 125, 128, 148). Höfer com-

plains: 'The inquiry into truth dies for the man who seeks to "understand" everything' (*Vom Leben zur Wahrheit*, 172).

60 See *Einleitung*, 26, and the Zusätze, I, 411n; see also 'Erkenntnistheoretische Fragmente,' XVIII, 198–9.

61 See 'Die Kultur der Gegenwart,' VIII, 204, and 'Das geschichtliche Bewusstsein,' VIII, 6.

62 See *Poetik*, 104, 126, 157; see also 'Die 3 Epochen der modernen Aesthetik,' VI, 242, 270.

63 The 'idealism of personality' is the 'soul of Christianity' ('Der Traum,' VIII, 222; see also *Philosophie*, 392; *Die Jugendgeschichte Hegels*, IV, 61; 'Das Problem der Religion,' VI, 292; *Weltanschauung*, 109–10; 'Friedrich der Grosse und die deutsche Aufklärung,' III, 143; *Leben Schleiermachers*, XIII–1, 178, and the Zusätze, p. 560).

64 *Der junge Dilthey*, 80, 146–7; see also 124.

65 See Groethuysen, *Introduction à la pensée philosophique allemande depuis Nietzsche*, 65.

66 'Zur Philosophie der Philosophie,' VIII, 207–8.

67 Dilthey uses a variety of names for the idealism of freedom, which found its 'sharpest expression' in Fichte (*Von deutscher Dichtung und Musik*, 447), its 'most convinced and powerful proponent' (*Die Jugendgeschichte Hegels*, IV, 48; see also the Zusätze, p. 268). He calls it subjective idealism, idealism of per-

sonality, of the person, of the moral person, of moral freedom, and of subjectivity (see 'Der entwicklungsgeschichtliche Pantheismus,' II, 314, 355; 'Leibniz und sein Zeitalter,' III, 46; 'Friedrich der Grosse und die deutsche Aufklärung,' III, 89, 143, 145, 147, 166; 'Die 3 Grundformen der Systeme,' IV, 547, 549; *Schleiermachers System als Philosophie*, XIV–1, 469–70; and *Weltanschauung*, 108, 111).

68 *Weltanschauung*, 99–100; see also the Zusätze, VIII, 150, 156, 160–1.

69 Dilthey's major treatment of the types of philosophical systems is his essay on the types of worldviews (VIII, 75–118). Also relevant are the following passages: *Philosophie*, 402–4; 'Der Traum,' VIII, 220–6; 'Die 3 Grundformen der Systeme,' IV, 547–8; *Schleiermachers System als Philosophie*, XIV–1, 47, 421; 'Jahresbericht über die nachkantische Philosophie,' XV, 334; 'Das Hegel-Buch Kuno Fischers,' XV, 350–1; 'Fragmente aus Wilhelm Diltheys Hegelwerk,' 122ff.

70 I have dealt with Hegel and Dilthey on the history of philosophy in my essay 'Dilthey's Philosophy of the History of Philosophy.'

71 Marquard writes that the typology of worldviews takes the place of a philosophy of history in Dilthey's thought and speaks of this as a 'latent ahistoricism' (see 'Weltanschauungstypologie,' 437–9).

72 See 'Das geschichtliche Bewusstsein,' VIII, 8.

73 See 'Der Traum,' Zusätze, VIII, 273.

74 *Weltanschauung*, Zusätze, VIII, 147; see also *Weltanschauung*, 80.

75 VIII, 235; see also 'Das Problem der Religion,' VI, 296.

76 'In the final analysis, reality cannot be logically explained but only understood. In every reality given to us as such, there is by nature something ineffable, something unknowable' ('Der Fortgang über Kant,' VIII, 174). Dilthey used the dictum 'Individuum est ineffabile' as the epigraph for his biography of Schleiermacher (see also *Einleitung*, 29; 'Die Entstehung der Hermeneutik,' V, 330; *Fortsetzung*, 256). At least one commentator denies that Dilthey was an irrationalist (see Cüppers, *Die erkenntnistheoretischen Grundgedanken Wilhelm Diltheys*, 113–15).

77 See *Die Jugendgeschichte Hegels*, IV, 55–6, 139, 179.

78 'Leibniz und sein Zeitalter,' III, 10.

79 'Oration on the Dignity of Man,' trans. E.L. Forbes, in *The Renaissance Philosophy of Man*, ed. Ernst Cassirer, P.O. Kristeller, and J.H. Randall (Chicago: University of Chicago Press, 1948), pp. 224–5.

80 'Der Traum,' VIII, 220–1, 223.

81 See Bollnow, *Dilthey*, 16–17, 29, 46, 191, and *Das Verstehen*, 37; Diwald, *Wilhelm Dilthey*, 209–10, 210n; Tumarkin, 'Ein Versuch, Diltheys Leben aus ihm selbst zu verstehen,' 264–5; Suter, *Philosophie et histoire*, 128, 181–2; Aron, *La philosophie critique de l'histoire*, 298; and Heinemann, *Neue Wege der Philosophie*, 186ff.

82 Nohl, 'Zur Neuausgabe der Werke Wilhelm Diltheys,' 624.

83 Groethuysen, 'Wilhelm Dilthey,' 69.

84 See *Briefwechsel*, 216, and 'Der Traum,' VIII, 220.

85 *Der junge Dilthey*, 139; see also 236.

86 Groethuysen, 'Dilthey et son école,' 2.

87 See 'Versuche einer Philosophie des Lebens,' 318.

88 See *Neue Wege der Philosophie*, 179. Dilthey's love of solitude, his reserved nature, and his need of contact with others combined to make him a somewhat puzzling person who did not always fit smoothly into social situations. This is reflected in the impression which he made on William James when he first met him in 1867 at the home of a mutual friend. James included an amusing account of this encounter with Dilthey in a letter to his sister (see *The Letters of William James*, Vol. I, ed. Henry James, London: Longmans, Green and Co., 1920, pp. 109–11).

89 *Einleitung*, 91. Meinecke also uses this term in connection with the work of the historian (see 'Ernst Troeltsch,' in *Zur Theorie*, 377).

90 VIII, 226; see also Dilthey's use of the term 'Hingabe' in 'Die Funktion der Anthropologie,' II, 482; 'Der moderne Mensch,' VIII, 235; *Die Jugendgeschichte Hegels*, IV, 38; and *Philosophie*, 410, 411.

91 Lukács writes: 'Thus the final note sounded in the lifework of Dilthey is one of resignation and despair' (*Die Zerstörung der Vernunft*, 385; see also 384).

92 'Carl Immanuel Nitzsch,' XI, 55; see also 'Frühe Aphorismen aus der Berliner Zeit,' XVIII, 208.

93 See 'Rede zum 70. Geburtstag,' V, 9.

94 *Weltanschauung*, Zusätze, 143; see also *Weltanschauung*, 80–1.

95 See *Leben Schleiermachers*, XIII–1, 78. Freud describes the death of one's father as 'the most important event, the most poignant loss, of a man's life' (preface to the second edition of *The Interpretation of Dreams*, trans. James Strachey, New York: Basic Books, 1965). Freud, of course, had reasons of which Dilthey was not aware for emphasizing the significance of this event. For Dilthey's reaction to his own father's death, see his letter to his brother in *Der junge Dilthey*, 245–8.

96 Dilthey's letter to Count Yorck on the occasion of the death of the latter's brother would seem to indicate that he left open the possibility of personal immortality (see *Briefwechsel*, 187). However, we must remember that Yorck was a (Lutheran) Christian, and thus Dilthey could hardly have avoided some such remarks in a letter of consolation to him. For Dilthey's own standpoint vis-à-vis the Christian faith, see the note on p. 20.

97 Dilthey lost sleep over this in later years (see *Aufbau*, 139, and 'Der Strukturzusammenhang des Wissens,' VII, 28). The deaths of various friends and acquaintances served as a reminder that his own time was limited (see *Briefwechsel*, 188). In 1911 he worried that his death would prevent him from enjoying Husserl's later philosophical work (see the Dilthey-Husserl correspondence, 437, 442). During that same year he died suddenly and unexpectedly, in the midst of uncompleted projects (see Misch, *Vom Lebens- und Gedankenkreis Wilhelm Diltheys*, 11, and Tumarkin, 'Wilhelm Dilthey,' 143, 151).

98 'Goethe,' in *Erlebnis*, 162. Heidegger mentions this passage in his discussion of 'Sein zum Tode' (*Being and Time*, 494n – p. 249n of the German edition).

CHAPTER 8

1 See Rodi, *Morphologie und Hermeneutik*, 9.

2 See, for example, Hodges, *The Philosophy of Wilhelm Dilthey*, 2, 23; Gadamer, *Wahrheit und Methode*, 205; Troeltsch, *Der Historismus und seine Probleme*, 509ff. Troeltsch speaks of the 'two souls in Dilthey's breast' (pp. 517–18) and writes: 'To combine Mill and Schleiermacher – that was the great paradox in the turn his thought took ...' (p. 512).

3 In his lectures on ethics, Dilthey speaks of Marx's *Kapital* as 'the most important writing of modern

socialism' (x, 15), and in his '26. Literaturbrief' he calls it a book '... which is mentioned much more than it is read and which must be characterized as the most important and basic book of socialism ...' He then goes on to add a few critical and historical comments (XVIII, 186–7). In the Zusätze to *Die Jugendgeschichte Hegels*, Marx and Engels are mentioned without being discussed. Yet Dilthey did conclude one of his published essays with a sharp denunciation of the 'frightful consequences' of capitalism: 'Within the modern legal order, mobile capital plays the same sort of role as it played within the Roman empire: it is unlimited in its power. Mobile capital can drop whatever it wishes to drop and pick up whatever it wants. It is like a beast with a thousand eyes and tentacles but without a conscience, a beast that can go wherever it wishes' ('Das natürliche System,' II, 245).

4 Erxleben, *Erlebnis, Verstehen und geschichtliche Wahrheit*, 20; see also 23, 26–7, 184ff.

5 *Kulturwissenschaft*, pp. xii–xiii; see also Husserl's comments on Dilthey (p. 168, note 42 above).

6 *Der Junge Dilthey*, 87; see also Misch's comments in his Vorbericht to Vol. V, pp. xiv–xv.

7 Morgan, 'Wilhelm Dilthey,' 351.

8 *Vom Lebens- und Gedankenkreis Wilhelm Diltheys*, 19.

9 Vorrede to Vol. V, 4.

10 See *Lebensphilosophie und Phänomenologie*, 23, 71.

11 See 'Friedrich der Grosse und die deutsche Aufklärung,' III, 99, 100, and *Die Jugendgeschichte Hegels*, IV, 124. In an early, unpublished manuscript Dilthey wrote that every philosophically inclined person feels within himself a need for some sort of total outlook or comprehensive view of the world and human life (see XVIII, 44–5).

12 See Ortega, 'A Chapter from the History of Ideas,' 170.

13 'Zur Philosophie der Philosophie,' VIII, 210.

14 'Der psychische Strukturzusammenhang,' VII, 6.

15 *Vernunft und Widervernunft in unserer Zeit* (Munich: R. Piper und Co. Verlag, 1950), p. 68; see also Bultmann's criticism of Dilthey above (p. 170 note 53, and p. 181, note 59).

16 *Der Historismus und seine Probleme*, 125. Perhaps Dilthey's preoccupation with individual historical phenomena could also be regarded as a manifestation of the 'universale Sammellust' which Hermann Glockner identifies as characteristic of German philosophical thought in general (see *Vom Wesen der deutschen Philosophie*, Stuttgart and Berlin: W. Kohlhammer Verlag, 1941, pp. 10–11; see also p. 170, note 53 above).

17 See Misch's Vorbericht to Vol. V, p. xcvii. Höfer writes: 'In philosophy of life, thought capitulates before the mystery of the world' (*Vom Leben zur Wahrheit*, 202).

18 Foreword to *Leben Schleiermachers*, XIII–1, p. xxxiii.
19 On the individual and Dilthey's individualism, see pp. 90, 111ff, 116, 134 above and the third section of Chapter 2.
20 See Misch, Vorbericht to Vol. v, pp. liii–liv.
21 See *Fortsetzung*, 199.
22 See Diwald, *Wilhelm Dilthey*, 152; Suter, *Philosophie et histoire*, 165; Höfer, *Vom Leben zur Wahrheit*, 70.
23 'See Rede zum 70. Geburtstag,' v, 9.
24 *Understanding and the Human Studies*, 39.
25 *Introduction à la philosophie de l'histoire*, 341, 343; see also 57, 337ff.
26 *Erkenntnis und Interesse*, 263.
27 Taylor, it should be noted, was not trying to deal with the war from Hitler's standpoint. He writes that what he tried to do was simply '... to tell the story as it may appear to some future historian, working from the records.' But he did proceed from an assumption that set him off from the conventional (Allied) understanding of the war: 'This is a story without heroes; and perhaps even without villains' (*The Origins of the Second World War*, London: Hamish Hamilton, 1961, pp. 16, 17).
28 See *Die Entstehung des Historismus*, 114.
29 *Fortsetzung*, 205; see also Binswanger's comment on this statement in *Grundformen und Erkenntnis menschlichen Daseins*, 660.
30 See Vorrede to Vol. v, 4.
31 See p. 94 and p. 181, note 59 above.
32 See *Dilthey*, 48.

Bibliography

An excellent bibliography covering Dilthey's works and the secondary sources dealing with his thought has been published by Ulrich Herrmann: *Bibliographie Wilhelm Dilthey: Quellen und Literatur* (Weinheim, Berlin and Basel: Verlag Julius Beltz, 1969). Also very helpful are the bibliographical section of Müller-Vollmer's book on Dilthey and the more recent bibliographies in Makkreel and Ermarth. Volume XVII of the *Gesammelte Schriften* includes a list of early articles by Dilthey (pp. 471–520).

DILTHEY'S WRITINGS

Most of Dilthey's works are available in the *Gesammelte Schriften*, which now include 18 volumes. Volumes I-XII have been published jointly by the B.G. Teubner Verlagsgesellschaft of Stuttgart, and Vandenhoeck & Ruprecht of Göttingen (1913–58). Volumes XIII-XVIII have been published by Vandenhoeck & Ruprecht alone (1966–77), and there are more to come. The titles and editors of the individual volumes are listed below.

Vol. I: *Einleitung in die Geisteswissenschaften: Versuch einer Grundlegung für das Studium der Gesellschaft und der Geschichte*, ed. Bernhard Groethuysen
Vol. II: *Weltanschauung und Analyse des Menschen seit Renaissance und Reformation*, ed. Georg Misch
Vol. III: *Studien zur Geschichte des deutschen Geistes*, ed. Paul Ritter
Vol. IV: *Die Jugendgeschichte Hegels und andere Abhandlungen zur Geschichte des deutschen Idealismus*, ed. Herman Nohl
Vols. V-VI: *Die geistige Welt: Einleitung in die Philosophie des Lebens*, ed. Georg Misch. First Half: *Abhandlungen zur Grundlegung der Geisteswissenschaften*. Second Half: *Abhandlungen zur Poetik, Ethik und Pädagogik*

Vol. VII: *Der Aufbau der geschichtlichen Welt in den Geisteswissenschaften*, ed. Bernhard Groethuysen

Vol. VIII: *Weltanschauungslehre: Abhandlungen zur Philosophie der Philosophie*, ed. Bernhard Groethuysen

Vol. IX: *Pädagogik: Geschichte und Grundlinien des Systems*, ed. O.F. Bollnow

Vol. X: *System der Ethik*, ed. Herman Nohl

Vol. XI: *Vom Aufgang des geschichtlichen Bewusstseins: Jugendaufsätze und Erinnerungen*, ed. Erich Weniger

Vol. XII: *Zur preussischen Geschichte*, ed. Erich Weniger

Vol. XIII: *Leben Schleiermachers*, ed. Martin Redeker (zwei Halbbände)

Vol. XIV: *Leben Schleiermachers*, Zweiter Band: *Schleiermachers System als Philosophie und Theologie*, ed. Martin Redeker. Erster Halbband: *Schleiermachers System als Philosophie*. Zweiter Halbband: *Schleiermachers System als Theologie*

Vols. XV–XVII: *Zur Geistesgeschichte des 19. Jahrhunderts*, ed. Ulrich Herrmann

Vol. XVIII: *Die Wissenschaften vom Menschen, der Gesellschaft und der Geschichte: Vorarbeiten zur Einleitung in die Geisteswissenschaften*, ed. Helmut Johach and Frithjof Rodi

Some of Dilthey's other works are available in separate published volumes, which are listed below.

Das Erlebnis und die Dichtung: Lessing, Goethe, Novalis, Hölderlin. Göttingen: Vandenhoeck & Ruprecht, 1970. This work has been reprinted many times.

Die grosse Phantasiedichtung und andere Studien zur vergleichende Literaturgeschichte, ed. Herman Nohl. Göttingen: Vandenhoeck & Ruprecht, 1954

Von deutscher Dichtung und Musik: Aus den Studien zur Geschichte des deutschen Geistes, ed. Herman Nohl and Georg Misch. Leipzig and Berlin: Verlag und Druck von B.G. Teubner, 1933

Grundriss der allgemeinen Geschichte der Philosophie, ed. H.G. Gadamer. Frankfurt am Main: Vittorio Klostermann, 1949. Gadamer adds a 'Vorwort' and an 'Anhang,' bringing the book up to date.

Schriften zur Pädagogik, ed. Hans-Hermann Groothoff and Ulrich Herrmann. Paderborn: Ferdinand Schöningh, 1971. Most of the material included in this volume is already contained in the *Gesammelte Schriften*.

'Fragmente aus Wilhelm Diltheys Hegelwerk,' ed. Herman Nohl, *Hegel-Studien*, Vol. I, 1961, ed. Friedhelm Nicolin and Otto Pöggeler, pp. 103–34

Part of the diary Dilthey kept in his earlier years has been published. Many of the letters he wrote and received have been published as well.

Der junge Dilthey: Ein Lebensbild in Briefen und Tagebüchern, 1852–1870, ed. Clara Misch. Stuttgart: B.G. Teubner Verlagsgesellschaft, and Göttingen: Vandenhoeck & Ruprecht, 1960. This volume includes all the material in *Ethica: Aus den Tagebüchern Wilhelm Diltheys*, published by the Literaturarchiv-Gesellschaft of Berlin in 1915.

Briefwechsel zwischen Wilhelm Dilthey und dem Grafen Paul Yorck v. Wartenburg, 1877–1897, ed. Sigrid v.d. Schulenburg. Halle (Saale): Verlag Max Niemeyer, 1923

Briefe Wilhelm Diltheys an Bernhard und Luise Scholz, 1859–1864, ed. Sigrid v.d. Schulenburg, in *Sitzungsberichte der Preussischen Akademie der Wissenschaften*, Philosophisch-Historische Klasse, 1933, pp. 416–71. Berlin: Verlag der Akademie der Wissenschaften, 1933

Briefe Wilhelm Diltheys an Rudolf Haym, 1861–1873, ed. Erich Weniger, in *Abhandlungen der Preussischen Akademie der Wissenschaften*, Philosophisch-Historische Klasse, 1936, No. 9. Berlin: Verlag der Akademie der Wissenschaften, 1936.

'Der Briefwechsel Dilthey-Husserl' (with an introduction by Walter Biemel), *Man and World*, Vol. I (1968), No. 3, pp. 428–46

Little of Dilthey's work is available in English translation. *Das Wesen der Philosophie* (Vol. V, pp. 339–416) has been translated by Stephen A. and William T. Emery as *The Essence of Philosophy* (Chapel Hill: University of North Carolina Press, 1954). The essay on the types of worldviews (Vol. VIII, pp. 75–118) has been translated by William Kluback and Martin Weinbaum as *Philosophy of Existence* (New York: Bookman Associates, 1957). H.P. Rickman has published a selection of materials from Vol. VII as *Meaning in History: W. Dilthey's Thoughts on History and Society* (London: George Allen & Unwin, 1961). The American edition of this work, by Harper and Row of New York, bears the title *Pattern and Meaning in History*. Rickman has put together a second volume of Dilthey in English, in which he includes material drawn from Vols. I, V, VII, VIII, XIII–1, *Die grosse Phantasiedichtung*, and *Das Erlebnis und die Dichtung*. The second Rickman volume is entitled *W. Dilthey: Selected Writings* (Cambridge, London, New York, and Melbourne: Cambridge University Press, 1976). H.A. Hodges has published a selection of passages from Vols. I, V, VII, and VIII in his book *Wilhelm Dilthey: An Introduction* (pp. 109–56). Dilthey's 'dream' (Vol. VIII, pp. 220–6) has been translated by William Kluback and is available in *The Philosophy of History in Our Time*, ed. Hans Meyerhoff (Garden City, New York: Anchor Books, 1959), pp. 37–43. A selection entitled 'The Understanding of Other Persons and Their Life-Expressions' (Vol. VII, pp. 205–20) has been translated by J.J. Kuehl and appears in *Theories of History*, ed. Patrick Gardiner (New York: The Free Press, 1959), pp. 213–25. Finally, a selection entitled 'The Eighteenth Century and the Historical World,' which is drawn from Vol. III and has been translated by James W.

Moore, appears in *Historians at Work*, Vol. 4, ed. Peter Gay and Gerald J. Cavanaugh (New York, Evanston, San Francisco, and London: Harper and Row, 1975), pp. 6–33.

SECONDARY SOURCES

Antoni, Carlo. *From History to Sociology: The Transition in German Historical Thinking*, trans. Hayden V. White. London: Merlin Press, 1962

Apel, Karl Otto. 'Das Verstehen (eine Problemgeschichte als Begriffsgeschichte),' *Archiv für Begriffsgeschichte*, Vol. I (1955), pp. 142–99

Aron, Raymond. *Introduction à la philosophie de l'histoire: Essai sur les limites de l'objectivité historique*, new edition. Paris: Gallimard, 1967

– *La philosophie critique de l'histoire: Essai sur une théorie allemande de l'histoire.* Paris: Librairie philosophique J. Vrin, 1969 (originally published in 1938 under the title: *Essai sur la théorie de l'histoire dans l'Allemagne contemporaine*)

Baring, Nina. *Wilhelm Diltheys Philosophie der Geschichte.* Dissertation, University of Freiburg, 1934

Bauer, Gerhard. *'Geschichtlichkeit': Wege und Irrwege eines Begriffs.* Berlin: Walter de Gruyter & Co., 1963

Berkhof, Hendrikus. *Christ the Meaning of History*, trans. Lambertus Buurman. Richmond: John Knox Press, 1966

Betti, Emilio. *Allgemeine Auslegungslehre als Methodik der Geisteswissenschaften.* Tübingen: J.C.B. Mohr, 1967

– *Die Hermeneutik als allgemeine Methodik der Geisteswissenschaften*, 2nd edition. Tübingen: J.C.B. Mohr, 1972

– 'Zur Grundlegung einer allgemeinen Auslegungslehre,' in *Festschrift für Ernst Rabel*, Vol. II: *Geschichte der antiken Rechte und allgemeinen Rechtslehre*, ed. Wolfgang Kunkel and Julius Wolff. Tübingen: J.C.B. Mohr, 1954, pp. 79–168

Binswanger, Ludwig. *Grundformen und Erkenntnis menschlichen Daseins*, 4th edition. Munich and Basel: Ernst Reinhardt Verlag, 1964

Bollnow, Otto Friedrich. *Dilthey: Eine Einführung in seine Philosophie*, 3rd edition. Stuttgart and Berlin: W. Kohlhammer Verlag, 1955.

– *Die Lebensphilosophie.* Berlin, Göttingen and Heidelberg: Springer-Verlag, 1958

– *Das Verstehen: Drei Aufsätze zur Theorie der Geisteswissenschaften.* Mainz: Verlag Kirchheim, 1949

Brands, Maarten Cornelis. *Historisme als ideologie: Het 'onpolitieke' en 'anti-normatieve' element in de duitse geschiedeniswetenschap.* Assen: Van Gorcum, 1965

Brock, Werner. *An Introduction to Contemporary German Philosophy.* Cambridge: At the University Press, 1935

Brunner, August. *Geschichtlichkeit.* Berne and Munich: Francke Verlag, 1961

Bultmann, Rudolf Karl. 'The Problem of Hermeneutics,' in *Essays Philosophical and Theological*, trans. J.C.C. Greig. London: SCM Press, 1955, pp. 234–61

Carr, Edward Hallet. *What is History?* London: Macmillan, 1962

Collingwood, R.G. *The Idea of History*. New York: Oxford University Press, 1956

Coreth, Emerich. *Grundfragen der Hermeneutik: Ein philosophischer Beitrag*. Freiburg, Basel and Vienna: Herder, 1969

Cüppers, Clemens. *Die erkenntnistheoretischen Grundgedanken Wilhelm Diltheys, dargestellt in ihrem historischen und systematischen Zusammenhange*. Leipzig: B.G. Teubner, 1933

Degener, Alfons. *Dilthey und das Problem der Metaphysik*. Bonn and Cologne: Ludwig Röhrscheid Verlag, 1933

Dietrich, Albert. 'Wilhelm Dilthey,' in *Die grossen Deutschen: Neue Deutsche Biographie*, Vol. V, ed. Willy Andreas and Wilhelm von Scholz. Berlin: Propyläen-Verlag, 1937, pp. 439–49

Diwald, Hellmut. *Wilhelm Dilthey: Erkenntnistheorie und Philosophie der Geschichte*. Göttingen, Berlin, and Frankfurt: Musterschmidt-Verlag, 1963

Donoso, Antón, 'Wilhelm Dilthey's Contribution to the Philosophy of History,' in *Philosophy Today*, Vol. XII, No. 3/4 (Fall 1968), pp. 151–63

Droysen, Johann Gustav. *Historik: Vorlesungen über Enzyklopädie und Methodologie der Geschichte*, ed. Rudolf Hübner. Munich and Berlin: Verlag von R. Oldenbourg, 1937

Ebbinghaus, Hermann. 'Ueber erklärende und beschreibende Psychologie,' *Zeitschrift für Psychologie und Physiologie der Sinnesorgane*, Vol. IX (1896), pp. 161–205

Ermarth, Michael. *Wilhelm Dilthey: The Critique of Historical Reason*. Chicago and London: University of Chicago Press, 1978

Erxleben, Wolfgang. *Erlebnis, Verstehen und geschichtliche Wahrheit: Untersuchungen über die geschichtliche Stellung von Wilhelm Diltheys Grundlegung der Geisteswissenschaften*. Dissertation, University of Berlin, 1937

Freyer, Hans. *Theorie des objektiven Geistes: Eine Einleitung in die Kulturphilosophie*, 3rd edition. Leipzig and Berlin: B.G. Teubner, 1934

Frey-Rohn, Liliane. *Die Grundbegriffe der Dilthey'schen Philosophie, mit besonderer Berücksichtigung der Theorie der Geisteswissenschaften*. Zurich: Ferrari-Buchdruck, 1934

Friess, Horace L. 'Wilhelm Dilthey: A Review of His Collected Works as an Introduction to a Phase of Contemporary German Philosophy,' *Journal of Philosophy*, Vol. XXVI, No. 1 (January, 1929), pp. 5–25

Gadamer, Hans-Georg. *Kleine Schriften*, Vol. I: *Philosophie, Hermeneutik*. Tübingen: J.C.B. Mohr, 1967

– *Le problème de la conscience historique*. Louvain: Publications Universitaires de Louvain, 1963

- 'Le problème herméneutique,' *Archives de Philosophie*, Vol. XXXIII (1970), pp. 3–27
- 'Vom Zirkel des Verstehens,' in *Martin Heidegger zum siebzigsten Geburtstag*, ed. Günther Neske. Pfullingen: Neske, 1959, pp. 24–34
- *Wahrheit und Methode: Grundzüge einer philosophischen Hermeneutik*, 2nd edition. Tübingen: J.C.B. Mohr, 1965. An English translation is available.

Groethuysen, Bernhard. 'Dilthey et son école,' in *La philosophie allemande au XIXe siècle*, ed. Charles Andler. Paris: Librairie Felix Alcan, 1912, pp. 1–23
- 'Idée et pensée: Réflexions sur la Journal de Dilthey,' *Recherches philosophiques*, Vol. IV (1934–35), pp. 371–6
- *Introduction à la pensée philosophique allemande depuis Nietzsche*. Paris: Librairie Stock, 1926
- 'Wilhelm Dilthey,' *Deutsche Rundschau*, Vol. XXXIX, No. 4 (January, 1913), pp. 69–92, and No. 5 (February, 1913), pp. 249–70

Gusdorf, Georges. *Introduction aux sciences humaines: Essai critique sur leurs origines et leur développement* (Publications de la faculté des lettres de l'Université de Strasbourg). Paris: 'Les belles lettres,' 1960

Habermas, Jürgen. *Erkenntnis und Interesse*. Frankfurt am Main: Suhrkamp Verlag, 1968

Heidegger, Martin. *Being and Time*, trans. John Macquarrie and Edward Robinson. London: SCM Press, 1962

Heinemann, F.H. *Neue Wege der Philosophie – Geist, Leben, Existenz: Eine Einführung in die Philosophie der Gegenwart*. Leipzig: Verlag von Quelle & Meyer, 1929

Herzberg, Guntolf. 'Wilhelm Dilthey in der heutigen westdeutschen Philosophie,' *Deutsche Zeitschrift für Philosophie*, Vol. XVIII (1970), No. 1, pp. 87–99

Heussi, Karl. *Die Krisis des Historismus*. Tübingen: J.C.B. Mohr, 1932

Hodges, Herbert A. *The Philosophy of Wilhelm Dilthey*. London: Routledge and Kegan Paul, 1952
- *Wilhelm Dilthey: An Introduction*. London: Routledge and Kegan Paul, 1944

Höfer, Josef. *Vom Leben zur Wahrheit: Katholische Besinnung an der Lebensanschauung Wilhelm Diltheys*. Freiburg: Herder, 1936

Hofmannsthal, Hugo von. 'Wilhelm Dilthey,' in *Die prosaischen Schriften gesammelt*, Vol. III. Berlin: S. Fischer Verlag, 1917, pp. 27–32

Holborn, Hajo. 'Wilhelm Dilthey and the Critique of Historical Reason,' *Journal of the History of Ideas*, Vol. XI (1950), No. 1, pp. 93–118

Hughes, H. Stuart. *Consciousness and Society: The Reorientation of European Social Thought, 1890–1930*. New York: Vintage Books, 1961
- *History as Art and as Science: Twin Vistas on the Past*. New York: Harper and Row, 1964

Hünermann, Peter. *Der Durchbruch geschichtlichen Denkens im 19. Jahrhundert: Johann Gustav Droysen, Wilhelm Dilthey, Graf Paul Yorck von Wartenburg – Ihr Weg und ihre Weisung für die Theologie.* Freiburg, Basel and Vienna: Herder, 1967

Husserl, Edmund. *Phänomenologische Psychologie: Vorlesungen Sommersemester 1925,* ed. Walter Biemel. ('Husserliana,' Vol. IX). The Hague: Martinus Nijhoff, 1962
– 'Philosophie als strenge Wissenschaft,' *Logos,* Vol. I (1910), pp. 289–341

Iggers, George C. *The German Conception of History: The National Tradition of Historical Thought from Herder to the Present.* Middletown, Connecticut: Wesleyan University Press, 1968

Kamerbeek, J. *Allard Pierson en Wilhelm Dilthey,* in *Mededelingen der Koninklijke Nederlandse Akademie van Wetenschappen,* Nieuwe Reeks, Deel 20, Afdeling Letterkunde, No. 2. Amsterdam: N.V. Noord-Hollandsche Uitgevers Maatschappij, 1957
– 'Dilthey versus Nietzsche,' *Studia Philosophica: Jahrbuch der Schweizerischen Philosophischen Gesellschaft,* Vol. X, ed. Daniel Christoff and Hans Kunz. Basel: Verlag für Recht und Gesellschaft, 1950, pp. 52–84

Katsube, Kenzo. *Wilhelm Diltheys Methode der Lebensphilosophie.* Hiroshima: Philosophical Institute of the University of Hiroshima, 1931

Klapwijk, Jacob. 'Over verschuiving van normen en historische filosofie,' *Philosophia Reformata,* Vol. XXXVII (1972), No. 1–2, pp. 26–41
– *Tussen historisme en relativisme: Een studie over de dynamiek van het historisme en de wijsgerige ontwikkelingsgang van Ernst Troeltsch.* Assen: Van Gorcum, 1970

Kon, I.S. *Die Geschichtsphilosophie des 20. Jahrhunderts,* Vol. I: *Die Geschichtsphilosophie der Epoche des Imperialismus,* trans. W. Hoepp. Berlin: Akademie Verlag, 1964

Kremer-Marietti, Angèle. *Wilhelm Dilthey et l'anthropologie historique.* Paris: Éditions Seghers, 1971

Kuypers, Karel. *Theorie der geschiedenis, voornamelijk met betrekking tot de cultuur.* Amsterdam: H.J. Paris, 1931
– *Verspreide geschriften,* Vol. I: *Mens en geschiedenis.* Assen: Van Gorcum, 1968

Landgrebe, Ludwig. 'Vom geisteswissenschaftlichen Verstehen,' in *Phänomenologie und Geschichte.* Gütersloh: Verlagshaus Gerd Mohn, 1967, pp. 34–45
– *Wilhelm Diltheys Theorie der Geisteswissenschaften: Analyse ihrer Grundbegriffe,* in *Jahrbuch für Philosophie und phänomenologische Forschung,* Vol. IX, ed. Edmund Husserl. Halle (Saale): Max Niemeyer Verlag, 1928, pp. 237–366

Lee, D.E. and R.N. Beck. 'The Meaning of "Historicism,"' *American Historical Review,* Vol. LIX, No. 3 (April, 1954), pp. 568–77

Liebert, Arthur. *Wilhelm Dilthey: Eine Würdigung seines Werkes zum 100. Geburtstage des Philosophen.* Berlin: Verlag von E.S. Mittler & Sohn, 1933

Litt, Theodor. 'The Universal in the Structure of Historical Knowledge,' in *Philosophy and History: Essays Presented to Ernst Cassirer,* ed. Raymond Klibansky and H.J. Paton. New York, Evanston, and London: Harper and Row, 1963, pp. 125–36

194 Bibliography

Lukács, Georg. *Die Zerstörung der Vernunft* (Vol. 9 of *Georg Lukács Werke).*
Berlin-Spandau: Luchterhand, 1962

Makkreel, Rudolf A. *Dilthey: Philosopher of the Human Studies.* Princeton: Princeton
University Press, 1975

- 'Wilhelm Dilthey and the Neo-Kantians: The Distinction of the Geisteswissenschaften and the Kulturwissenschaften,' *Journal of the History of Philosophy*,
Vol. IV (October, 1969), pp. 423–40

Mandelbaum, Maurice. *History, Man and Reason: A Study in Nineteenth Century
Thought.* Baltimore and London: The Johns Hopkins Press, 1971

- *The Problem of Historical Knowledge: An Answer to Relativism.* New York,
Evanston, and London: Harper and Row, 1967.

Marquard, Odo. 'Weltanschauungstypologie: Bemerkungen zu einer anthropolo-
gischen Denkform des neunzehnten und zwanzigsten Jahrhunderts,' in *Die Frage
nach dem Menschen: Aufriss einer philosophischen Anthropologie* (Festschrift für
Max Müller zum 60. Geburtstag), ed. Heinrich Rombach. Freiburg and Munich:
Verlag Karl Alber, 1966

Masur, Gerhard. *Prophets of Yesterday: Studies in European Culture, 1890–1914.* New
York: Macmillan, 1961

- 'Wilhelm Dilthey and the History of Ideas,' *Journal of the History of Ideas*, Vol.
XIII (1952), No. 1, pp. 93–107

Meinecke, Friedrich. *Die Entstehung des Historismus*, ed. Carl Hinrichs (Vol. 3 of
Meinecke's *Werke).* Munich: R. Oldenbourg Verlag, 1965. An English translation
is available.

- *Zur Theorie und Philosophie der Geschichte*, ed. Eberhard Kessel (Vol. 4 of
Meinecke's *Werke).* Stuttgart: K.F. Koehler Verlag, 1959

Mekkes, J.P.A. 'Wilhelm Dilthey's "Kritik der historischen Vernunft" in de wending der eeuw,' *Philosophia Reformata*, Vol. XX (1955), No. 1, pp. 7–45

Miller-Rostowska, Alice. *Das Individuelle als Gegenstand der Erkenntnis: Eine Studie
zur Geschichtsmethodologie Heinrich Rickerts.* Winterthur: P.G. Keller, 1955

Misch, Georg. 'Dilthey versus Nietzsche,' *Die Sammlung: Zeitschrift für Kultur und
Erziehung*, Vol. VII (1952), pp. 378–95

- *Lebensphilosophie und Phänomenologie: Eine Auseinandersetzung der Diltheyschen
Richtung mit Heidegger und Husserl*, 3rd edition. Darmstadt: Wissenschaftliche
Buchgesellschaft, 1967

- *Vom Lebens- und Gedankenkreis Wilhelm Diltheys.* Frankfurt am Main: Verlag
Gerhard Schulte-Bulmke, 1947

Morgan, George A. 'Wilhelm Dilthey,' *Philosophical Review*, Vol. XLII, No. 4 (July,
1933), pp. 351–80

Müller-Vollmer, Kurt. *Towards a Phenomenological Theory of Literature: A Study of
Wilhelm Dilthey's 'Poetik.'* The Hague: Mouton, 1963

Nietzsche, Friedrich. *The Use and Abuse of History*, trans. Adrian Collins. Indianapolis and New York: Bobbs-Merrill ('Library of the Liberal Arts'), 1957

Nohl, Herman. 'Der junge Dilthey,' *Germanisch-romanische Monatsschrift*, Vol. XXII, No. 3–4 (March-April, 1934), pp. 139–44

– 'Wilhelm Dilthey,' in *Die grossen Deutschen: Deutsche Biographie*, Vol. IV, ed. Hermann Heimpel, Theodor Heuss, and Benno Reifenberg. Berlin: Propyläen-Verlag, 1957, pp. 193–204

– 'Zur Neuausgabe der Werke Wilhelm Diltheys,' *Die Sammlung: Zeitschrift für Kultur und Erziehung*, Vol. XII (1957), pp. 618–25

Ortega y Gasset, José. 'A Chapter from the History of Ideas – Wilhelm Dilthey and the Idea of Life,' trans. Helene Weyl, in *Concord and Liberty*. New York: W.W. Norton, 1963, pp. 129–82

– 'History as a System,' trans. William G. Atkinson, in *History as a System and Other Essays Toward a Philosophy of History*. New York: W.W. Norton, 1962, pp. 165–233

Palmer, Richard E. *Hermeneutics: Interpretation Theory in Schleiermacher, Dilthey, Heidegger, and Gadamer*. Evanston: Northwestern University Press, 1969

Philipson, Morris. 'Dilthey on Art,' *Journal of Aesthetics and Art Criticism*, Vol. XVII, No. 1 (September, 1958), pp. 72–6

Plantinga, Theodore. 'Dilthey's Philosophy of the History of Philosophy,' in *Hearing and Doing: Philosophical Essays Dedicated to H. Evan Runner*, ed. John Kraay and Anthony Tol. Toronto: Wedge Publishing Foundation, 1979, pp. 199–214

Rand, Calvin G. 'Two Meanings of Historicism in the Writings of Dilthey, Troeltsch, and Meinecke,' *Journal of the History of Ideas*, Vol. XXV (1964), No. 4, pp. 503–18

Renthe-Fink, Leonhard von. *Geschichtlichkeit: Ihr terminologischer und begrifflicher Ursprung bei Hegel, Haym, Dilthey und Yorck*, in *Abhandlungen der Akademie der Wissenschaften in Göttingen*, Philologisch-Historische Klasse, Dritte Folge, No. 59. Göttingen: Vandenhoeck & Ruprecht, 1964

Rickert, Heinrich. *Die Grenzen der naturwissenschaftlichen Begriffsbildung: Eine logische Einleitung in die historische Wissenschaften*, 5th edition. Tübingen: J.C.B. Mohr, 1929

– *Kulturwissenschaft und Naturwissenschaft*, 6th and 7th edition. Tübingen: J.C.B. Mohr, 1926

– *Die Philosophie des Lebens: Darstellung und Kritik der philosophischen Modeströmungen unserer Zeit*. Tübingen: J.C.B. Mohr, 1922

– *Die Probleme der Geschichtsphilosophie: Eine Einführung*, 3rd edition. Heidelberg: Carl Winters Universitätsbuchhandlung, 1924

Rickman, H.P. 'General Introduction,' in *Meaning in History: W. Dilthey's Thoughts on History and Society*, ed. and trans. H.P. Rickman. London: George Allen & Unwin, 1961, pp. 11–63

- *Understanding and the Human Studies.* London: Heinemann Educational Books Limited, 1967

Ricoeur, Paul. *Le conflit des interprétations: Essais d'herméneutique.* Paris: Editions du Seuil, 1969

Rodi, Frithjof. *Morphologie und Hermeneutik: Zur Methode von Diltheys Aesthetik.* Stuttgart and Berlin: W. Kohlhammer Verlag, 1969.

Rothacker, Erich. *Einleitung in die Geisteswissenschaften.* Tübingen: J.C.B. Mohr, 1920

- *Logik und Systematik der Geisteswissenschaften.* Munich: R. Oldenbourg Verlag, 1965

Scheler, Max. 'Versuch einer Philosophie des Lebens: Nietzsche-Dilthey-Bergson,' in *Vom Umsturz der Werte: Abhandlungen und Aufsätze,* 4th edition, ed. Maria Scheler (Vol. 3 of his *Gesammelte Werke*). Berne: Francke Verlag, 1955, pp. 311–39

Schleiermacher, F.D.E. *Hermeneutik,* new edition by Heinz Kimmerle, in *Abhandlungen der Heidelberger Akademie der Wissenschaften,* Philosophisch-Historische Klasse, Jahrgang 1959, 2. Abhandlung. Heidelberg: Carl Winters Universitätsverlag, 1959

Schmidt, Ferdinand Jakob. 'Das Erlebnis und die Dichtung,' *Preussische Jahrbücher,* Vol. CXXIII (1906), pp. 201–19

Schmied-Kowarzik, Walthar. 'Diltheys und Sprangers verstehende Psychologie in ihrem Verhältnis zur erklärenden (naturwissenschaftlichen) Psychologie,' *Archiv für die gesamte Psychologie,* Vol. LVIII (1927), No. 3–4, pp. 281–306

Schopenhauer, Arthur. 'On History,' in *The World as Will and Representation,* Vol. II, trans. E.F.J. Payne. New York: Falcon's Wing Press, 1958, pp. 439–46

Sommerfeld, Hans. *Wilhelm Dilthey und der Positivismus: Eine Untersuchung zur 'Einleitung in die Geisteswissenschaften.'* Dissertation, University of Berlin, 1926

Spranger, Eduard. *Lebensformen: Geisteswissenschaftliche Psychologie und Ethik der Persönlichkeit,* 5th edition. Halle (Saale): Max Niemeyer Verlag, 1925

- 'Zur Theorie des Verstehens und zur geisteswissenschaftliche Psychologie,' in *Festschrift Johannes Volkelt zum 70. Geburtstag.* Munich: C.H. Beck'sche Verlagsbuchhandlung Oskar Beck, 1918, pp. 357–403

Stein, Artur. *Der Begriff des Verstehens bei Dilthey,* 2nd edition. Tübingen: J.C.B. Mohr, 1926

Stein, Ludwig. 'Historical Optimism: Wilhelm Dilthey,' *Philosophical Review,* Vol. XXXIII, No. 4 (July, 1924), pp. 329–44

Störring, G. 'Die Frage der geisteswissenschaftlichen und verstehenden Psychologie: Eine Streitschrift,' *Archiv für die gesamte Psychologie,* Vol. LVIII (1927), No. 3–4, pp. 389–448; Vol. LXI (1928), No. 3–4, pp. 273–354; Vol. LXII (1928), No. 3–4, pp. 443–80

Suter, Jean-François. *Philosophie et histoire chez Wilhelm Dilthey: Essai sur le problème de l'historicisme.* Basel: Verlag für Recht und Gesellschaft, 1960

Tapper, Bonno. 'Dilthey's Methodology of the *Geisteswissenschaften,*' *Philosophical Review*, Vol. XXXIV, No. 4 (July, 1925), pp. 333–49

Trill, Barbara. *Kunstphilosophie als Metaphysik beim späten Dilthey.* Dissertation, University of Münster, 1969

Troeltsch, Ernst. *Der Historismus und seine Probleme* (Vol. 3 of his *Gesammelte Schriften*). Tübingen: J.C.B. Mohr, 1922

– 'Die Krisis des Historismus,' *Die neue Rundschau*, Vol. XXXIII, No. 6 (June, 1922), pp. 572–90

Tumarkin, Anna. 'Ein Versuch, Diltheys Leben aus ihm selbst zu verstehen,' in *Festschrift für Karl Joël zum 70. Geburtstag.* Basel: Helbing & Lichtenhahn, 1934, pp. 255–67

– 'Wilhelm Dilthey,' *Archiv für Geschichte der Philosophie*, Vol. XXV (1911–12), No. 2, pp. 143–53

Tuttle, Howard Nelson. *Wilhelm Dilthey's Philosophy of Historical Understanding: A Critical Analysis.* Leiden: E.J. Brill, 1969

Wach, Joachim. *Das Verstehen: Grundzüge einer Geschichte der hermeneutischen Theorie im 19. Jahrhundert.* Tübingen: J.C.B. Mohr, 1926–33, 3 volumes

Walsh, W.H. *Philosophy of History: An Introduction.* New York: Harper and Row, 1960

Windelband, Wilhelm. *Präludien: Aufsätze und Reden zur Philosophie und ihrer Geschichte*, 5th edition, Vol. II. Tübingen: J.C.B. Mohr, 1924

Index